DANCING IN PARADISE, BURNING IN HELL

Women in Maine's Historic Working Class Dance Industry

TRUDY IRENE SCEE

D1319600

Camden, Maine

Published by Down East Books
An imprint of Globe Pequot
Trade division of The Rowman & Littlefield Publishing Group, Inc.
4501 Forbes Boulevard, Suite 200, Lanham, Maryland 20706
www.rowman.com

Unit A, Whitacre Mews, 26-34 Stannary Street, London SE11 4AB, United Kingdom

Distributed by NATIONAL BOOK NETWORK

British Library Cataloguing in Publication Information Available

Library of Congress Cataloging-in-Publication Data Available

ISBN 978-1-60893-509-3 (paperback)
ISBN 978-1-60893-510-9 (e-book)

♾™ The paper used in this publication meets the minimum requirements of American National Standard for Information Sciences—Permanence of Paper for Printed Library Materials, ANSI/ NISO Z39.48-1992.

Dancing in Paradise, Burning in Hell

For My Mentors:

Harold Duane Hampton, who taught me the history of the American West,
and allowed me to play with words,
Edwin Charles Woodward, who fostered my love of nature and of frolicking,
David C. Smith, who taught me the history of the American East,
set me a high production goal, and whose extensive memory
and knowledge I can never hope to reproduce,
and for
Paula Petrik, who bridged the American East and the American West in her
studies and classrooms in Montana and Maine, and whose classroom—
if not the photograph of a hurdy gurdy girl I brought to Hampton
so many years ago— was the starting place of this book.
And for my dance partners, April Michelle and Jim, and Mariah and Bub.

CONTENTS

Acknowledgments ix
Introduction: Dancers for Money xi

CHAPTER ONE: The Road to Perdition. 1
CHAPTER TWO: Scandal on the Stage and the Search
                 for Much More 29
CHAPTER THREE: Oh, for the Satin Slippers and the
                 Gold and the Silver Purses 67
CHAPTER FOUR: And the Victrola Played On 93
CHAPTER FIVE: Dancing in Paradise, Burning in Hell. 111
CHAPTER SIX: The Dance Didn't Go On, and They
                 Really Weren't Strippers. 147
CHAPTER SEVEN: Bring Back the Hootchie-Cootchie. 185
CHAPTER EIGHT: "Little Egypt" Grows Up and Becomes
                 the Queen of the Coast 203
CHAPTER NINE: Conclusion 229

Notes 233
Selected Bibliography 253
Index 257

Acknowledgments

As always, there are other people whose work and lives have affected my life and my work, including this study of, primarily, the working-class female dancers of Maine and elsewhere. Those who have so affected me go way back to when my mother used to take me to the library when I was four and five years old and I could choose my own books, which I consider the start of my reading and writing career, if it may be called that. And, even before that, when I watched my big brother teach my mother how to jitterbug in our tiny apartment, and then he would let me climb up on his feet and he would dance with me and around and around we would go, came the start of my love of dancing. Even as adults, we would dance together at family gatherings. I hope somehow that I can see him dance again one day. And my sisters too would dance with me when I was little, and then came my friends, and Jim, who would always tie up my dancing shoes for me, no matter where the world took me.

Academically, as noted in the dedication, there were several professors whom I greatly admired and who have influenced my life and my work. Other writers and historians and sociologists and the like who have studied dancing have in turn piqued my interests and inspired me. And, as importantly as ever, I owe gratitude to the librarians of Maine and to the Bangor Public Library, the Portland Public Library, the University of Maine, the Old Orchard Beach Historical Society, the Maine Historical Society, and to others who have preserved historical materials and made them available to the public, including me. And I owe thanks too to all my dance partners, from my mother to my brother to my sisters to my daughter, and to my friends, and to my teachers: Terri and Dick, Katriana, Kitty, Lorienne, and the others. And thank you everyone who let me interview them for the book, and to those dancers who appear in the book, both those who are living and those who have passed on. And thank you Michael Steere, for help with this and other projects, and to the teams at Rowman & Littlefield, and at Down East Books. Thank you all, and of course, all mistakes herein are of my own doing.

Dancers for Money

America Meets the New Dancing Women of the 1800s, Recoils in Shock, and Yet Whispers "Come a Little Bit Closer"; The Hurdy Gurdy Girls, Burlesque Women, Little Egypts, and Taxi-Dancers of the 1800s–1940s

WHEN I WAS FIFTEEN YEARS OLD, I STOWED AWAY ON A TRAIN FOR New York City. When I arrived, my best friend's aunt sent me right back, on a Greyhound bus. During a layover in Syracuse, New York, I noticed a woman approaching. She sat down directly across from me and placed a little green suitcase at her feet. And as I wrote in my upcoming book, *Finding Shelly*:

> *She was dressed in jeans, boots, and a tight t-shirt. She smiled at me, and we started talking.*
>
> *"Where are you going?" she asked me.*
>
> *"Home," I said. I then told her something about my adventures of the last thirty-two hours and she laughed.*
>
> *"Where are you going?" I asked her in return.*
>
> *"Oh, just to another city for another job."*
>
> *"What do you do?"*
>
> *"I'm a dancer. A stripper."*
>
> *"Oh." I didn't quite know what to say to that.*

"It's kind of sad really," she continued. "My whole life is in that little suitcase." She opened up the suitcase—it was one of those rectangular hard-backed numbers. Inside I could see just some feathers and chiffon and some high-heeled shoes, all sort of jumbled up.

"See," she said. "Just little bits of things I throw on, and then throw off. That's it. That's all I do."

"Do you like your job at all?" I asked her.

"No. I hate it. I hate every friggin' asshole in every friggin' bar."

I didn't know what to say to that either. We sat in silence until my bus was called. Then she wished me luck and we said good-bye.

Four years later, my best friend April Michelle would come to me with a proposal. She said,

"I've got this routine with beads. It's really good. It's classy. You could dance with me. We'd be on stage together again. We could be really good together."

Oh no. I couldn't even think of it. Couldn't stand the thought of it. Couldn't think of her up there, dancing for money, stripping for money, the act hurting her . . . I knew it was hurting her . . . I couldn't understand it. I didn't know how to stop it. . . . She was my best friend and she was only nineteen. How could I make it stop?

As it turned out, I could not make it stop, and within the year my friend was dead. She died of a gunshot wound to the chest. And I hated every part of what had put her there, including the stripping. As teenagers, we had shared many a stage, but never that one. And as the years went by, I looked at some parts of our story, and of other women's, and I conducted a few studies of dancers—of taxi-dancers and marathon dancers as a historian, and of ballet and gymnastics as a student of them years before, and little bits about the West's hurdy gurdy girls and the like—but I didn't want to look at the stories of strippers. That would be much too raw, much too difficult. And besides, I tend to become immersed in my research projects, and I had no intentions of ever being—or playing at being—a stripper.

And yet, not long ago I packed up a little green suitcase of my own, a rectangular hard-backed one, with little bits of this and that—dancing shoes and silk-chiffon, a sequined bra and bangles and beads—to dance in a downtown bar. I didn't intend to strip, oh not too much, just a little burlesque in the background before my real number started. It was just going to be a little insertion of my own sense of humor, but hoots and howls soon filled the place, and well, it was pretty much a striptease that followed: my back to the audience I shimmied my hips and then my chest and pulled off my velvet overdress and then the opera gloves, one by one. The hair came down, and I turned. With my sequined bra flashing, a hip-scarf from Egypt sparkling, a long skirt swaying, and coins and beads jingling, I strutted out to CeeLo Green, the music full of sex and anger. It was a Halloween party, and I was one of the belly dancers. It was comedy, but it wasn't. It was traditional, yet modern. It was once of the oldest female dances in the world transformed by cultural and historical changes and the experiences of the dancer. No one threw money at my feet, but in another venue, were I pleasing enough, they might well have done so. People do throw money at belly dancers. Or quietly leave it on the stage. They do not touch the dancers, not even in public performances.

So why was I there that Halloween night, or at another show, two months later, at which I danced again before a larger audience, on a formal stage, first alone to a sad contemporary song dedicated to my brother, and then segueing with two friends to an upbeat Motown song? I was there because in spite of many suspicions to the contrary, belly dancing is very different from stripping and not part of that dance industry I so despised. I was there because belly dancing has survived, and of late has started to flourish, unlike some of the earlier forms of women's dance that were viewed as immoral, or at least of questionable morality, and their performers sometimes accused outright of prostitution. And I was there because belly dancing is hard work but fun and offers a unique blend of historical depth and modern adoptability. And it has become women-centered.

When Farida Mazar Spyropoulos—also known as Fatima—appeared at the 1893 World's Fair held in Chicago—in flimsy clothing and sans corset, stockings, and shoes, and with her long hair left natural—dancing a style that eventually became known as belly dancing, people were scandalized. The exhibit was meant to give fairgoers a glimpse into the Middle East and Morocco, but for many the first "Little Egypt" exhibition was instead a view into a new avenue for vice. When Ashea Wabe performed a similar dance at a bachelor party on New York's Fifth Avenue in 1896, a vice squad raided the party, having been informed that Wabe might dance naked. Even as Americans confronted this new threat to morality, some burlesque dancers were becoming more brazen, or so some people commented, while others were transitioning into a new form of performer—one who would appear in the new films as well as in major stage productions. Belly dancers would soon start filling the places that smaller burlesque performances and the declining numbers of hurdy gurdy girls (who had been paid by the dance generally, sometimes up to a dollar per dance, with the men handing them the money directly) were leaving, as well as creating their own niches.

A decade later, as was true in some California cities and many other urban areas, Chicago's downtown area saw a growth in taxi-dancing—wherein women would be paid by the minute for dancing with men. At "ten cents a throw" men could buy a dance with the woman of their choice. Residents protested that the "girls" were dancing inappropriately (although they generally specialized in ballroom-style dancing), and were perhaps performing other services for money. In some places, police raided the halls, and in other cities the halls were outlawed as supposed fronts for prostitution.

In the 1920s and 1930s, many Americans lamented the rise of marathon dancing, through which some women managed to secure lodging and cash awards, sometimes thrown onto the dance floor, especially during the Great Depression. Marathons provided entertainment, yet some people deemed them inappropriate. In 1933, when fire swept through the Hampden Dance Pavilion outside of Bangor, Maine was brought into the national spotlight regarding marathon dancing, and not for all the right reasons. Even before the fire erupted, local police had raided the dance hall and made several arrests, the charges being violations of Maine's blue laws. However, that same year, Americans flocked to watch Sally Rand perform her fan dance at the Chicago World's Fair. People looked as closely as they could; she was rumored to be naked during part of her routine although she was actually wearing a bodysuit behind her feathers. Rand was better received than Fatima had been forty years earlier, and more warmly than were the contemporary "Little Egypts," a name by then regularly given or taken by belly dancers, whose numbers had been growing over the previous decades.

Then a new strain of vaudeville came over the nation, followed by new forms of belly dancing, and other, more risqué, burlesque came to stage and screen, and the misconceptions continued. Women worked in these newer industries in Maine and elsewhere to help pay the bills and to earn a living.

Perhaps only a few women reached the fame of Sally Rand, but many women performed as taxi-dancers, marathon dancers, belly or hootchie-cootchie dancers, hurdy gurdy girls, and in other forms of dancing for money. Many—if not the vast majority—of these women were working class and danced in small or in large part for the money. As opposed to the more respected dance genres, these women were generally paid or otherwise remunerated by the individual dance or an individual performance, not by a paycheck or salary from a company or other sponsor. And most of them during the late 1800s and well into the 1900s were condemned for their work, with the validity of their work as even being a true form of dance often called into question. Misconceptions abounded as to what the women actually did, and why they did it. They were often compared with strippers (who by the mid-1900s had their own niche) or prostitutes, and although some may have crossed the boundaries, the vast majority did not, and most remained well clothed, or, for some women, unclothed only as much as a contemporary woman might be in her bathing suit. It is these women who are discussed in the following pages. In some cases a great deal is known about the individual dancers, dance halls, or theaters or clubs; in other cases, only small bits of their history survive.

I was a working-class girl, as was my friend April Michelle, although as a child I did not see it quite like that. Her family had more education and money than mine, but her mother was a single mother during part of the time when we were growing up, with six kids to feed and clothe, and April Michelle drifted into a world I could not enter. So did other girls I grew up with, and some of them died also, and some would ply their bodies for money, some through dance, some through prostitution. That was in northern New York state, but the same stories have been repeated elsewhere, including in Maine. And Maine has long enjoyed a tourist industry, as well as shipping, lumbering, and other industries, that have made the stage that much more beckoning, if it may be called that. So here are some of the stories of working-class and other women (and, in some cases, men) in the dance industries in Maine—and to some degree elsewhere, as the women and the dances often traveled from place to place.

CHAPTER ONE

The Road to Perdition

*The Early Barroom Dancers, the Hurdy Gurdy Girls,
the Circus and Fair Come to Town, Native Americans
Perform, and the Dance Hall or Whorehouse Riot of 1849*

DISCOVERING THE DANCERS OF EARLY MAINE HISTORY IS TROUBLE-some. That women danced, and that some danced for money, is not in question. The question is, how many did so, where did they dance, and what dances did they do? In most cases, what happened in Maine reflects trends elsewhere in the nation. Although in some ways the trends were closer to those of New England in general, in other aspects they were more like those of the American West, as broad expanses of Maine remained wilderness and boom town areas reminiscent of those found in the West could still be found well into the 1800s and even, in places, the early 1900s.

In general, dancing and public "entertainment" in almost any form was harshly condemned by the Puritan society of Massachusetts, which governed Maine until 1820. The Puritans who had control over early Massachusetts "regarded the playhouse as the direct road to perdition and they would countenance no such levity," as one study determined.[1] And dancing was seemingly even further along that road to Hell. Maine residents might wish to dance, and some did—indeed, some members of society held dancing parties and even balls in the revolutionary era, but they still risked being persecuted for such amusement. For example, in Portland (or Falmouth as the community was initially called) in 1766, two of the community's couples were indicted for dancing. After the war, early theater did come to Maine in October 1794, to Portland, and the theatrical company risked including some "songs and impromptu dances" in at least a few of its shows. It performed at the Assembly Hall and called it the "New Theater." A few other theatrical companies came to the community over the next few years.[2] By the mid-1790s, after the infamous witch trials at Salem and other related terrors and developments, the Puritan hold on Massachusetts had clearly loosened, many Maine residents were clamoring for freedom from Massachusetts, and public entertainment would appear with increasing frequency in the cities and towns of Maine in the early 1800s.

In Portland, the old Union Hall became a theater or playhouse during 1820–1829. Then, a small theater opened its doors for a brief period on Free Street, followed by a theater on Union Street soon thereafter. The newest playhouse burned down in 1854. Some performances were held, after 1866, the year of Portland's Great Fire, at the new City Hall. Theater was now acceptable under certain guidelines, but female dancers were still scarce. However, in 1897 the Jefferson Theater opened in Portland at the corner of Oak and Free Streets, at a site that had once housed a convent. It initially offered primarily plays, but within a few years it would begin offering something else.[3]

Farther north, in the heart of Maine's other population center located in Bangor (which at the time some people thought would come to rival Boston in terms of its population and commerce), women did dance in numerous shows staged at the Bangor Opera House, which opened in April 1882. The citizens and the local press gave the Opera House a warm welcoming, packing its seats for its initial shows. Some of the first offerings were amateur productions staged by locals, but traveling shows also appeared in various performances. These performances, however, were generally considered of higher moral content than were those of the backwoods saloons and stages and of the traveling circuses and fairs that became part of the nineteenth-century culture in Maine as elsewhere.[4]

Previous to the opening of the Opera House, in 1838 the Bangor Theater had opened and brought numerous productions in from Boston and other cities during spring through autumn of each year. Hard times in the 1840s eventually caused the theater to close for a time—and be used as a stable—until another person purchased the venue and staged the show "Ten Nights in a Bar Room." Other people subsequently owned or managed the theater, which eventually changed its name to the Bangor Athaeneum. The theater burned down in the 1850s in a fire caused by "fireballs which boys were throwing into the air." A new theater was built on the same site, not as large as the previous one but still capable of seating 800 people with room for another 200 to stand. The newest theater also burned down after a short period. Then City Hall and a few other locations housed other shows until Norombega Hall opened in autumn 1855. It began shows for the general populace in 1856, and served as "the chief hall for amusements, and the number of traveling companies that have played within its walls [was] legion," according to the *Bangor Whig & Courier* of 1882.[5]

In 1877, the Buskin Club was organized and brought to Bangor "nearly two-hundred leading combinations." The Opera House on Main Street would essentially replace that organization, which had started plans for the new venue in 1879. The Opera House was ultimately funded by subscriptions, a popular means of raising funds in the 1800s. The brick building could seat up to 1,100 people, with standing room for hundreds more. Dancing was part of the opening night's play, *Rosedale*, and young dance students performed at the venue in the following days, dancing a variety of folk and other dances, including Turkish and Spanish numbers. In addition to these venues, musical performances and dancing were regular offerings of Bangor's Music Hall.[6]

However, it was outside of the theaters and playhouses of Maine that the working-class women's dance industries made their greatest impact or, at any rate, provided the most controversial entertainment. One form of dance that likely came to Maine in one semblance or another in the mid- to late 1800s was that of the hurdy gurdy girls.

Hurdy gurdy girls may have been new to America in the 1800s; they were not new to the world. The hurdy gurdy girls had come out of Europe and initially served essentially as an advertisement venue. As Hessian farmers in Germany in the 1820s began making "wooden brooms and fly-whisks" during the winter months for sale, they found that using young women to sell their wares during the warmer months increased sales. The girls so employed would play the "hurdy gurdy"—an older string instrument that was said to resemble the bagpipe in sound but played by means of a hand-cranked wheel rubbing against the strings—while dancing. The hurdy gurdy instrument had fallen out of favor in the 1700s as it was considered vulgar, but then it experienced something of a comeback in the late seventeenth and the eighteenth centuries.[7]

The new marketing scheme worked, and the practice of using dancing girls to increase sales spread through other parts of Germany, then to England and France. In many places, the dancing became the dominant feature of the performances, instead of the instrument. The sales of brooms and whisks then ended as the dancers moved to America and other places outside their homelands. A male agent often negotiated with families to secure permission for the family's young women to travel and perform with him. The girls were then to send part of their earnings home, but the recruiters would take a good slice of their earnings.[8]

The hurdy gurdy dancers were usually young and attractive, and generally traveled in groups, sometimes in family groups. As they moved into the American West (and some boom towns of the East, including Maine—which had a booming lumber industry and some mining towns just as did the Trans-Mississippi West), the hurdy gurdy girls made their money by dancing with men in a direct exchange for money. As the decades passed, other women entered the business, many with no ties to the older traditions of Europe, and the price per dance sometimes reached as high as seventy-five cents to one dollar per dance or dance session. Tickets were frequently used, and a session might last five to fifteen minutes. The dancer generally had to share her earnings with the owner of the bar or the dance hall where she performed, and would often be expected to encourage alcohol sales as well as to entertain the men, who generally far outnumbered women in the general population. Instruments might be played by the dancers, but they often played violins or, more likely in terms of the style, fiddles, which the hurdy gurdy itself did resemble except for the crank-wheel and covered strings. And the fiddles might be played by people other than the dancers, generally by male musicians. The women's partners were often rambunctious and sometimes lifted the young women up in the air as they danced.[9]

The young women were generally pictured with their hair long and down, sometimes with puffed sleeves, sometimes with bare arms, their tops were generally low cut and their skirts calf-length, and their attire altogether was often considered scandalous. The women frequently wore makeup, sometimes dyed their hair, and their cleavage was evident. In some places, they may have had more of a peasant-type dress with a peculiar form of headdress one newspaper said looked like "the top-knot of a male turkey." The reporter thought it hideous.[10]

Yet, as author Jacquie Rogers, drawing on other research, has stated, "Hurdy gurdy girls were considered 'good women' by men, but usually not by 'respectable' ladies, the schoolmarms and bankers' wives of the town." As Idaho governor William McConnell expressed it in 1913, "These girls were pure women, who simply did the work they had bargained to do." And, he stated, "The[se] poor girls, and they danced only because they were poor, had kind hearts and wonderful patience and forbearance." What he did not explicitly state but did imply was that what the women had to endure was both the condemnation of the wider culture and the clumsy attentions of the men.[11]

Another source, the *Sentinel*, focusing on the Cariboo gold rush in British Columbia, concurred that the dancers were "from 'poor' but honest parents and normally speaking, are not what they are generally put down for."[12] And the male author did not seem to mean "put down at the end of a dance for." As the years passed, more and more assumptions were made that the women were prostitutes, and in some cases this may have been true. However, dance halls sometimes had rules to try to safeguard the women both physically and from slander, including forbidding the girls from accompanying the patrons to their lodgings, forbidding any fighting, mandating that they all appear on the stage after a show or dance session, and requiring that they secure permission to leave their house (hence, they could not easily disappear with a customer). In some ways, their living situation sounds a bit like those of the young women and girls employed in textile mills in the East. The hurdy gurdy girls and their experiences had their counterparts in Maine, in the state's many saloons and more disreputable dance halls, be the female dancers called "hurdy gurdy girls" or not.

In Maine, there were dance halls from at least the mid-nineteenth century. Exactly what dances the women who worked in them performed is largely unknown, but they were clearly there and clearly a concern of local populations. City and town directories generally did not list dance halls—which, in the timber producing regions, might be considered quite similar to those in the western camps and young settlements where the hurdy gurdy girls performed. Women did dance for woodsmen and for sailors and shipbuilders along the Atlantic coast and along the larger rivers of Maine, and some for pay, but detailed evidence is scarce. One newspaper (the *Bangor Daily Whig & Courier*), however, indicated that hurdy gurdy girls did come to Maine and made at least an appearance or two in the early 1880s. Other dancers may have shared the same forms of dance and pay but were not identified specifically as hurdy gurdy girls. In the case of lumbering, some women might have gone to the camps to perform, but the population in any one camp or settlement was fairly small, and the evidence for this is lacking. However, men often traveled the rivers down or "over to" places like Bangor, which supported a larger year-round population and saw large numbers of sailors and lumbermen coming in regularly, and their antics appeared in local papers continually.[13]

In the larger cities, although they might not be found in directories, dance halls and saloons clearly existed by the mid-1800s and were often associated in the public mind with prostitution. Bangor had its "Devil's Half Acre" with numerous saloons, dancing halls, and houses of prostitution, and Portland had its waterfront area—portions of it now known as the Old Port—which sported some of the same types of "immoral activities." Arrests for some of the women of the dance halls or saloons appear in local police records.[14]

Other Maine towns and settlements, especially those where large numbers of single men—or men away from their families—lived or visited undoubtedly saw women dancing in their midst, and not just the accepted dance forms that existed prior to and during the 1800s. The coastline of Maine with its shipping activities, and the northern woods with their lumbering industries, were particularly open to such activities. The trains also brought in more customers, and dancers, by the last third of the century. Although the vast majority of women discussed herein were women simply looking for a way to make a living, a few probably did enter the nether regions of stripping and, as is discussed later, prostitution.[15]

Augustus King of Portland fits into a broad spectrum of issues in Maine related to rum and other forms of alcohol—especially beer—during the 1800s, as well as to working-class dance women and prostitution. Maine legally became a dry state in 1846, via legislation that would be strengthened a few years later. The 1846 law sought to end sales of liquor in Maine, but liquor remained widely available in one form or another just the same. Medicinal alcohol remained legal under the new laws, and some people made use of this loophole, while others smuggled alcohol in or made it on their own.[16] Houses of ill repute were notorious for violating the liquor law, and, of course, were themselves illegal. Dance halls were essentially suspect no matter their other possible connections.

Augustus King, like the more well-known—and a bit later—Fan Jones farther north in Bangor, owned a Maine brothel. The clientele of his brothel, as was true for Jones's, included sailors. Both were located near the waterfront, Jones's not far from the Penobscot River, King's just up the hill from the ocean in Portland. Unlike Jones's, however, King's brothel included a dance hall or, rather, the dance hall was supposedly his true business, and the prostitution business was purportedly conducted nearby, in a hotel and sometimes in the so-called dance hall or King's house. The two endeavors had a rather shady obfuscation, with the dance hall purportedly being the legitimate business while prostitutes and sailors and other men spilled from the one into the squalid hotel next door. King's businesses were located on Munjoy Hill, in a neighborhood later demolished to secure gravel and fill for city streets.[17]

The dance or prostitution business was not always peaceful. On July 4, 1849, a group of seamen created a disturbance at the dance hall, and King supposedly ran them off by shooting at them. Three weeks later, the men returned and fired five cannon balls into his house. King, his wife, and their child were sleeping together in one bed, and one of the cannon balls crashed through its headboard. On September 7, sailors returned yet again. This time there was a larger number of men involved, and they attacked King's business with a swivel cannon. King returned fire, and as one local newspaper, the *Eastern Argus* noted, "In a better cause he would be quite a hero." In this instance, the editor wrote more than once that the events on the hill were a "Disgraceful Outrage."[18]

King might not have been a hero—although his actions may indeed have protected some working girls from rape and other violence, and the *Argus* even noted that he asserted that "Providence" was protecting him and his house, and "he bears himself as a martyr rather than an offender"— but he was unique on the landscape. King had settled in Portland with his white wife, but he was a black man or, as the paper identified him, "this colored man who unquestionably has been keeping a house of prostitution on Munjoy."[19] The paper seldom mentioned the dance hall portion of King's business in its coverage of the attacks and counterattacks.

When he returned fire in September, King did so in earnest and wounded fourteen men and killed one. King's "Disgraceful Outrage" was discussed for a couple of days running by the newspaper, as it sought to sort out just what had happened. At first, in spite of the offended tone of its coverage and not knowing the severity of the damage, the paper in a sense joked about the event, stating rather tongue in cheek that "it is high time this amusement in experimental gunnery was abated.

The authorities better see to it at once—our notoriety in this matter is unavoidable."[20] Certainly it did make Portland seem a bit like a frontier city, which in some ways it still was.

The *Argus* reiterated the events the next day, September 9, after the severity of the September 7 exchange was known, including the death of one of the men who had attacked King's place. The *Argus* reminded readers that two months previously, when his house was attacked, King had fired back with buckshot, and stated that when the men returned they had placed their cannon in close range of King's "den" and "came within an inch of destroying several lives in the house." The guilty parties, in terms of the cannon shots, had not been apprehended to date. However, the *Argus* asserted, "Still King continued his nefarious mode of livelihood" even though "he ought to at once [been] taken in hand by the authorities." Instead, the previous Friday, the "second round of this tragedy" had started.[21]

On that Friday, "some sea-faring men, belonging to coasters lying in the harbor," had gone to King's establishment in the late afternoon or early evening, and had some further disagreement with King. They returned later looking to fight, and King had fired on them and wounded two of their number. A fire alarm was sounded, people rushed to see what was happening, and King, the paper stated, started firing on the crowd, irrespective of who was friend and who was foe. Several young men were wounded. One was initially presumed dead, but he apparently survived. However, before midnight, the attackers regrouped, secured a swivel cannon and powder, "and they fired two broadside" into King's house. King and a couple of cohorts returned fire, were able to take control of the cannon, and kept firing until "the besiegers withdrew from the Hill." While the fight was on, however, a Captain Snow had gone to the scene to find his men and was wounded so severely that he died that morning. His schooner soon left port, even before the coroner could be brought in, "with colors half-mast."[22]

Another local paper, the *Portland Advertiser*, also published news of the events. Not only did it note that several people had been wounded in the foray, it stated too that "a young lad . . . was shot badly in the back, and one of the women in the house received a shot in the arm, and a colored relative of King had the ends of his fingers shot away." The paper noted that part of the crowd drove the "occupants from one of the houses, stove in the windows and doors, and, ripping open the straw beds, set the straw on fire." Those small fires were extinguished "without doing material damage." But another portion of the crowd, "finding the victory still doubtful, proceeded to the wharves, where they obtained a 6 pounder iron gun," and brought it to the houses, where King and a few of "King's adherents" remained, loaded the gun with stones, and shot it at the house two or three times, by which time King and the others had purportedly abandoned the property. The original crowd, the paper noted, was comprised primarily of sailors, and they had acted out of a "spirit of revenge" after being shot upon from King's or a neighboring house. After King and his "adherents" had left the house, they had "skulked round in the outskirts of the crowd and fired whenever they got an opportunity." Many of the wounded had been wounded rather far from King's establishment, some down on Congress Street about a quarter of a mile from King's place.[23] The mayhem had not been contained to its original site.

A crowd gathered on the Hill Saturday afternoon, according to the *Argus*, and at about 3:00 the city marshal and his deputies arrived and arrested King "and a co-adjuror named Thomas." The marshal and his men also arrested "five bad girls, inmates of the house." The girls were taken to the House of Corrections (a common New England institution in those days, where people who did not present a severe threat were housed). The *Portland Advertiser* stated that eight women had been arrested or removed from the two houses, along with King and his father-in-law. On Saturday afternoon, according to the *Argus* in its minute-by-minute coverage, rumor was circulating that "the bad houses in that vicinity will be razed tonight." For the good of the city, the paper hoped that no such violation of law and order would occur.[24]

Occur, however, they did. Or, at least one did. A mob assembled on Munjoy Hill, and in its notes from 6:00 p.m., the *Argus* noted, "The incendiary's torch has been applied to King's Dance Hall, (near his house) and it is now in flames." According to the *Advertiser*, both the dance hall and King's home had been attacked, the one set afire and the other had its windows smashed and sustained other damages.[25] (There was no mention of what happened to any dancers who might have remained therein.) The mob fought back both the police and the firemen who tried to intervene. The crowd wanted to set fire to King's house also but was forcibly restrained. By this time, the mob was estimated to number in the thousands, as people had continued to rush up the hill to see what was happening. The Portland Light Infantry (which had only recently been established and which just days before had marched through the streets showing off their new uniforms as part of a ceremony celebrating their organization[26]) was then called out to help local police quell the riot, later known as the Whorehouse Riot of 1849. "Missiles thrown by the crowd" injured some of the soldiers, and various other people were wounded as well. The following morning, Sunday, the fire continued to burn—a rather demented beacon upon a hill—as people continued to wander up to see the destruction.[27]

The *Bangor Daily Whig & Courier* (*BDW&C*) covered the news from Portland on its news page—the paper had essentially one of its four pages devoted to "news" at the time—and these entries were often "bullets" of a sort, brief pieces with a hand and finger pointing at the news paragraph. "The Riots in Portland" received more space than most state items, the longer items generally dealing with political or national issues. The paper stated that "On Saturday King and an accomplice named Thomas were arrested and committed to jail. Five girls were also arrested and sent to the House of Correction." The paper, whose news brief came from a Portland source, did not categorize the girls as "bad" as had the *Argus*, but did note their arrests along with the men's, as well as stating that the fire had been discovered at about 6:00 p.m., and that "in the evening a mob of about 1,000 or more assembled, intending to pull down King's house." Accompanied by the sheriff and the mayor, the police had been able to disperse the crowd without any further acts of violence, "further than the throwing of some volleys of stones, by which, is stated, a few of the soldiers were hurt, though not very seriously." The *Portland Umpire*, a short-lived city newspaper, further noted that "the temperate but firm course of the authorities reflects much credit on them, and gives assurance that mob law will not be permitted to rule in our city."[28]

After his release from jail, King left the state, never—as far as is known—to return. The *Advertiser* was pleased to report on September 17 that King's house had been sold. According to the paper:

> *We have learned that the house and land on Munjoy belonging to Mr. King that has been the source of the late disturbances, has been purchased by Chas. Q. Clapp Esq. King will not again occupy the premises. Our city is thus relieved of the fear of further disturbances on account of this obnoxious place, and hope that we shall hear of no more violations of order and law under pretenses of punishing this odious offender.*[29]

In the short term, the *Advertiser* would be granted its wish, but the Whorehouse Riot of 1849 would have something of a sequel in another mob revolt involving a dance hall almost a century later.[30]

Maine was in some ways still a frontier state in the 1840s, especially its northern and western sections. As one quip in the *BDW&C* noted in May 1849:

> *The Kennebec papers caution people to beware not to expose themselves to highway robbers on the road between the two sister villages of Augusta and Hallowell. It is very kind to give the warning but it would be better to maintain a watch until the danger be removed.*[31]

Individuals taking measures to protect their own property were not unheard of at the time Augustus King took matters into his own hands. Augusta, Maine, did not become the state capitol until 1827 and in 1849 was still considered a village. By 1890, Augusta would have a little over

10,500 residents and then grow to almost 11,700 people in 1900, whereas Bangor had over 19,000 people in 1890 and almost 22,000 in 1900, plus 3,000 to 4,000 more people lived just across the river in Brewer. Portland had over 36,000 people in 1890, and by 1900 some 50,000 people lived in Portland while another 6,000 people resided in South Portland. Lewiston had over 21,000 people by 1890 with another 11,000 people living across the river in Auburn. Houlton's population in northern Maine was about that of Brewer, where Ellsworth and the Downeast coastal communities had fewer people than Houlton. The Portland and Bangor regions had the largest population bases when one included the surrounding towns and cities, and generally attracted the largest share of working-class dance industries in the 1800s and into the 1900s and beyond. The Lewiston–Auburn area, perhaps because of its purportedly more conservative culture for much of the era but also because one could take the trains and other vehicles down to Portland and Old Orchard Beach quite easily, did see dancers perform throughout the period, but not in the numbers one might otherwise have expected based on its population.[32]

Saloons, taverns, and dance halls dotted the Maine landscape. However, Augustus King had the distinction of defending what appears to have been a bordello, and what certainly was a dance hall, one where women clearly were paid to dance for or with the men. Yet King's may not have been the first dance hall—although it may well have been the first of its type—to be established by an African American on Munjoy Hill. By at least the 1830s, according to one source, there existed a "Negro Dance Hall" on Munjoy Hill. No details were provided. Years later, the Kemp family, some of whose members had escaped slavery in the South, would perform songs, dances, and skits in Maine and other New England locations. Soon thereafter, when vaudeville arrived, numerous black entertainers, including female dancers, would appear in the state. None, however, would become as notorious as Augustus King and his female dancers, except, perhaps, the women at the center of a 1943 riot.[33] However, many famed black musicians and singers would bring their talents to Maine, to vaudeville houses, theaters, dance halls, and clubs.

Even after the riot on Munjoy Hill, Portland had problems with lawlessness. Perhaps augmented by events on Munjoy, as reported in Portland and Bangor, "The number of criminal cases before the Municipal Court, Portland, since January last, thus far exceeds four hundred, being larger than the number for the whole year previous." A number of men were arrested involving the events on the hill, but certainly many others swelled the number of prosecutable cases to that number of four hundred.[34]

Elsewhere, while King was having his original skirmish with the sailors in July 1849, other people in the state were more concerned with the cholera epidemic, especially in Bangor where cholera killed some 258 people in 1849 alone. The *BDW&C* published accounts every day it published (six days per week) on the latest death tolls and the numbers of cases as reported by the city health officer, and Portland covered the epidemic as well, publishing some of the Bangor deaths as well as those in other states. These reports would continue to come in subsequent years, as disease continued to exert a high toll on the population. Other news items were upcoming elections and the celebrations held for the Fourth of July, which in Bangor included a march by local youth and those who might wish to join them, a talk and a song on temperance, a performance by the Bangor Brass Band, and in Portland, fireworks were set off from Munjoy Hill—not far from King's establishment—after a procession through the major streets ended on Munjoy.[35]

What all Maine newspapers reported continually were arrests for drunkenness, even though a general prohibition on alcohol had started in Maine even before the 1849 events on Munjoy Hill. Events such as the Whorehouse or Dance Hall Riot only strengthened the desire of prohibitionists to crack down harder on those who drank and those who supplied alcohol to them. Calls for cleaning up disreputable houses and strengthening the 1846 liquor law resulted in the passage in 1851 of what became known as the Maine Law, considered the first truly statewide prohibition law in the nation and one upon which numerous other states modeled their prohibition legislation. Americans drank an astounding amount of alcohol in the 1800s, as they had in the 1700s, and, not surprisingly, problems with enforcing prohibition continued, especially with farmers and others continuing to produce hard cider and wine from apples, and skirting the law in other ways. The Maine Law allowed for the production and sales of "mechanical" and "medicinal" liquor, which produced a few more loopholes. In addition, corruption was not unheard of, even within the various law enforcement agencies. More than one supposed Maine law-keeper in the 1800s was discovered seizing liquor from citizens and then reselling it for personal profit, and others were accused of shaking down citizens who legitimately possessed medicinal alcohol prescribed by a physician and provided by the city agent of their community.[36]

Following the "Portland rum riot" in 1855, in which anti-prohibitionists stormed City Hall thinking that leading prohibition advocate and politician Neal Dow was illegally selling legal alcohol stored in the basement, resulting in the death of one person and the wounding of several others, the Maine Law was repealed but then reenacted in 1885. In the meantime, yet more saloons and liquor out-lets (including pharmacies or apothecaries) had opened up; even after 1885, the saloons, taverns, and other hospitality establishments were never truly suppressed in providing patrons with spirits. For a time, under the so-called Bangor Law, saloon keepers and the like would pay a large "fine" every year and then nonchalantly carry on selling liquor.[37] And prohibition in Maine resulted, among other things, in concerns that women and men were drinking in the dance halls and other venues where women performed. As in drinking, just what was moral—or, in some cases, legal—was not always clear when it came to female performers.

Part of the problem with the very existence of female dancers in the late 1800s was simply that even if fully covered in terms of the amount of skin showing, they were still scandalously underdressed in terms of traditional female attire. Schools of women's "hygiene" and "fitness" sprang up concerning just how constricting the middle-class and upper-class garments of the day were. Women wore five, six, seven, or even eight layers of clothing on their lower bodies, as well as rigid corsets that constricted them yet further, in the mid- to late 1800s. Some young girls (many already outfitted with corsets) could not even lift their arms above their heads, according to one study.[38] Underskirts and outer dresses dragged on the floor, and sometimes in the mud and filth of city streets, although the women avoided this as much as possible. And most of the lower body garments were "fastened" by overlapping layers of fabric, making the layers around the waist number ten to sixteen, and sometimes more. Corsets constricted not only the waist and upper hips but also the rib cage. In addition, women often wore fake hair—wigs and "rats"—that often hid their natural tresses, creating further problems with hygiene and sometimes obscuring even the shape of their heads. In order to dance anything but the most acceptable quadrilles and waltzes (in the mid-1800s, still a little less acceptable), a woman simply *had to* take off some of that clothing and fake hair.

By the late 1800s, however, not all dancing was deemed disreputable, and those who wished to learn the acceptable social dances, while properly attired, could take lessons. In 1867, in Portland, one could study dance with Joseph Craig or with George Wilson. By 1908, Wilson's, located at 519 Congress Street, advertised dancing and deportment lessons. Twelve lessons for female beginners cost $3.00; for "gentlemen" the price was $5.00. At the same time, in Bangor, one could study dance at the Memorial Parlors on Main Street with Miss Emily F. Lee, or at Society Hall with "Pullen's Classes in Dancing." At least one more option also existed.[39]

Advertising for dancing schools was not common, so it is difficult to ascertain just how many there were in a city except where they showed up in city and town directories. By 1907, for example, when the city directories began to include them, there were three dance instructors listed in Bangor. However, dancing societies, which no doubt helped members and guests learn formal dances, existed long before 1900 in the Bangor area, just as they did in southern Maine. For example, in the Bangor region, a dancing society was established by the late 1830s such that by 1868 the Bangor Dancing Fraternity was able to issue a certificate for an

"Honorary and Diploma Member" card to John Martin in April 1868 for "30 years' service as a Benefactor." John Martin was actually one of the founders of the fraternity, which admitted women to its affairs. He was considered an "avid dancer" who worked primarily as an accountant and a shopkeeper. And he recorded many of his life experiences. Martin's dance repertoire—and one no doubt shared by his dancing contemporaries— included "waltzes, polkas, schottisches, and other new forms of dance," according to the Maine Historical Society.[40]

That dancing schools and societies existed is important in that although some female dancers made up their dances or performed folk-type dances in Maine's taverns, dancing halls, and other stages during the 1800s, as did some men, some had studied the more traditional dance forms and then taken them (or versions of them) to other venues. This would also be true in the 1900s and beyond, and, in the last few decades of the 1800s, a montage of changes in the dance world developed in America, or came to America and then changed, including the dancing styles and clothing the hurdy gurdy girls had brought with them.

That there were many, many saloons in Maine in the late 1800s into the early 1900s is evident. And they were not just in the larger cities such as along the Portland waterfront and on its Munjoy Hill. For example, in 1868, the year John Martin was issued his "membership card" (and after the 1856 repeal of prohibition), there were nineteen saloons listed in Bangor alone. There was a slight decline in those listed in city directories a decade later, but in 1890 (after prohibition was reinstated) there were forty-three listed, in 1895 there were fifty-three, and by 1901 Bangor had at least sixty-five saloons. Most of the saloons in Bangor were located along the waterfront and in the downtown area, the same area that housed the infamous "Devil's Half-Acre," the prostitution business. Not all the women who frequented the area were prostitutes and not all the men were "Johns"; some just went to the area to have fun, drink, and to dance. Many were lumbermen and sailors, but citizens of the city also went to the saloons as well as the brothels. Arrests for public intoxication, immoral acts, and disturbing the peace were common. Unfortunately, as noted, just which dances the women were performing for money is unknown, but there were concerns that women performed lurid or indecent dances. And police had a hard time keeping track of all the activities in all the saloons.[41]

Hurdy gurdy girls did make at least one big appearance in Maine in the early 1880s: They danced in Bangor. This was later echoed when a play about the hurdy gurdy girls opened a new season at the newly renovated Bangor Opera House in 1907. The playwright had undertaken his project when a song had come into his possession some three years earlier about the hurdy gurdy girls. When Bangorites and visitors came to watch "the hurdy gurdy girl and her companions" in 1907, they came, the *Bangor Daily News* reported, to see "plenty of good-looking girls, with plenty of fine clothes (not much of a great plenty, either), bright music, and all the fun that can be stirred into the mixture." *The Hurdy Gurdy Girl* of 1907 was a musical comedy.[42] The hurdy gurdy girls of the 1800s may have offered comedy, they did offer dance performances and chances to dance with them, and they did present a costume of sorts to those who wanted to dance or just to watch.

Another possible venue at which hurdy gurdy girls (or some version thereof) might have performed was at the fair: at the Eastern Maine Fair held in Bangor; the Waterville, Lewiston, or Skowhegan State Fairs of the late 1800s; the New England Fair in Portland; as well as the smaller fairs throughout the state. Circuses also came to town, and some offered female dancers. Of the fairs and circuses, the Eastern Maine Fair in particular allowed various types of dancers to perform, often under the cover of the tents on the midway. Some midway dances were deemed respectable, others were not. Of the circuses, one that came to town in 1897 may serve as an example.

The *Bangor Daily Whig & Courier* and other Maine newspapers were just beginning to offer space to "amusements" as they were generally called in the late 1890s. Paid advertisements had been available before then, but they generally provided few details. In 1897, however, a bit of space was turned over to one circus that came through Maine. In 1897, not long before the Eastern Maine Fair opened, the "Adam Forepaugh & Sells Brothers' Greatest Shows Consolidated" circus came to town. James A. Bailey, "Sole Owner [of] the Barnum & Bailey Greatest Show on Earth," sent in a testimonial stating that the Forepaugh & Sells Circus "is the only Big or First-Class Exhibition of the kind that can or will visit any section of New England this year." Of course, lesser shows might have visited Maine that year, as well as previously. In the days before the show opened, "Great Train Loads of Exclusive Features" came into Bangor carrying the various animal and human acts. A plethora of animal acts came, including "3—Great Herds of performing Elephants—3," "the only trained sea lions and seals in the world," "two horned Sumatra rhinoceros," "black-maned lions," and the "snow white polar bear." All "1001" attractions of the show apparently came to Bangor. Human acts included clowns and a Japanese "circus." Unfortunately, few other mentions of humans, including dancers, appeared in advertising for the circus. Seating capacity was 15,000.[43]

The circus received press just as the fairs did, but less of it. Over 300 people came from the Caribou and Fort Fairfield area alone for the big show, and attendance overall was high. The trapeze and high-wire acts were particularly popular, including a woman who "danced" on a high wire, as well as other women performing on the trapeze and in aerial acts.[44] Although not generally perceived by later generations as "dancing," contemporaries did see many of the aerial artists as dancers, and they certainly employed dance moves, and almost everyone in the state had a chance to see such dance art performed.

At the same time that the circus came to Bangor, the New England Fair opened in Portland, at Rigby Park, running from August 16 to August 21 in 1897. It featured many of the same types of attractions of the Bangor and other Maine state fairs, but a rivalry of sorts had sprung up between the cities of Portland and Lewiston. The state fair currently (in the late 1890s) located at Lewiston had previously been moved there from Portland, and Portland wanted the fair back. In the meantime, the New England Fair proved popular with an estimated crowd of 20,000 on its governor's day, when the governor and other officials visited. Other days saw 15,000 to 20,000 visitors. The fair offered numerous circuslike events, as well as other entertainments. One of these entertainments was clog dancing, which both women and men performed.[45]

Then, the Eastern Maine State Fair opened in Bangor on August 31, 1897. It billed in advance its "high-wire walking" and "blindfold trapeze act," as well as a "blood–curdling slide for life" in which a woman would slide diagonally to the earth from 100 feet in the air, harnessed only by a collar around her neck. The advertising overall was for acts much like those featured at the fair in Portland, and indeed, many of them likely were the exact acts, including the clog dancing in the "Irish Village," which had housed the dancers in Portland also, and various military performances and a parade by the "F Troop" or "Troop F" of the US Cavalry. The fair included a number of "song and dance" routines. A vaudeville performance would also be staged at City Hall during every evening of the fair, and vaudeville meant women, not just men, and generally dancing women at that. Bicycle and horse races, poultry exhibits and art displays, ascending balloons and fireworks, would be present, and there would be a band concert every night. Advertising suggested that the fair had added such acts just recently, building upon the agricultural aspects present from the start of the fair in the early 1880s. The midway would offer "amusing entertainment and is expected to cover considerable territory," the *BDW&C* announced. In addition, the fairgrounds at Bangor's Maplewood Park had undergone some renovations. A large contingent of people was expected to come up from Bar Harbor, as well as thousands of visitors from throughout northern and central Maine.[46]

In 1897, the Maine State Fair at Lewiston opened on August 30, while the Maine State Fair in Bangor opened on the 31st. The estimated peak of attendance at the Lewiston Fair reached about 5,000 people on opening day, while that in Bangor was higher. On governor's day in Lewiston, an estimated 20,000 came to the fair; in Bangor, September 1 saw perhaps 30,000 people on the grounds. Steamships and trains brought large crowds to Bangor, while buckboards poured in from the countryside, and carriages brought some city people into the gates. On the midway, as the people passed by, the fakirs called out "persuasive and eloquent," selling both goods and entertainment. The promised vaudeville troupe performed at the grandstand on governor's day in Bangor with a crowd of roughly 18,000 to 20,000 people on the grounds.[47]

The largest continuously held state fair in Maine at the time, the Bangor or Eastern Maine State Fair, established in the early 1880s, had, by the mid-1890s and possibly from the get-go, had female dancers perform—if not in the more respectable auditorium and exhibit areas, then on the midway. Unfortunately, details once again remain scarce. The local papers did not devote much coverage to the "lesser" entertainment acts into the 1890s. However, it is clear from the coverage of the fair in 1899 that something less than respectable had been going on. In 1899, a year that also brought vaudeville to the region in a new way, the *BDW&C* and the fair's management apparently believed that it was worth informing the public about what would *not* be happening on the midway that year. The newspaper reported, "The spaces along the 'Mid-Way' have nearly all been let to the fakirs. There will be no 'houchie couchee' dances *this year* [emphasis added]. There will be plenty of fun to make the 'Mid-Way' interesting without vulgarity." One amusement mentioned specifically was "the merry-go-round, that never ending source of pleasure to both young and old." Also to be included was a vaudeville show from—or at least arranged in—Boston.[48]

The Bangor State Fair was highly touted for its horse racing and agricultural exhibits, but other forms of entertainment had long been offered, including more recently, "houchie couchee" dancers. The much-heralded "Scenes in the Klondike" of 1899, featuring scenes from the Klondike mining operations and "camp life," might also have included hurdy gurdy girls or similar dancers, as they were widely present on the western mining frontier. However, they were not discussed in fair advertisements or coverage. The local paper did say that "the midway is extensive and will be vociferous." It would be in the tents of the midway that the "Little Egypts" and other "exotic" dancers would perform a few years later, if they had not done so already.[49]

By 1899 the Eastern Maine State Fair (or, more accurately, the city) had added fencing around the grounds such that one could visit the auditorium and its exhibits as well as the midway at one price, and readily move from one to the other more easily, and with less scrutiny, or so it might seem. In addition, as was true for previous years, the Maine Central Railroad brought special trains filled with visitors from its routes encompassing Mt. Desert Island, Aroostook, Bucksport, and other locations. The regular trains from other railroads, plus streetcars, also brought in fair-goers, as did ships—largely steamships—and private boats and yachts. The governor of the state, some of his aides, and other politicians visited the fair on governor's day, and in 1899 an estimated 10,000 people attended the fair on that day.[50]

The "houchie couchee" dancers referred to in 1899 may have performed at the fair the year before, or earlier. Unfortunately, the dancers were located along the midway, and little notice was given of such performances. As noted, newspapers were just beginning to provide details in general. However, the *BDW&C* did note in 1898 that the midway was "extensive and the fakirs are humorous. They are an entertainment in themselves and their orations would go down in history as epics of the fair if they could be reduced to manuscript and cold type." It was often the fakirs—the barkers as a later generation would call them—who drew people into the tents where generally sanctioned—but sometimes not—performances took place. (The "fakirs" of the fairs were not the holy fakirs of other cultures, but rather the appellation seems taken from the "fake" or "swindling" meaning of the word.[51])

Held at Bangor's Maplewood Park, the 1898 fair did feature "The Famous Japanese Troya from Mikado Land." The group may have offered dancing performances but was more gymnastically oriented, according to fair coverage. At least two women performed gymnastic routines at the fair. No acts billed or advertised individually were referred to specifically as Eastern, Oriental, or "hoochie couchie." The paper did note that one "Princess of the Tarrantines" appeared on the midway that year, but this may well have been a young Penobscot performer who would eventually travel much of the nation to great acclaim.[52]

In the late 1890s, the midway was lighted at night, the Bangor Band played, manned balloons often made ascents, and fireworks exploded. Police roamed the premises, but opportunities for indecorous acts continued to exist, as the 1899 statement that "there will be no 'houchie couchee' dances *this year*" implied. And, if they had not already visited, within a few years there would indeed be dancers of the hootchie-cootchie (the preferred spelling) at the fair. With an estimated crowd of 15,000 people on one day alone at the 1898 fair, not every tent could be closely monitored. And, just after the Bangor Fair closed, the Skowhegan Fair began, so any dancers appearing at the one may well have appeared at the other. So, too, did the Waterville Fair open within days.[53]

Although some women traveled into the state to perform, some Maine working-class dancers performed their own styles of dance, their own traditional dances, just as the hurdy gurdy girls had brought theirs to the towns they visited. As the American West continued to open to nonnative peoples in the 1800s, the interest in native peoples grew. Although their communities were frequently decimated, and some tribes were relocated to smaller and smaller (and less desirable) plots of land and later to reservations, nonnatives became fascinated with native life. In the American West, trains would be decorated with native motifs, and Native American women clothed in some semblance of traditional dress were hired to serve and entertain in the deluxe cars. P. T. (Phineas Taylor) Barnum included native exhibits in his museum from the 1840s on, and he incorporated female dancers of different genres into his shows. He added Native American dance acts specifically to his shows by the 1860s, as well as including them when he opened his famed circus in the early 1870s to take his various acts on the road. Likewise, he included native and other dancers in his Wild West Show established in the early 1880s. This interest spread, and various other shows and later films exploited this interest. On their end, Native Americans sometimes participated in such performances out of economic necessity.[54]

In Maine, the four tribes of the state—the Micmac, Passamaquoddy, Penobscot, and Maliseet—found themselves subjects of interest as the fascination for natives in the West extended to the Eastern tribes as well. Members of the Wabanaki or Abanaki tribes participated in some traveling shows by the 1840s, often using them as venues to sell their medicinal herbs, baskets, and other traditional goods. Although the Passamaquoddy were known for their musical and dance talent, the most active of the Abanaki tribes of Maine in the entertainment business were the Penobscot of Old Town and Indian Island.[55] The state's most well-known female Native American dancer to date was a member of the Penobscot nation, as was a singer and dancer who became most celebrated as a vocalist.

In the 1840s, Penobscot Frank Loring ("Chief Big Thunder")—in addition to signing up with P. T. Barnum's museum in New York City for several months along with his sisters—served as an agent, first signing up a Micmac and then a Penobscot group to tour in a traveling show in which he himself also acted. A few years after Loring took his show on the road, Penobscot member Clara Neptune performed in some of the country's early vaudeville shows. Then, near the turn of the century, Lucy Nicolar (also spelled Nicola and less often as Nicholas), performing under the name Princess Watawaso or Watahwaso, sang her way from the East Coast to Chicago and was highly received at every entertainment hall along the way.[56] She also danced.

Native Americans appeared at local fairs by the 1890s, and in 1898 an exhibit at the Eastern Maine Fair, just down the river from the Penobscot nation, included an "Indian camp" and an "Indian wigwam" made of birch bark. The local press reported, too, that "The Indian Girl, Miss. Nicolar, and Mrs. Joe Nicolar," both "received much attention." Miss "Nicolar" may well have been Lucy Nicolar, or one of her sisters, and she may well have been the young woman billed at the fair that year as the "Princess of the Tarrantines," the Tarrantines being a name given local peoples (both

Micmac and Penobscot) during the earliest days of European exploration and settlement in what would become the state of Maine. Unfortunately, the paper did not note if the young woman sang or danced, or exactly what she and the other Native Americans did at the fair. Evidence suggests that they were demonstrating native life, likely selling some of their handiwork, and offering entertainment, perhaps musical or dance. The Nicolar family of Indian Island did sell their baskets to tourists in Kennebunkport on a regular basis during the era.[57]

Moreover, tourists found their way to Indian Island (visitors had to ferry across the Penobscot River to reach the island, which had a population of about 400 people in 1900) and, more frequently, to Old Town by the first decade of the 1900s if not earlier. They would "reward" Penobscot dancers with change and sometimes—for children—candy. According to anthropologist and author Bunny McBride's work, one Penobscot, who was a child in the early 1900s, stated, "Tourists used to come across to the island on the bateau. We'd be waiting for them, and we'd start dancing as soon as they got close. We'd get candy and small change." Various road shows, early vaudeville acts, and then filmmakers also made it to Old Town and the island to sign up promising talent, including dancers. Various acts, including dancers, performed there. Summers on Indian Island especially became "the season of road shows and ballyhoo"—ballyhoo being a term used by at least one local woman to describe not just the dancing but the whole buildup behind it, including trumped-up advertising and often unauthentic native costumes.[58] Native American women, not just men and children, became part of the dancers-for-money shows in Maine and elsewhere in the 1800s and the 1900s at the same time as locals were able to see entertainers from far away perform their acts. How many Native Americans and Abanaki men, women, and children performed through these venues is unknown, like so many things about the working-class dances of the era, but exist and dance they certainly did.

While Native Americans brought their arts to America, and in particular to Maine, in some cases the changes in dance came from far away. For example, ballet was first seen by the American public in general in the mid-1800s. Women ballet dancers were by then traditional in some European countries, but not in America. Their tights and tutus, although often covering the dancers' legs down to the knee, still revealed more than most American audiences were used to seeing. And, more importantly for working-class women, once ballet started to appear in less-populated American cities as well as traveling in some spectacular shows presented by circuses and via other venues, local women were often hired to fill out the ranks of the dance or chorus line. They were dressed as dancers but had little training except for the drills and brief lessons given to them by people sent out by a given company in advance. Being hired to perform in the chorus line was generally deemed unrespectable, even as ballet's lead dancers began to earn some respectability.[59]

These less respected women—sometimes disparagingly called "ballet girls"—and those who simply wished to have more freedom in their dance and lives would often transition into vaudeville or to other forms or venues of dance, also initially seen as morally questionable. At the same time, some women took ballet and other moves and made them their own, without the years of training a Russian or other European ballet company would have demanded of them, added more sinuous motions, and—especially when presented with materials and ideas from other cultures—created something new.

Two working-class women illustrate part of what was happening in the American dance world in the late 1800s. Ruth "St." Denis (the "St." added by her impoverished religious mother, partly in view of Ruth's pursuit of various religion-inspired dances) was one of them. Born in the rural East Coast, St. Denis danced in vaudeville in the 1890s—which increasingly celebrated the female solo dancer—then developed a Japanese and theater-inspired "Madame Butterfly" dance, followed by her Hindu-based Nautch, snake, and Radha (an Indian girl loved by the god Krishna) dances after studying Hindus in New York circa 1905. (She had wanted to study Egyptian life and dance but could not finding a source for that, and realizing that most Americans lumped Egyptian and Hindu cultures together, she built several dances on what she knew of Hindu culture.) St. Denis next danced in Europe, developing a Nautch and a yogi dance there, and returned after three years to America.[60]

Isadora Duncan, a working-class daughter of the West Coast—who did have some training in dance through her family and was familiar with "Wild West" productions—performed as a fairy and a gypsy in a few New York theater performances, then developed her "little Greek tunic" circa 1897 and taught herself to emphasize the solar plexus or upper ribs in her dances, something that would have been much impeded by ten or twelve layers of clothing and a corset binding her ribcage. By the turn of the century, Duncan often performed these dances in a silk tunic. She, too, moved to Europe, as did St. Denis and a few other American female dancers in the 1890s and early 1900s, but Duncan elected not to return to American audiences.[61]

St. Denis and Duncan helped develop what would become known as "free," "interpretive," and later "modern" dance.[62] All of this makes defining exactly who was doing what in the late 1800s into the early 1900s even more difficult. Often, genres of dance overlapped greatly, as did the venues in which women, and sometimes men, performed them. And some women slipped from one dance form or venue to another.

Hurdy gurdy girls were paid by the dance; saloon dancers by the dance or through "tips" and perhaps offered money or lodging by the venue owners; Native Americans were paid by the dance or the appearance (and sometimes for a longer-running show tour); ballet chorus line dancers by the show or local tour; dancers of various sorts at local fairs could slip in and be paid by the money the barker brought in as well as by tips, or go on short-term tours for low salaries; and the taxi-dancers who came to public attention a few decades after the hurdy gurdy girls were going strong were paid by the dance, and their venue was generally not the isolated boom towns but instead the larger cities—although they did sometimes work in the lumbering and mining towns of the nation.

First, however, vaudeville came to Maine and the rest of America. It came to the cities and in a more limited way to rural areas. And it came to more than the Abanaki people—the "People of the Dawn"—and the "modern" dancers. It came in ways that the more limited shows of the 1800s had not seen. Vaudeville made an appearance before the turn of the century, but not in the way it would for the decades thereafter. Vaudeville was considered too risqué for women to attend as audience members in many places during the 1800s (but not as performers), but in the early 1900s that would change, at least until in some venues vaudeville became burlesque. And that, too, happened in Maine.

CHAPTER TWO

Scandal on the Stage
and the Search for Much More

*Early Vaudeville Comes to Maine, the Midways Beckon,
the "Wiggle Dance" Shocks, and Other Vice
Concerns of the Early 1900s*

VAUDEVILLE, FIRST SEEN IN THE 1800S, WOULD DEVELOP INTO THE all-time everything-in-one-show type of entertainment of its era during the early decades of the 1900s. Comedy, music, dance, magic, and human and animal tricks were all popular components. Eventually, some of the music and dancing would transition into burlesque, especially during certain years, with partial and sometimes almost total nudity either implied or presented. The nude or seminude entertainers, of course, were women. And the vaudeville acts that brought entertainers to various towns and cities in Maine provided the performers with subsistence living, if not something a level or two above that. Like the hurdy gurdy girls of previous years, and later the marathon women, many of these female performers would travel from place to place in order to make their living. And, especially late in the era of vaudeville, their work would make them objects of public censure, the most dramatic example of this being a riot that broke out in Portland in 1943, when the women dancers on stage did not do as the male audience anticipated: They did not take off all their clothes. In retaliation, close to 1,500 men tore up a theater and blocked city streets.

The riot of 1943 was far away in 1908, however, when a new theater offering vaudeville opened its doors in Portland. Keith's Theater opened that year and started advertising regularly in local papers. Located at 20 Preble Street, under manager James E. Moore, the venue purportedly suffered a few economic setbacks during its first year or so of operations but soon became one of the city's most popular venues. The managers of the Keith's line of vaudeville houses had helped make vaudeville more acceptable in the early 1900s and had promised to keep their shows "clean" in Maine[1]; however, in the following decades, vaudeville offerings would again become scandalous.

Keith's in Portland was part of the B. F. Keith Theater of Boston. Although some of its own early advertisements identified it as such, those references slipped away over the decades.[2] The early original building for the vaudeville house in Boston—the Boston Bijou Theater—started new operations on July 6, 1885, under Benjamin Franklin Keith and his then-partner Edward Franklin Albee II. Benjamin Keith of New Hampshire had had experience in museums and in the circus—including serving a stint in the more famous P. T. Barnum circus as well as in one or two others. At the Bijou Theater the two men (Albee had recently been engaged in selling circus tickets) adopted the "continuous variety show," which at the Bijou would operate from 10 a.m. to 11 p.m., every day and night. A patron could enter the theater at any time and simply stay until the show reached the point at which he or she had arrived.[3]

A few years later, in 1896, Keith and Albee secured the American rights to the *Lumiere Cinematographe*, and in June 1896 showed their first moving picture film at the new theater, the Union Square Theater in New York. They next opened theaters for their moving pictures in Boston and Philadelphia, and then established them throughout the East and in the Midwest, buying out competitors if necessary. In 1896 the two men signed a contract with Biograph Studios as their film supplier, and in 1905 switched to the Edison Studios for their films. (Thomas Edison was himself interested in dance and filmed a young Ruth St. Denis in an 1894, two-minute film or kinetoscope he called "Ruth Denis, Skirt

Dancer." She wore skirts and performed a variety of movements on stage, sometimes blending clog dancing, ballet steps, swirls, and curtsies together, which were popular in vaudeville in the 1890s.[4]) In June 1906, not long before Keith's in Portland, Maine, opened, vaudeville giants Keith and Albee joined their theater circuit with that of Frederick Freeman Proctor.[5] Keith's in Portland would see both vaudeville acts and movie offerings, often merging both in a combined presentation, especially as the years passed.

The entire Portland region celebrated the opening of the new Keith's in Maine. The venue advertised and received notice in various papers. In Lewiston, the *Dailey Sun* not only noted the opening of Keith's in Portland, it even carried a complete schedule for "**Keith's New Theater, Portland, Me.**" With the word "VAUDEVILLE" running alongside vertically, the paper listed every feature act on the venue's opening bill, as well as the theater's schedule. Keith's would hold a matinee daily at 2:30 p.m. and every evening at 8:15. Prices ranged from fifteen cents to fifty cents a ticket. Advance tickets would go on sale on Thursday, January 23, at 9:00 a.m. Keith's would hold its grand opening on January 27. Seven major acts were listed, and two of these starred women and at least one featured "dancing experts."[6] One could easily catch a train down to Portland to buy a ticket or to see the opening, or drive a car if one had one. (However, with the first commercial gas station not opening until 1913, one would have to carry one's own extra gas, or purchase more gas at a general store.) In Portland, the new vaudeville house received an incredible amount of public attention.

A week in advance of the grand opening, the *Portland Evening Express* carried news of the venue in its "Theater" section. On January 24, 1908, the paper noted, "Vaudeville is king. Not a single person in Portland needed to inquire about the sweeping line yesterday morning that stretched in unbroken length from Steinert's Music Store [where the advance tickets were sold] from the Casco Street entrance clear down Congress to Brown Street. Everyone who saw this chain of people intuitively murmured, 'Keith's opening.'" The number of advance sales exceeded those for Keith venues elsewhere, including in much larger cities. According to the manager of the new theater, "In my many years [of] theatrical experience, I never heard of such a tremendous call for tickets. It all signifies one thing: that Portland appreciated vaudeville more than ever, and the demonstration is a gratifying criterion for the success of the new theater." The manager, James E. Moore, had limited sales of tickets to five per person, which "gave all a chance" to secure a seat. As the paper noted, "The house for the opening was soon sold out, but the line remained unbroken, and a steady call for seats continued throughout the day." Some of the opening acts had been heralded across the country, and in addition to these, moving pictures would be shown on the theater's kinetograph.[7]

Fire swept through the streets of downtown Portland the week Keith's opened, destroying City Hall, or the "City Building," as well as other prominent buildings, and fire erupted more than once. The freezing temperatures added to the destruction, and photographs of burning and destroyed buildings crowded the city papers. Yet the front pages of the January 27 papers still made room for the opening of Keith's.[8]

"Celebrities of Theatrical World Here" ran the subtitle of the *Express*'s front-page coverage on January 27. Not only would crowds attend the opening night that evening, but so, too, would various "stars" of the vaudeville world. Chief among these was B. F. Keith himself, the "Father of Vaudeville." His son, A. Paul Keith, who at the time served as assistant manager of the company, would attend also, as would the manager of the company's New York theater, Percy Williams, plus William Hammerstein of the Hammerstein Theater of New York, S. Z. Poll of the Poll Vaudeville Circuit, and F. F. Proctor, "noted theater manager"; last, but not least, E. F. Albee, identified as the "general manager of the Keith Syndicate," was on hand. Other notables of the theatrical world would also attend the evening show as B. F. Keith's guests. During the matinee show that day, some 2,000 people filled the theater, which E. F. Albee attended.[9]

Albee informed the press that "the theater which we are opening in your city today is unexcelled in the world. It is possibly equaled only by three other theaters, Mr. Keith's Boston and Philadelphia houses and another New York theater. It is one of the 20 largest theaters in the United States. These are broad statements, but they are true." Albee stated that he had opened Keith theaters in "Boston, Providence, Columbus, Cleveland, Philadelphia, and New York," and although they had each been designed to be "the best possible," the new Portland theater "in every aspect of its interior decoration, finish, safety, comfort, acoustic properties, stage equipment, scenery, and in fact everything" exceeded those of the other theaters. The Portland venue would remain open every day of the year except Sundays, and remain open "every year in the future, so long as it shall last." The theater had been planned for the present and the future, and the future would do very well for Keith's of Portland. The new theater had cost more to build than its predecessors, except for the cost of the land itself, which was less expensive than that in the larger cities. Albee had to leave the theater before the grand opening that night, but he noted that everything was ready to go.[10]

A separate, full-page article extolled the appointments of the new theater. Construction had cost close to $250,000, and the venue had a seating capacity of 1,800. The electrical and lighting systems were state-of-the-art for 1908. The stage itself had 150 footlights, plus 1,000 "electric lamps" or bulbs, providing general stage lighting. Ornate chandeliers and over 2,000 additional "lamps" lit the theater in general. Adding outside lights and signage increased the "lamp" count to over 5,000. Preble Street and Congress Streets had large signs, as well as flaming arc lights on either side of the main entrance, located on Preble Street. In addition, "complete systems of telephones" connected every department of the theater. Decorated entrances, foyers, corridors, stairways, and the like added to the luxury of the venue.[11]

The auditorium itself included balconies and private boxes. The auditorium measured eighty-six feet by eighty-seven feet, with a seating capacity of 700. A gallery held 500 more seats, and a balcony seated another 600 people. The stage measured thirty-eight feet by eighty-seven feet, and measured seventy-four feet from the stage floor to the ceiling. The main auditorium was decorated in the Rococo style, as was the building in general. The general color scheme was "Nile green." Marble columns as well as mahogany floors, doors, and wainscoting and marble mosaic tiles, provided further decoration. Smoking rooms, a ladies' parlor, restrooms, a cloakroom, and other amenities added to the comfort of theater patrons. A 200-foot-long "subway" with marble floors and mirrored walls provided access from Congress Street. An asbestos curtain and a sprinkler system added to the safety of the production and of the public. In the event of fire or other disaster, some fifteen exits could be accessed.[12]

On January 28, the press declared the opening night of Keith's a brilliant success. Over 2,000 people attended (apparently exceeding the seating capacity of the venue), and the opening matinee of the 27th saw only slightly fewer people. The mayor of Portland and various city and state officials attended opening night. All acts received good reviews, including a dance act that featured four men and one woman.[13] As the years passed, more and more women would dance on the stage at Keith's.

In the meantime, at the close of its opening year, which had seen a variety of shows and acts, the *Portland Evening Express* gave the new Keith's theater another enthusiastic review. It stated that "January 1st, 1909 will be a red letter day on the theatrical calendar, for the bill at Keith's represents the best product of the 1908 vaudeville output and will serve as the fitting offering for the beginning of the new year." Keith's was to hold "two big houses" on New Year's Day, and during the matinee there would be special "holiday prices." These particular shows may have had vaudeville dancing by women, especially a production that included Venus losing her goddess status for a brief time and romping with a bellboy who promised to take her to Coney Island, but such dances were not featured in the newspaper's review. Rudy Raymond and Her Boys, another act playing at the turn of the year, might also have included dance.[14]

Vaudeville had appeared in Maine before Keith's came to town, however. By 1907—and indeed by the mid-1890s—most towns and cities of any size had seen at least one vaudeville troupe pass through, and by 1899 they were beginning to make formal appearances. And they included female dancers. In Hampden, at Riverside Park, established just the year before, "Miss Stella Lee" had danced before a local audience (but not for the first time) in August 1899 as part of a vaudeville troupe she had recently joined. Of the vaudeville show in general, the press noted, "This is the first company of its kind to visit Riverside, and the park audiences welcome it as a change" from previous offerings, and added that the park managers intended to bring in more vaudeville acts during the season.[15] The performance Stella Lee danced in that August was part of her company's (J. W. Gorman's Operetta Company) "Gypsy Festival." It featured "elaborate and intelligent costumes" and may well have had some somewhat "exotic" or "free" forms of dance, as gypsies—who made their own appearances in Maine in the 1800s and 1900s, provided another venue for female dancing, with the women likely being remunerated only by the money thrown at them or offered at tent entrances—and, not surprisingly, were rumored to have scandalous dancing. Later that month, Gorman's New York Vaudeville Club performed at Riverside, and other vaudeville acts would follow.[16]

Moreover, at about the same time that Keith's was opening in Portland, farther north, on Indian Island, just across the Penobscot River from Old Town, a little girl was just beginning to dance. She danced first in Native American ceremonies on her island homeland and then began to dance for tourists. Born in November 1903 and named Molly Alice (pronounced Molliedellis by her family) Nelson, the girl would one day, under the name Molly Spotted Elk, dance across the nation and in Europe. She would dance on stage and on film. She would also dance for a few nights at Keith's in Portland, three decades after the venue opened, as well as at a nightclub in Bangor, one opened decades after Keith's started its Maine shows. Like many dancers who did not fit into the traditionally acceptable avenues of female dance, Molly Spotted Elk would be considered something of a scandalous dancer by many people, but also as a talented, beautiful dancer by perhaps just as many others. Her roots were in Maine, and she would become the state's most well-known dancer to date.[17]

Molly would not be the first to venture out into the entertainment world from the Abanaki peoples, however. In addition to earlier people, Lucy Nicolar, born in 1884, was taking her dancing slippers on the vaudeville circuit at about the time Molly Nelson was born. As a child, Lucy had gone with her parents to sell baskets, in Kennebunkport and other places, to tourists and would sometimes perform native dances and songs at such venues. She started to dance publicly as a teenager at sportsmen's shows and other events. She then landed a position as a stenographer to a Harvard administrator, who had long had a passion for Native American life, and he helped sponsor her to enter Radcliffe College in 1901. That year, the *Cambridge Chronicle* published an article about the young woman, stating that Nicolar was "the first young woman of her tribe to leave the community for that of the world." Although that may have not have been strictly accurate, she may well have been one of the first to enter a major university, and she would travel much more than most young women of her day, be they Native Americans or not. An accompanying photograph showed Lucy with her long hair down, wearing a fairly simple top with short, capped sleeves and native necklaces.[18]

In its interview with Nicolar, the paper asked her what her intentions were. She responded, "I cannot tell you now. I want to do something for my people, for the world. I want to accomplish something worth the while, and I want to accomplish it in the best and most lasting way. If a college education will help me, I want it; if working with my hands is best, then I shall continue that." The paper stated that the young woman "has indomitable energy, and perseverance, and lets no opportunity escape her." She had already visited a few major cities.[19]

Lucy soon commenced a life in music. She traveled with the Redpath Chautauqua Bureau and then with the Keith Vaudeville Circuit for a time, using, as she had been already, the name Princess Watawaso (also spelled Watahwaso). She danced, but would make her way primarily as a singer, and she would eventually start a couple of Native American troupes; Molly Nelson would perform with her troupes for a time. Lucy soon signed on with Victor Records, and the company sent her on a promotional tour. She sang opera arias as well as native songs. She would eventually return to Indian Island and work on a variety of issues, just as she had stated as a young woman that she wanted to do: help her people and the world.[20]

In the meantime, Molly Nelson was just getting her dancing feet. She performed her first solo at the age of six at a St. Patrick's Day celebration doing an Irish jig, and then as a young teenager landing her first paid gigs. She danced for the nickels tourists would shower her with, and she won $10 at "Native Night" in a Bangor theater contest.[21]

In the early 1910s, as the two Penobscot women were bringing their music and dance to the world, the Keith's circuit continued to bring new acts to Maine, sending some of them farther north. However, the city of Portland had already had vaudeville performances before Keith's opened. The Jefferson, the Nickel, the Savoy, and the Congress Theaters each presented vaudeville acts at the close of 1908, in a time when the area was not even at the height of its entertainment season, which by 1900 was the summer season, when people arrived from other parts of the state and throughout the nation to enjoy the Maine woods, the ocean, and the tourist spirit that had been developing over the past few decades. People might also watch films, and sometimes live acts, at various other local venues. The Dreamland in particular had offered another option in Portland. The dancing that women performed in the early vaudeville acts seems to have been much less risqué than some later performed. Yet vaudeville in general—if not its dancing elements in particular—was not unanimously welcomed and was considered more than a bit crude by some members of society. As one theater, the

Jefferson, described it in 1908, or rather labeled its own offerings, what they had to offer was "polite vaudeville," implying that some vaudeville was indeed "less than polite."[22]

Keith's, as was true of some of the other theaters, presented a wide range of acts, even in terms of vaudeville, even in 1908. For example, late 1908 saw spiritualism on the stage and orphans from St. Elizabeth's Orphan Asylum and St. Joseph's Home invited for a special feature—likely an animal show in which horses played a tune on chime bells, and dogs rode the horses around the ring for a finale. Not far away, the Nickel presented female acrobats, a comedy film, and assorted other acts as 1908 ended, and seemed to be doing quite well.[23]

The Nickel, however, was not strictly competition for Keith's. Perhaps it was locally, but not to Keith's parent company. The Nickel, located at 469-1/2 Congress Street, was actually another avenue or line of the larger Keith's circuit. Although it did have vaudeville performers, including dancers, its focus was more on films and "illustrated songs" in which local singers would perform between short films, and sometimes during the films—while the main Keith circuit concentrated more on live acts. In a sense, the "Nickels" on the Keith circuit were essentially part of the thousands of "nickolodians" opened in America from about 1903 to 1910, offering patrons films and, sometimes, live shows or musicians. However, the Nickels in Maine were not long lived.[24]

In Portland, the Nickel opened circa late 1907 shortly before Keith's and would be augmented by the coming of Keith's, achieving record-breaking ticket sales in early 1908. Farther north, the Nickel Theater of Bangor had opened in August 1907. Anther Nickel had opened in Lewiston, as would one in Biddeford, and the circuit of Keith's and Nickels would also, at least at some junctures, include Gardiner, Waterville, and Fairfield, Maine, plus cities across the border in lower Canada as well as other cities in New England.[25] As some of the theaters did not last and others had been taken over—sometimes for a very short time—from existing venues, determining just when all the cities and towns were actively part of Keith's overall enterprise, and just how large the acts they acquired were, remains rather obscure. The heyday of the houses in Maine, however, did start in about 1907 and began to fade a few years later. And the largest vaudeville acts presented were not at the many Nickels.

In Lewiston, in case there was any confusion in early 1908, the parent company, in a sense, clarified the situation. In one combined advertisement, "The Nickel Company Theater" listed two individual theaters in the city. "The Nickel" was advertised as having formerly been "Keith's" and was located in the Music Hall Block, while the "Nickelet" had formerly been "The Majestic" and was located on Lisbon Street. Both theaters advertised, together, having the "Latest Moving Pictures and Illustrated Songs." Admission to "each house" cost five cents, and these two houses offered "continuous performances, afternoon and evening." A perusal of some of their offerings shows that they did indeed offer some of the same films seen at some of the other Nickels in the state. Moreover, the *Lewiston Dailey Sun* reported, "Nothing can stop the run of good houses at the Nickel and the Nickelet." Their films and their singers were both top-notch. Meanwhile, the Empire Theater of Lewiston was showing both films and some live vaudeville, while the Crystal Theater just across the river in Auburn offered "moving pictures and illustrated songs."[26]

Vaudeville in general was highly competitive in its early years of the 1880s to the 1920s before B. F. Keith and his associates coalesced and then bought out—and ruthlessly drove out—some of its major competitors. Maine communities saw shows presented not only by the Keith circuits but also those on the early Albee, Schubert, Loew, and other vaudeville circuits. Sometimes individual performers, including female dancers, came to the state not as part of the various circuits but as individuals, or after leaving one circuit to join with another.

In terms of films, in 1907 the first "talkie" came out, but silent films remained the norm for many years. A few years after Keith's in Portland opened, in 1912–1913, the now combined Keith-Albee-Proctor circuits tried using Thomas A. Edison's early film system that produced "talkies." The resulting films were not properly synchronized, however, in terms of images with sound, and after the initial excitement about them wore off, audiences quickly became irritated with the audiovisual problems, and the talking films were cast to the side for the time being.[27]

In Bangor, the coming of its Nickel Theater was met with great public excitement, as were those of Keith's and the Nickel in Portland. Bangor was particularly pleased, however, as the Nickel was unique for the city in several regards, and what happened in Bangor was mirrored in other Maine communities as the theaters arrived.

The now-combined *Bangor Whig & Courier–Bangor Daily News* (or simply the *BDN*), included news from throughout the state, especially focusing on towns north of Augusta, much as the Portland papers covered southern Maine, and discussed various stages of the renovations for the new Nickel every few days before the theater opened. The paper, as others in Maine, had evolved since the late 1800s to include more than just "bullets" of events in the region, including individual news columns from each of the communities it served. Previous to 1900, only the "largest" news items (outside of politics) warranted more than a brief paragraph, if that. Patrons from Houlton, Bar Harbor, Ellsworth, Belfast, Greenville, Calais, and Machias, as well of those from the immediate area including Brewer, Old Town, Orono, and so forth, could both read about the opening and, transportation being well developed by the early 1900s, could attend it, as long as they bought tickets on time. Augusta was also covered by the Bangor papers, although these readers fell between both the northern and southern larger papers and were also served by the *Kennebec Journal* and other Augusta area papers, and were midway in terms of the larger entertainment centers.[28]

The Bangor newspapers not only covered cosmetic renovations but also addressed comfort and safety improvements for the new Nickel. These included "fireproof floors and walls, broad exits, perfect ventilation, and big electric fans." In addition, asbestos curtains (a nightmare for later generations) would be lowered when the stage was not in use. Movies would, the *BDN* boasted, "not be thrown upon a sheet—as has always been the custom in this city—but instead thrown upon a solid background of cement coated with white." New alternating electrical current wiring would—like the new solid wall—help end the appearances of flickering views of the shows.[29]

The first presentation at the Bangor Nickel included three short films, and advertising for the same started days before the grand opening. The Nickel billed its presentations as "Moving Pictures and Illustrated Songs," running continuously from "12 to 6 [in the afternoon] and 7 to 10:30 [at night]." Tickets cost five cents, and the advertisements included the slogan "Nothing Cheap, but the Biggest Five Cents Worth of Entertainment in Maine."[30]

The new theater opened on August 12, 1907, and on August 13 accolades poured in. The *BDN* reported that the city was most pleased with the theater and so, too, should its parent company be. The opening in the Graham Building along Franklin Street should have "satisfied" them "that they did the right thing in coming to Bangor.... The opening on Monday was more than a success—it was a gigantic ovation, and proved beyond all reasonable doubt that this city, with its more than 50,000 people" (the paper included the surrounding communities in its population tally) was ready to support anything "clean and cleaver [*sic*] and of worth in the amusement line." Lines had formed for the shows, and by 1:30 p.m., the manager remarked on behalf of the parent company, "We've had more paid admissions now than we had on the opening day in Lewiston, evening and all." By night, the crowds had swollen yet further. Within five minutes, every seat for the opening show had been sold out. "By eight, a big, good natured, perspiring crowd was jammed before the entrance. It couldn't get in, so it waited as patiently as possible for those inside to come out." The sidewalk was now blocked, as well as the street. The first show ended at 8:15, and as hundreds came out of the theater, hundreds surged in, and hundreds more waited still for an opportunity to enter. Patrolmen kept the crowd peaceful but were hard pressed to keep them from surging forward. "The day, in every sense, had been a record breaker." It had succeeded—in cash takings—beyond openings "on the same circuit of moving picture playhouses embracing Manchester, Portland, St. John, Montreal, and Halifax," and also the one recently opened in Lewiston.[31]

The initial offerings of the theater would include films suitable for children as well as dramas more suited to adults. Two local singers, a male and a female, performed at the opening night, and the film *Struggle for Life*, according to the local press, "a drama without words—introduc[ed] some of the most remarkable and superbly blended color effects which can be imagined, and posed for, evidently, by some real actors." "Prominent citizens" were numbered among the many patrons. When the finishing lights and other touches were added, the theater was anticipated to truly light up the night in Bangor.[32] Still, some people wanted something else. They wanted more vaudeville, they wanted more dancing women, and they wanted more risqué dancing women.

Two weeks after the Nickel opened in Bangor, the Bangor Opera House reopened after going through extensive renovations. Its first offering, although quite likely a toned-down version for the stage, was a show about hurdy gurdy girls. The *Hurdy Gurdy Girl* was a musical comedy, and it sold out. The theater's seating capacity had been enlarged to 1,200, and the nearby Nickel Theater continued to pull in the people, but no seat remained empty as the curtain went up at the Opera House. The crowd enjoyed the beauty and gyrations of the female dancers, and the press noted of the play that there were "plenty of good looking girls," women who were not wearing as much clothing as they might, which also apparently pleased the crowds. The lead hurdy girl, played by Mae Botti, was deemed "a delight, physically and in every other way." She both sang and danced.[33] And, to add even more spice, a new group of women danced the following day, and not in a sedate theater.

"Little Egypt" came to town on August 27, 1907. And she did not come alone. The day after the reopening of the Bangor Opera House, the Eastern Maine State Fair opened in Bangor at Maplewood Park. The fair had started in the late 1800s, bringing exhibits and various acts to the region. And, in 1907, it once again brought dancers, this time women who were still known as "Little Egypts," but also as hootchie-cootchie dancers with various spellings and perhaps named for the Indian province of Cooch Behar, as Americans sometimes interchanged Hindu and Egyptian cultures. Americans later called them Oriental or Eastern dancers, and then belly dancers. The women who danced at the fair in Bangor in 1907 may or may not have been from the Middle East or Eastern European countries that enjoyed a history of belly dancing. The women who came to Bangor and performed on the newly enlarged midway (and likely at other fairs in the state) were described as "Egyptian ladies from East Boston, who are said to be bad but are not," according to one member of the local press who unfortunately gave no further information.[34]

However, a second article about the fair noted that, as with other acts on the midway, "The East Boston Egyptians also played to the crowded houses and some of our first citizens were noticed filing in and out under the flame torches." The journalist aimed more than a bit of sarcasm at these "first citizens" who visited tents many people might have found disreputable.[35] The journalist continued:

> *It's a great treat to watch the good men of the town enter these tents. They generally wait until the out of town visitors have all disappeared inside the canvas, and then they saunter along and make a quick duck. Of course they don't think anybody sees them, but there is always a sarcastic gallery observing things from afar.*[36]

The writer noted that there was not really "anything inside the tent that they shouldn't look at. Not unless they are very thin skinned. So it is somewhat on the side of laughter to watch the maneuvering to get in unobserved."[37] Such furtiveness and "thin-skinness" may also have come into play regarding a minister who a few years later filed a formal complaint about the dancing he had seen on the midway.

In addition to the presence of the women and the men watching them, the writer mentioned the musicians who accompanied the

43

women and who, with their instruments, formed "a foreign orchestra." The orchestra "consists of a bass drum and a queer sort of reed instrument which, under proper conditions, probably gives a strong influence to the dances of which these are alleged to be imitations." So the Little Egypts were indeed dancing, and to instruments culturally common to belly dancing—possibly the *zumara* (a reed instrument), a *zurna* (a horn instrument that sounds rather like a modern tuba), or a *nay* (a flute type of instrument), plus perhaps an *oud* (a stringed instrument considered the forerunner of the lute), and a *tar* (a smaller drum that resembles a tambourine) or another, tallish, deep-sounding drum common in the Middle East and Eastern Europe. Dancers also sometimes used *zils* or *zagats* (finger cymbals). (Spellings for each of these vary, in part by ethnicity and era, and other instruments are also used by or to accompany belly dancers.[38])

Mainers already knew about the Eastern dancers by 1907, however. Eastern dancer Fatima had appeared at the World's Fair held in Chicago in 1893, and belly dancers had possibly appeared in front of American audiences earlier. One or more hootchie-cootchie dancers had performed right in Bangor circa 1898 at the fair. At least one belly dancer had danced in New York City in the late 1890s to the consternation of many people, and Little Egypts had danced again at the St. Louis Exposition in 1904, which one source stated had involved "a relatively normal routine of gyrations of the torso," to which some dancers had later added various "bumps" and the "spinning of the breasts and rump."[39] The latter is worded a bit peculiarly, but belly dancers do use their stomach, chest, hip, leg, and other muscles to control various movements of their torsos. And in 1910, one "thin-skinned" Bangorite would indeed have an issue with a Little Egypt, finding her movements highly immoral.

In 1907, in the meantime, more than Little Egypt came to the fair. Various other acts also appeared on the Bangor midway in 1907, including two vaudeville companies, one of them with "25 girls," seemingly dancing girls. Another company or act consisted of "Gorman's Alabama Troubadours, a troupe of 25 colored people" scheduled "to give a different performance every afternoon."[40] Diversity was present in Maine at its larger fairs, even in the late 1800s and early 1900s. Belly dancers came to the state, as did other dancing and singing women and men, in vaudeville at theaters as well as at the ever-popular fairs, which although they may have been largely agricultural did have entertainments that challenged at least some observers.

The following year in Bangor, in 1908, in addition to the Nickel—which was more of a short-movie house than not, in terms of what it showed most—a larger vaudeville house, Union Hall, opened its doors to much fanfare on October 26. It was located on Union Street across from the Bangor House—a long established hotel and restaurant combination that in following decades would also see a few dancing women perform, including strippers. The *BDN* called the newest venue a "tasteful little vaudeville house," a slight against some vaudeville houses that offered more risqué—for the time—performances. The manager, Harry M. Gardner, as quoted in the *Bangor Daily Commercial* (*BDC*), stated that the theater was an independent one, and thus the house was free to engage acts directly, implying that it had more artistic freedom than those houses on circuits such as Keith's. Gardner also stated, "I believe Bangor has long needed a vaudeville theater and this demand I intend to supply. I intend to supply it the right way, too. Everything as clean as it is up-to-date." He wanted to bring more women and children in to see the performances than vaudeville houses traditionally had as patrons, and to introduce various "novelties."[41]

Union Hall would be a "continuous" venue, with its doors opening each day at noon. Programs would be printed with gilt letters on their covers, "similar to those carried by the vaudeville houses of the big cities." Tickets sold for ten cents, twenty cents, and thirty cents, the same as the general prices in Portland. Moreover, the street entrance, once complete, would feature a "big electric sign" to usher people into the building.[42]

The new management had remodeled the interior of Union Hall, adding new furnishings and decorations, a stage large enough for all sorts of vaudeville acts, and seating room for up to 1,000 people. Female attendants dressed all in white and a female master of ceremonies ushered people in on opening night, while the orchestra also featured female musicians. Opening night was by invitation only. At least one female dancer was included in the first show, Cassie Clifford, "A Singing and Dancing Soubrette, Who Compels You to Sit Up and Take Notice," as advance advertising billed her. (A soubrette, in terms of dance, generally referred to an energetic solo female performer, sometimes wearing wooden clogs and sometimes performing a skirt dance.) In addition, Raymond Mason, "a Bangor boy who has worked on the Keith's Circuit and is as good a wooden shoe dancer as can be found on the stage today," also performed. Local citizens were excited, the venue was packed in its first weeks, both local papers sang its praises, but the Union Hall vaudeville house survived for only a year. It was replaced by Acker's Family Theater, part of a Canadian company, and then after the Great Bangor Fire of 1911 destroyed much of downtown, the Nickel Theater moved into the building. It, in turn, burned down in 1963. But 1963 was decades into the future when Bangorites poured into Union Hall in 1908 to watch and listen to vaudeville, "Advanced Vaudeville" at that, as the theater proclaimed its offerings.[43] And some of the vaudeville they would experience over the next year was pretty much the same as that experienced by citizens in and visitors to other communities in Maine.

With the Nickel and Union Halls recently opened, other changes came to the entertainment scene in Bangor. The Gem Theater had opened on February 7, 1908, and soon began "playing to capacity houses." Therefore, in early October of that year, work began on renovations and, ever optimistic about such things, the *BDN* declared, "The new theater will not only be the handsomest of its kind in Bangor, but it will be safe to say that it is one of the finest east of New York." With a 40- by 100-foot addition, the Gem would seat over 1,000 people. It would serve primarily as a movie house.[44] However, just a few weeks after the immense addition and renovation to the Gem began, a true vaudeville venue seemed to be coming to the city on the Penobscot. Another, fifth venue would also open.

In October 1908, Bangorites learned that a new theater was to be built in Bangor, on York Street, with a large arched entryway opening on that street and a luxurious foyer opening on the more traveled Exchange Street. It would seat 1,000 people and hopefully open in time for Christmas. It was anticipated to feature both moving pictures and vaudeville acts.[45]

However, the headlines on October 27, 1908, included more than just the news about the new theater on York Street. As the opening paragraph of one local news article stated:

> *It was time, and not so very long ago, when Bangor had but one theater. Now there are four doing business here—the Opera House, Nickel, Gem, and Union, while a fifth is in progress of construction and still another is promised.*[46]

This particular article focused on the fifth, the York Street venue, which would become the Graphic. Another article focused on the sixth. And the sixth could have become the most popular theater of all, and the one with the most risqué dancers. Headlines announced, "**KEITH HAS TAKEN THE NOROMBEGA.**" By that, the article meant Norombega (or Norembega) Hall, an older amusement venue, built in 1855 and the center of culture for the city for decades. The announcement had just come in that "B. F. Keith has taken the Norombega, and will at once begin the work of fixing it up." However, the purported announcement was not officially that; no one "intimately connected with the [Keith's] enterprise" would go on record with it. But the *BDN* insisted that it had it on "excellent authority that a five year contract has been signed." The article concluded, "The Keith vaudeville is famous all over the country, and would doubtless be welcomed here."[47]

The following day, the paper's headlines read: "**KEITH IS SURE TO TAKE NOROMBEGA.**" But again, "official confirmation" had not been obtained. The newspaper asserted, however, that developments of the day before had left little doubt about the matter, and that work would commence within thirty days "converting old Norombega into a Keith vaudeville palace."[48]

Moreover, over the past three to four years, "at frequent intervals," "announcement has been made that the Keith interests were coming into Bangor in one location or another—but every time they fell through before papers had been drawn and signed." Now, however, the press reported that the paperwork, signed and ready, affirmed that Keith's planned to take over the old hall and build new entrances to it, including a bridge leading from it to Central Street or Harlow Street, into the heart of downtown Bangor. The newest addition would ensure that "Bangor will be on the Portland Circuit, and this assures as fine a class of vaudeville as can be found anywhere in the country."[49]

On December 15, the *BDN* announced that Central Street would soon become "The Great White Way." The manager of the newest venue, now to be called the Gaiety, not Keith's, had received new plans. With a sixteen-foot lavishly lightly sign mounted on a twelve-foot pillar above the venue duplicating "those before the New York Theater and the new Keith Theater in Montreal," a second large sign mounted above the main entrance, and "five gigantic arcs" plus a few more to be placed in front of the Nickel, "Central Street will surely become the Great White Way of Eastern Maine." Indeed, nothing else would "compare with it in any other New England city of this size."[50]

The Gaiety opened on February 16, 1909, and received the praises of the local press. According to current plans, the theater would change films three times a week, on the same schedule as that at the Nickel, and songs and vaudeville acts would change twice a week. Two of the initial acts that appeared on the opening bill—one of the singers and a dance and entertainment group known as "the colored whirlwinds"—had performed in Bangor before. The singer in question had been "transferred" from his illustrated song performances at the Nickel. Another performer, a woman, also danced at the opening. All seats cost ten cents, and no reservations would be taken.[51]

Even before the theater opened that Monday in February, on the Saturday before, according to the *BDN*, "the whole front of the Norombega, now called the Gaiety, burst into a flood of light when Manger Forrest threw on the switch controlling the electric signs. The display was gorgeous. It lit up the entire section of the city, and hundreds passing through Central Street stopped to gaze and admire." Just the one major sign had 600 lamps, and the one over the entrance—spelling out "Vaudeville and Motion Pictures"—had another 220 lights. Colored streams of light flared up to even better illuminate the signs and building. It was beyond compare. And at the new venue, as at the Nickel, patrons could "go and come as they please" as the shows were "almost continuous." The *BDC*, which generally did not go into as great coverage of entertainment as did the *BDN*, pronounced the programming "excellent" and "balanced."[52]

The Nickel (asserting that it was "Turning Over a New Leaf,") and the Gaiety, with an umbrella company in common, began running their advertisements together, placed one above the other in the *BDC*, and side by side and part of one integrated block in the *BDN*, the two sections united by a column or pillar on which in large block quotes was written: "**ON THE GREAT WHITE WAY**." One of the acts featured on the Gaiety's side of the advertisement of March 1, 1909, was for "Vesta Gilbert, Who Knows How to Sing and Dance." At this point, the column between the two sides said simply, the letters printed one atop the other, "**WHITE WAY**," while above the block the lettering stated, "Where Thousands Will Stop This Week:" and the bottom stating, "And They'll Stop More Than Once."[53]

Meanwhile, the Graphic Theater opened at York and Exchange Streets with hundreds in attendance and bringing yet more lights in the downtown area, causing the *BDN* to comment: "It's about time to change the name of Exchange Street to 42d." All 900 seats in the new theater had sold out. The theater would feature "moving films." Dancers might appear there, but it would not be a major venue for them.[54] And, if all this were not enough, the Union Hall held an amateur vaudeville night in which any dancer could get up and perform, and the city also held one that January. Public participation was high.

And, of course, people were on the move in Maine during the 1800s and 1900s. The citizens of Bangor, Portland, Lewiston, and other communities could visit various vaudeville and other entertainments locally, or they could travel elsewhere to see them. Bangorites, for example, had their new theaters and the fairs and circuses, but by the last decades of the nineteenth century, especially by the 1880s, they could easily take a steamship or a train ride down to Portland, Old Orchard Beach, Bucksport, or Mt. Desert Island, as well as to other locations. "Excursion Trips" were advertised in all the larger papers from the 1870s on. And they went both ways. One advertisement for the Eastern Maine State Fair in the late 1800s proclaimed, "Excursion Rates on all Railroads and Boat Lines. It will be cheaper to come than to stay away!" Other venues could almost as easily pull in the audiences. Bar Harbor had a Music Hall, whose offerings were regularly posted in the Bangor papers as well as in the *Ellsworth American*. During one week alone in 1907, the Bar Harbor Music Hall sold some 2,900 tickets for its current "moving picture show," and these sales were boosted by tickets to dances. Tickets to the movies cost five cents, tickets to the dances twenty-five cents. In addition, other venues closer by were more accessible, ones reachable by trolley cars or streetcars by the early 1900s, those linking Bangor, Old Town, Hampden, and other communities. For example, Riverside Park in nearby Hampden opened in 1898 and by 1905 offered both a dance hall and vaudeville performances to visitors and residents of the area. It had brought its first vaudeville acts to the area in 1899, with much fanfare.[55]

Entertainment offered at Riverside Park—which people could easily reach from Bangor, or from points southward such as Bucksport, Belfast, Rockland and the like, received both regular reviews and advertising space in the local papers in the early 1800s. For example, at the same time as the Nickel was gearing up in early August 1907, Riverside Park Theater presented *Priscilla*, which included "A Fine Singing and Dancing Chorus of Pretty Girls." The *BDN* gave the play a favorable advance notice, as it did *Blue Beard, Jr.*, which included "several fine singing and dancing numbers," and in July *The Belle of New Hampshire* had been billed as "A Whirling Revelry of Mirth and Melody," and included "Vaudeville's Best Singing Quartet" and "A Dancing Chorus of Pretty Girls in Gay Attire." Other performances, quite often with dancing women, followed over the next months and years.[56]

And, just as it became increasingly easier for audiences to go to shows in Bangor, Ellsworth, Hampden, Portland, Old Orchard Beach, and so forth, female dancers and other performers had the same transportation means available to them to reach most sections of the state. However, except for perhaps the hundreds of saloons in the backwoods, performers generally visited the more populated areas. That was, after all, where much of the money was to be made.

Vaudeville became a major concern for some citizens in the urban areas, but the old circuses and fairs continued to come to Maine, and to bring their own forms of dancing entertainment, which also, some people worried, might cross moral boundaries. There may have been vaudeville-type performances, but along the midways and in the side tents, the fairs and circuses sometimes offered something else.

One of the most amusing anecdotes of the Bangor region involved the Eastern Maine State Fair. In 1910, a local minister saw something that caused a bit of a scandal and an amusing diversion in the winter of 1911. Reverend Wilbur F. Berry of Waterville stated that on August 25, 1910, at eleven in the morning, he had seen something immoral at the Eastern Maine State Fair. He saw a two-part act, the first act purportedly featuring a "Spanish Dance"—but sounding more like an Eastern dance—performed by a young woman. He stated that the woman's costume was sufficiently modest, but that her dance movements were immoral. He apparently watched the performance twice. He said that the barker on the midway had yelled out that for another twenty-five cents, a person could "see the dance as it was danced when John the Baptist was beheaded." Being a highly moral man himself, he paid the fee and entered the tent. There, he recounted, a girl was doing "some poses"—theatrical poses for dances were rather common at the time—in pink tights and a flounced skirt, and he had no complaint with that.[57]

The good reverend did, however, complain in writing that September: "'The Eastern Maine Fair management allowed' a grossly immoral show on their grounds," as reported in the *BDN*. He filed the complaint with the commissioner of the Maine Department of Agriculture, Augustus W. Gilman. He was informed that a hearing would be held and that he needed to furnish "a list of names of witnesses against the fair." Reverend Berry had problems furnishing witnesses. He simply wanted to testify by himself. At the hearing, held on December 20, 1910, in Bangor, he came by himself and decided to withdraw his allegations against the fair managers, and to pursue the complaint now only against a vaudeville troupe, the troupe that had brought the dancer who had so offended him with them. Berry, however, could not bring anyone in who would testify they had watched an "immoral act." (That, of course, might have caused a few eyebrows to lift in *their* direction, as it would imply an immoral or indiscreet act, perhaps an inadvertent one, on their part.) Berry himself found the entertainment "grossly immoral." Yet he stated that he had purchased a photograph of the dancing women at the immoral show, and produced it at the hearing.[58]

The president of the fair introduced fourteen witnesses, including the city mayor and members of the local police, who testified that they had not seen any immoral acts at the fair. The police and another individual had been charged with monitoring exhibitors "for the selling of liquor, gambling, or any immoral show whatever." (A few exhibitors who might indeed have brought in immoral acts were turned away.) The reverend stated then that his complaint was now against a sole person, the female dancer. He had seen in that midway tent something "immoral, indecent, suggestive of evil, and shocking." He did not enter any complaints to the fair on the day in question. The possibility was raised that the act might have been introduced clandestinely. Berry then yielded in his complaints against the fair but said that he could not condone any such dance, no matter popular opinion. The commissioner made his decision at the outset of January 1911. In bold headlines, the *BDN* announced, **"THE WIGGLE DANCE WASN'T IMMORAL."** The *BDC*'s headline was a more subdued **"COM'R GILMAN DISMISSES CHARGE AGAINST FAIR."** Both articles, however, were largely the same, being essentially the report rendered by the commissioner.[59]

The problem was, Reverend Berry had complained against the dancing, but Commissioner Gilman had said that he could not tell if the dance had been immoral if he could not see the dance. The minister initially refused, due to the presence of a stenographer, but later complied and tried to replicate the dance. The commissioner decided the dance was not immoral.[60] Of course, the minister may not have had all the moves and attributes of the dancing girl. And then again, the fair's representative—a well-known Bangor civic leader, stated that the dance in question was actually "one of science and skill." Moreover, he had received only one other complaint against the dancers, and that from a woman who did not think the dance immoral but did request that part of it be cut out.[61]

The source of the complaint might have been an act billed as "The Great Golden Troupe, Whirlwind Dancers from the Kingdom of the Czar" in advertisements for the fair, which ran August 23–26, 1910. However, there was also one Lew Walker, who among other acts brought in "his dancing girls," as the press described them. Both groups performed on the midway rather than in the more genteel auditorium or at the grandstand. The so-called Russian Act received at least one favorable comment in the press; Walker's act did not. The Whirlwind Dancers were reported to have been "a big hit," but one act—which was unidentified but included women—received a few unfavorable quips. On August 25, 1910, a *BDN* reporter stated that it was difficult to watch "a leading citizen of East Weedybumps separating himself from his hard and honestly earned and modest savings to gaze up on the mysterious beauties of the Orient, who probably live in one squalid room near the Gas House Patch in South Boston." The woman might have been both beautiful and poor, and both Eastern in ethnicity and a resident of Boston.[62] But this does seem to have been the group that so upset the minister.

And if so, it was one of Lew Walker's acts, as Walker was identified specifically at the December hearing. Berry said that he had seen "six girls dancing upon the platform." Then, "one girl gave an immodest dance after the management had requested that the two women and children, who were among the audience, to leave the tent." The man in charge of the show had then said that for twenty-five cents the men could watch a woman dancer "who would not wear the proper amount of clothes."[63]

As estimated 5,000 or more people attended opening day alone in 1910, and how many might have watched the various women dancers perform at the Eastern Maine State Fair is unknown. And then, just as Mainers recovered from the Eastern Maine Fair, the Waterville Central Maine Fair opened on August 30. Some of the acts would go from one fair to another, but in the case of Walker's dancing girls, in 1910 that was not the case. They may have appeared elsewhere in Maine before the Bangor fair, but Reverend Berry stated in December that after he saw the dance performed in Bangor, he prevented it from going on the stage at Waterville, Lewiston, Norway, and Gorham. Berry was apparently willing to take his objections on the road.[64] And, of course, he had his photograph of the dancing women to show around if need be.

Reverend Berry was not the only man in America to complain about such dancing. The same year that Berry protested about the "Wiggle Dance," Samuel Payne Wilson of Chicago, one of the city's "first men" stated that

The performers [of burlesque], mostly women of the underworld, are paid to amuse the audiences by kicking up their heels. The higher they kick, the more they are paid. The hootch kooche and the Salomé dances are here given in all their rottenness. . . . These shows are liberally supported by all classes of men. Price of admission is low, and the performance suited to the taste of the audience.[65]

Wilson tied burlesque to the "hootch kooche and the Salomé dances," and both dances were used to describe the "Little Egypts."

In 1910, when Berry and Paine took umbrage with female dancers, the first movie *Salomé* came out, and J. P. Morgan, the financial giant, tried to pay to halt production, not because he objected to the Dance of the Seven Veils in the film but rather because it showed a woman fondling a man's head, without the rest of the man's body attached. In a nine-and-a-half-minute movie, John the Baptist's head was shown to Salomé only in the last half-minute. She "caressed it" for a much shorter period. And she remained well covered in the film.[66]

Morgan had already helped cut short the play *Salomé* by Richard Strauss, on January 22, 1907, after the play had gone on stage just once. In that instance, he, along with W. K. Vanderbilt and August Belmont, had been the play's backers, and *Theater* magazine had stated that the shedding of the seven veils and the "prima ballerina's" caressing of the severed head of John the Baptist had "sickened the public stomach." Having had just a one-night run, the lead dancer then took her dance to another theater and was quickly branded a "kootch dancer." She then opened a school to train "Salomés" who then went out on the vaudeville circuits. At about the same time, Florenz Ziegfeld brought his version of *Salomé* to a high-class vaudeville house in New York. Salomé was not to be eliminated from the public eye, and with the head of John the Baptist in the play—and the "Dance of Salomé" often very close to Ruth St. Denis's "Radha" dance—it is likely that it was this dance that so upset the Bangor minister in 1910. And it was at this point, in 1909, that Ruth St. Denis burst back onto the American stage and outdid the other performers, opening her show *Egypta* in New York in 1910, and then touring with parts of it across the nation.[67] She would later work with a woman who would help America rediscover Eastern dance in the 1970s.

As well as in Bangor, fairs brought female dancers to various communities in the state, and vaudeville theaters or houses in addition to those in operation by 1908 would also open in Portland, as they did in other towns and cities in the state. Various changes were underway. In early

1911, when the state commissioner of agriculture rendered his decision regarding the "Wiggle Dance" at the Eastern Maine Fair, the *Portland Sunday Telegram* reported that the Jefferson Theater of Portland was soon to present a large musical performance that was an act of one of the big "syndicates." As the owner of that theater also owned "the one in Lewiston," it raised questions about what the Lewiston theater would do. Furthermore, as the current manager or booker for the new Union Hall venue in Bangor was now resuming booking acts for those two theaters, Bangorites were uncertain what would happen in their city. Apparently, being an "independent" house, but one that was also open to circuit acts, it had not actually been getting many circuit acts, as the two under discussion in Portland and Lewiston had been strictly "independent," and it had been considered poor form to "jump a show from Boston to Bangor for one or two performances." Moreover, the *BDC* pointed out, "If high class productions continue to come here to empty houses, neither the 'syndicate' nor the 'independents' will tumble over themselves in sending big attractions to this city." Theaters were apparently suffering in the city of Bangor, but one dancing act did stand out that week: the dancing of one of the three "Dancing Mitchells," at the Acker's Family Theater at Union Hall, who was reportedly "one of the most beautiful Creole women on the stage" and whose dancing was deemed "eccentric" but of "blue ribbon quality."[68]

Not long after the positive review at Acker's, destruction came to downtown Bangor. Just as the opening of Keith's in Portland had been ushered in by fire, the Keith's Gaiety in Bangor was crushed by fire. Fire ripped through downtown Bangor on April 30, 1911. The Great Fire of 1911 destroyed Norombega Hall, much as it burned down other city landmarks. Union Hall (where Acker's had been located) and the Bangor Opera House survived the inferno, which killed two people and seriously wounded others, but the "Great White Way" of Bangor was gone. The Gaiety was destroyed, and the Nickel Theater burned as well. City Hall survived, and a few books that people had carried out of the Bangor Public Library survived, but not much else—except ruins—remained standing in the immediate area around Norombega. Hundreds of buildings were simply gone.[69]

Most other changes in entertainment in the early 1910s were less drastic. In Bangor, the Nickel soon took over Union Hall, in effect removing the second "true" vaudeville house from the city. The Bijou Theater replaced the Gem, but like the Graphic and the Nickel offered primarily movies. The Bangor Opera House did continue to see live female dancers, but they were not as frequent as would have been the case with the Gaiety and Union Hall vaudeville houses. Nor were they, especially in following years, the same types of dancers as those who might have danced at the other venues. The changes that had only started a few years previously in live shows effectively ended, at least for the time being.[70] In other communities, other changes occurred.

By 1913, Greely's Theater had started to offer vaudeville in Portland, including dance numbers. A "review" of one of its entertainers that November stated, "Dorothy Knowles pleased greatly with her dainty offering of songs and dances. Miss Knowles wears some pretty and most fetching gowns that enhance her act to no small degree." The comment seemed to be meant to titillate, albeit gently.[71]

Another 1913 "review," one clearly identified as an "Advertisement" but printed in a regular column format, stated of one of the acts at Keith's:

> *One of the most pleasing novelty acts that has been introduced here is a big special production entitled "The Belles of Seville." Six exceptionally talented young lady dancers are introduced in a series of novelty terpsichorean feats of the most fascinating and delightful order, the feature of which is their presentation of the Argentine Tango.*[72]

The tango would be one of the dances often seen as risqué, although it could also be seen as perfectly acceptable depending on the venue, the dress, and the exact way the dance was performed. In Spokane, Washington, the mayor banned both the dance and the film *Tango Dancing Lesson* because, he stated, "I won't let my daughter do those dances!"[73]

The female dance numbers in the local vaudeville houses may not have been extremely risqué or the dancers paid by the dance—although they may well have been paid by the show or day of a given performance. As the women, except for a few leading actresses and singers, were seldom billed individually, they likely made less money than some of the other acts. But they still made as much of a living as they could through their dance work, and like some earlier and later dancers often went from venue to venue. In addition, some local vaudeville houses, as least as early as 1908, offered "Amateur Nights" where local women and men, including single female dancers, could perform for prizes, including monetary prizes. The Jefferson in Portland may have been the first theater to do so.[74]

A number of female dancers would garner national attention in films, and some of them first appeared on the vaudeville and dance stages in the 1910s. For example, in 1912, Mae West reached the stages in some of the larger cities (but not, as far as can be determined, Maine), and her dancing was what first drew in the crowds. As one theater promoter described her act in Philadelphia, "She does a muscle dance in a sitting position. It is all in the way she does it, and her way is all her own." Mae West was also known to employ a "trick strap" on her performance dresses, such that the strap would seemingly break, and show off her nude breasts in the process. When the opportunity came to bring not just her body but also her sultry voice and sensuous moves to a wider audience via the movies, she took it.[75] Years later, when Mainers saw Mae West advertised as an exotic dancer in the movies, there was truth behind the advertising. Although more women dreamed of making the transition than actually did so, Mae West was not alone in making the move.

One news item that made the Maine newspapers in 1913 was the filing of a $300,000 legal suit against United Booking Offices of America. The suit was filed under the Sherman Antitrust Act, by H. B. Marinelli, Ltd. of New York, London, and Paris. The Marinelli Company was in the business of hiring vaudeville performers and alleged that the defendants controlled the vaudeville business in America and blacklisted "performers at theaters not in the Keith and Orpheum circuits." The defendants named in the suit were, in addition to United Booking Offices, "the Central Vaudeville Promotion Company, Benjamin F. Keith, A. Paul Keith, Frederick F. Proctor, Edward F. Albee, John J. Murdock, Morris Meyerfield, Jr., and Martin Beck."[76] Of the men listed, at least the first four, and the last one named, Martin Beck, who had previously operated his own vaudeville circuit, had been in Portland for the opening of Keith's. And the men were responsible for booking many of the women who came to Maine to dance in the 1910s and 1920s, not just at the Portland Keith's but also at a number of the smaller theaters in the state, the large Gaiety when it had been in operation, and at some of the fairs in Maine.

By the time the suit was filed, B. F. Keith had essentially removed himself from his business pursuits. He retired in 1909 and remarried in October 1913 to a woman just twenty-six years of age to his sixty-seven. It was just a month later that the suit was filed. Keith died in 1914, his son Andrew Paul—who had taken over his end of the business when the elder Keith retired—would die four years later. Control of the company would then pass to Albee.[77] Other company changes would follow in the 1920s.

The situation with the B. F. Keith circuits would have the most impact on southern Maine. Farther north, while the lights had gone out on Bangor's "Great White Way," vaudeville acts and dancing girls did continue to come to the city and the region. The Bijou Theater began holding live plays and some other performances during the summer season in the later 1910s, and these included dancing women. The Gorman Company sent up a few shows, and these proved especially popular. Other live plays and acts presented on the stage likewise included female dance numbers.[78]

The fairs, and to a lesser extent, circuses, also brought female dancers before the public during the era. For example, Walter L. Main's "Fashion Plate Show" circus came to Bangor in July 1918, after having come there for several years, and brought aerial dancers, if they might be called that, women who performed on the high wire and trapeze with dance as well as acrobatic moves. And, just the week before, the Robinson Circus had come to town (again, not for the first time) and had had a few of the same types of performers. The Robinson Circus also came with a Wild West show that summer; female dancers were a standard part of such presentations, and the circus also had unspecified side shows. Moreover, the Robinson Circus played not just to a Bangor audience but also to "all the nearby towns and cities."[79]

People likewise continued to flock to fairs like the Bangor Eastern Maine State Fair into the 1920s, and the fairs were advertised in numerous towns, not just in the community that hosted them, or, more accurately, arranged for them. For example, the Bangor fair advertised in the *Ellsworth American*, as did a number of smaller local fairs, and in Bangor, advertisements for the Waterville Fair, the Lewiston Fair, the Northern Maine Fair in Presque Isle, and other fairs appeared in its two major papers. The Bangor State Fair billed itself as "By Far the Biggest and Best Fair in Maine!" in 1918, doing so not just in Bangor but in other communities also. Its "free entertainment" that year included "clever metropolitan dancers, acrobats, high divers, vocalists, fun makers, etc." (Twin sisters who had previously performed at the Bijou Theater also presented an aerial dance act.) There would be free vaudeville every day in front of the grandstand. The fair ran for six days. Railroads continued providing reduced rates to the fairs as they had for decades, and horse transportation remained popular as did boats, but in 1918 the fair management also let it be known that there was "plenty of automobile parking space."[80]

In addition, of course, there was the midway, home of the dancing girls since the 1800s. The fair advertised that the midway that year had "long lines of tents where Mirth and Marvels reign supreme." Newspaper reporters added to this.[81]

The *BDC* reported on the first day of the fair that "the midway is attractive with many side shows of interest, and almost innumerable booths where good food, confections, ice cream, etc. are displayed in the most inviting fashion." After the fair had started, the newspaper expanded on this coverage. It noted that two troupes of dancers had arrived. Of one, the Zubelda Dancing Girls, the paper stated that they had "a very attractive booth and all the tawdriness of the usual show of this type is missing." The members of this group, the reporter stated, "appear to have a graceful and pleasing and first class act." The other group of dancers, Sam Cohen's Golden Girls, also "give an act in dancing and they are well advertised and apparently their tent is being well patronized." The writer did not have anything positive to say about the Golden Girls; perhaps they had some of the "tawdriness" of the type just mentioned. At any rate, they seem at least to have been popular. The other local paper, the *BDN*, simply noted that the fair had dancing girls on the midway.[82] Even in the late 1910s one sees repeated assertions that there were or would be no bawdy or immodest dancers *this year*. But the very fact that fair managers felt the need to assure the population that there would be no immodesty on the midway implies that there repeatedly was. The fair may have tried to keep such dances out, but there were always dancers, and the concern remained that at least some of them might do something they ought not. Female dancers had an ongoing presence in Maine fairs in the early to mid-1900s, and fairs provided a source of money for the women as they traveled from fair to fair. Some may have performed only in a limited geographic area, going from Maine city to city, while others, with the bigger shows, likely moved from state to state.

Circuses and fairs continued to provide entertainment into the 1920s and beyond, and in the 1920s would continue to feature vaudeville and some other dancers, although the focus of dancing in Maine was beginning to shift elsewhere. In 1923, both the circus and the fairs that came to Bangor highlight these changes and continuities. The Spark Circus, which proclaimed that it had "tripled in size and will be the only big circus to visit Maine this summer," came to Bangor in July. The circus, still staged at Maplewood Park, which would soon become known as Bass Park, was known largely for its animal acts, but it also advertised its "350 arenic artists." One public relations illustration featured an elephant adorned for the show in a headdress and fancy blanket with a young woman in a dance costume and ballet shoes balanced on his trunk. At the two shows presented on the circus's day in Bangor (and at other stops in the state), the company presented Eastern musical instruments and dances, as part of a grand show it called "Echoes from the Reign of King Tut." There was also a "flapper" who danced her way up to the men in the audience and was later revealed to be "a female impersonator," and a "female tightrope dancer" named Nadia Miller performed in the ring. As a review of the circus described her act, "She danced as gracefully on her tight wire some six feet above the grandstand as others do on their smooth glass-like surface of the ballroom." Dancing girls also were part of a horse show in the big tent.[83]

The Bangor State Fair had vaudeville performers in the early 1920s, but the midway offerings did not incite any great comment. In 1925, the word "barker" was heard instead of "fakir," and although local papers did not mention dancers specifically, they stated that the midway was an exciting one, and that it had "a riot of color and music galore."[84] Some of that music no doubt accompanied dancing women. The fair held public dances, too, as did other fairs in the state in the 1920s. Dancing halls were exploding in number, and in what they offered.

In general, vaudeville dancing at fairs—and it was in these shows that women likely made more money and had longer engagements—remained fairly subdued during the 1910s and 1920s, even if the dancing outside the purview of the grandstand did not always do so. Vaudeville advertisements for theaters also remained rather low key, compared to what they would be for much of the 1930s. The flapper made her appearances in advertising, and not just at the fair. For example, during the same season that the female impersonator danced her way up to audience members at the 1923 circus, the Bijou Theater, still staging live acts during the summer, advertised the appearance of the James Carroll Players in *The Vamping Venus*. And their flapper was their female impersonator, Howard Blair, billed as "America's Foremost Female Impersonator." He was back in Maine once more. He was likely the inspiration for the sketch in the advertising: a woman dancing in high heels and a longer, three-quarter-length, flapper-style dress and headdress, her arms up, one leg kicked back. He also appeared in the show as a grandmother, and as himself. The show was in town one week, and the company presented other shows for another two weeks, closing out the season.[85]

Dancers and dancing had started changing in the early 1910s, and these changes would be seen in vaudeville, at the fairs and other such venues, in the movies, and in dance halls. Blair's performances were just one example of such changes, as modern dance as developed under such terpsichorean artists as Ruth St. Denis and Isadora Duncan continued to evolve, and as some of the dances performed by the public became more active, more participatory, and sometimes more energetic. By the late 1910s, although vaudeville would try to embrace some of the new modern or interpretive dance, and many female dancers would make ample money in the American West on the largest circuit there—the Pantages Circuit under the management of Alexander Pantages, who paid up to three times what dancers on the Eastern circuits received—modern dance under the guidance of such dancers as Ted Shawn (the much younger husband of Ruth St. Denis) and the celebrated Martha Graham, would, especially under Graham, start moving in new directions.[86] Vaudeville, too, would undergo its own problems in the late 1920s and 1930s, eventually, at least in Maine, finding part of its answer in upping the stakes, in bringing in the more risqué dancers. Much as under the management of the Keith's circuit it had earlier cleaned up its houses, it would increasingly bring in burlesque dancers, although burlesque in the 1900s meant something a bit different than it had in the 1880s and 1890s, when all acts in a vaudeville production would appear in one grand "burlesque" at the end of a show. The new burlesque acts of the twentieth century would bring sauciness to a new level.

Dance halls would also continue to cause debate and concern in the Maine community, as a whole. However, more pressing matters would soon catch the eye of the public, as the 1920s progressed into the 1930s, including—but not limited to—what vaudeville was doing.

Meanwhile, Keith's and other Portland and Maine venues continued to hold vaudeville shows, some of them featuring dancing, some of them getting close to burlesque, which they would indeed become in following years. The show at Keith's the week the 1913 antitrust lawsuit made the news featured "HIGH CLASS VAUDEVILLE-EXCLUSIVE MOTION PICTURES." The theater noted that at least its lead act came "Direct from B. F. Keith's Theater, Boston." In addition to this, the show featured some "Fascinating Dancing Numbers Including the Brazilian Tango." The theater had three shows daily, at 2:30, 7:15, and 9:00 p.m. The Portland Keith's did not have a continuous show as seen in some of the original company offerings elsewhere and at many of the Nickels. And in case there might be any doubt, especially when the entertainment started leaning toward the burlesque side, in the 1910s and the 1920s, Keith's regularly noted that "ALL ACTS APPEAR IN PERSON."[87]

On January 28, 1928, the Keith's chain underwent some changes in management when the B. F. Keith circuit united with the Orpheum Circuit. The merged company became known as the Keith-Albee-Orpheum Circuit, or KAO. A few months later, the company became the Radio-Keith-Orpheum, or RKO. It became a major motion picture studio, surpassing in scope those of the individual companies pre-1928, and opened the B. F. Keith Memorial Theater—also known as the RKO Keith's Memorial Theater—on October 29, 1928, in Boston, featuring vaudeville acts and first-run films, and the RKO Keith's Theater in Flushing, New York, on Christmas Day 1928, also as a vaudeville house and film theater.[88]

In general, the Keith's vaudeville venues were considered "higher class" than those of the Marcus Loew circuit (which eventually became a movie house, as in some ways did Keith's) and some of the others, with Keith-Orpheum shows aimed at the types of people who might attend Broadway plays—had there been such in Maine—and the Loew circuit designed for a "mass audience," according to Joe Laurie and Abel Green in *Show Biz, from Vaud to Video*. As America entered the 1920s, Keith's remained the largest and most profitable vaudeville circuit. In addition, the Shubert vaudeville circuit had competed with Keith's in the early 1900s (some of its performers would come to Maine), reached an agreement with Keith's to stay out of vaudeville for ten years, then reestablished competition for a short time in the 1920s, and then left the field again. This consolidation helped boost the sagging position vaudeville held in the entertainment business after the late 1920s, but by the 1930s even the larger circuits were being decimated by the film industry and other changes in the entertainment world.[89] This may be why some of them not only embraced the film industry but became an active part of it.

Burlesque, which would also come to Maine in its newest incarnations, was under attack in some regions by the late 1910s for its "indecency" in New York and other cities where partial, and later total or almost total, nudity was common.[90] In Maine, Keith's and some other venues would push the limits with burlesque in the 1930s, and, to some degree, beyond.

In Maine, Keith's continued to feature both vaudeville acts and motion pictures, something that had become common to vaudeville houses across the nation, as the earlier live-acts-only shows gave way to a combination of live acts and film shows. In addition, other Portland area venues started staging vaudeville acts featuring female and, in fewer numbers, male dancers. A whole new venue was under construction in September 1928. The State Theater was slated for opening in February 1929, and was to be operated by New England Theaters Operating Corporation of Boston. The theater would seat 2,500 people and be built in a Spanish style with Spanish decorations. The plan was to make it "the finest theater east of Boston."[91] It would offer standard films but also some vaudeville as the years passed.

In addition, Portland's Strand Theater offered vaudeville in the late 1920s, including dance offerings. A show on the last week of the month of September 1928 featured musical numbers and "Devalery's 12 Dancing Tambourines, a chorus of pretty girls, beautifully costumed." They offered "several dance numbers that are very well done." The women danced in groups and in solo routines, "full of intricate turns and twists that are done in winning style."[92] They may have also been doing the "shake," which many burlesque chorus lines did that year wherein all the women—both feature dancers and the chorus line—were required to "shake," in particular to shake their breasts, in unison. And then came the striptease act. Before this, in 1921, Mae West "brought down the show" with her "very wiggly shimmy." Dances were changing, with versions of the shimmy and jazz dancing coming to the general population, with the public starting to dance more vigorously, sometimes cheek-to-cheek, sometimes in separate but energetic dances like the Charleston, and the lines between which dances to watch and which to perform becoming blurred.[93]

It was at about this time that Sally Rand stepped out of the chorus line, much as Mae West had years earlier. She had changed her name in 1927 from Billie Beck and started working for Cecil B. DeMille. Within a short period, she developed her "fan dance," which set the audiences ablaze. From earning $125 a week at the Chicago World Fair in mid-1934, she was soon bringing in a $6,000 paycheck performing at the Paradise Club in New York in late 1934. Not long after this, Rand would "invent" another dance, the bubble dance, which she copyrighted. She danced with a huge bubble she had designed herself, hiding her body from the audience via the balloon, and like she did with her fan dance, she often wore a flesh-colored body stocking or a filmy Greek-style short garment. But, as with the strippers in cities like New York, exactly what she had on, or did not have on, varied. Perhaps the most scandalous part was when she laid on her back on the floor, and rolled or bounced the huge bubble between her legs or on her torso. And, as with striptease and burlesque dancers during the era, Sally Rand was arrested and tried for indecency. At the time of her sentencing, she stated that other women could do her dances, she had only done them for the money and a chance to go to Hollywood; she had made money, and Hollywood had beckoned. She would star in a couple of movies.[94]

Meanwhile, at Keith's in Portland, in September 1928, the theater proclaimed its dual offerings of both live acts and films once again. A review of the current show at Keith's stated of the female dancers that "the dancing is as good as has been seen in Portland in a long time." And, just one column over and slightly below one of Keith's advertisements that month, on September 5, an advertisement appeared for something else that would entrance the state: a marathon dance.[95] But first, there were other dances to be had. And they, too, blurred the lines quite nicely.

Chapter Three

Oh, for the Satin Slippers and the Gold and the Silver Purses

Scandal in the Dance Halls, Taxi-Dancers, Lucy Nicolar Retires as Molly Spotted Elk Dances Out, and the Early Dance Contests of the 1920s

Vaudeville tended to make its more prominent appearances in the larger dance halls, ballrooms, and theaters, but concerns about morality in the smaller dance halls remained a concern in the early 1900s, as it had been over the previous decades. For example, in the early 1910s some citizens complained of immorality occurring in Maine's dance halls, and a citizens' commission in Portland sent private investigators into seven such establishments. The commission published its findings in a 1914 pamphlet that included current ordinances and called for stricter ordinances and licensing for all dance halls.[1]

Although the report was specific to Portland, it raised concerns voiced elsewhere in the state as well. The Citizens' Committee of Portland was incorporated in 1913 "to promote the public good and remove corrupting and undesirable agencies in the city of Portland." It claimed in 1914 to have "the moral and financial support of nearly one-hundred subscribers," and anticipated increasing those numbers as well as gaining additional moral support among the general public. Following its first chapter, "The Social Evil Upon the Streets," was a second chapter that was simply titled "Dance Halls." Unfortunately for later historians, the report did not identify the actual names of the dance halls investigated but rather developed its own code for the various dance halls, "regular houses of ill-fame," and other questionable establishments and locations it investigated.[2]

Although dance halls were the focus of the second chapter of the Citizens' Committee report, they appeared in the first paragraph of the first chapter and were discussed from time to time throughout the report. In the first mention of dancing in the body of the booklet, the commission reported that their investigators "witnessed soliciting in restaurants and dance halls, and saw men and girls making appointments." Dance halls were clearly designated as morally dangerous, but restaurants did not have their own chapter, as did dance halls. (Hotels and the like did, however, warrant a short chapter.) Such solicitations were not limited to establishments in the more rugged areas of the city. "It was no means confined to the waterfront or to the haunts of sailors and soldiers." Rather, "such soliciting was found on streets and corners centrally located in respectable neighborhoods," the commission determined. The second paragraph of the booklet specifically mentioned solicitation along the area beginning at Monument Square and extending into the city's piers and wharfs. The report focused primarily on teenage girls and young women.[3]

The seven dance halls investigated by the commission, according to the group, were those "seven dance halls constantly in use for public dances, centrally located in the city of Portland and immediate vicinity." The halls were referred to by a letter and a number: from X36 to X43, although not all in that order and not all-inclusive. These were not the cabarets that started opening in New York and other large cities in the early 1910s—offering both food and drinks and entertainment. Rather, these were the older-style dance halls of which Portland had many and the entire state had in abundance. They were generally working class, but not always.

At the first dance hall described, X41, investigators initially saw dates made openly, "pick-ups" arranged both inside and outside the establishment, and "liquor fumes" were readily detected. On the initial visits by the investigators, patrons were seen dancing in the "one-step" dance, in which the young men and women generally danced quite closely, the male often putting his right knee between the girl's legs. As the night progressed, the dancing got even closer with "the rag," an especially suggestive or blatant dance, being done. On or about October 20, 1913, "police regulations prohibiting extreme dancing were made public," and soon after that the dance hall came under new management. This occurred again on October 28, and the place was "clean," but by November 8, 1913, new management allowed the objectionable dancing once again, and at least one known prostitute as well as other objectionable patrons of Dance Hall X38 were in attendance.[4]

Dance Hall X40 proved to have even more objectionable dancing even though often frequented "by young people coming from better families." "Indecent dancing" was observed, with every third dance being a "moon-light" dance, in which all lights except a few red lights were turned off. Purportedly, on October 10, 1913, police informed the managers that "the dancing would have to change." That seemed to make little difference, however, and "the patrons laughed about the police interference."[5]

The next hall listed, X42, saw the "latest dances . . . in full swing." Some "ragging did occur, but overall the dance hall passed muster, with no "extreme dancing." Dance Hall X38, however, was judged as "one of the worst places in the city." The worst offenders from X41 made X38 their home base, and "the dancing was vile." The investigators deemed prostitution evident. The investigators visited this hall a number of times, as they did the others, at one visit deeming "the dancing licentious and vulgar in the extreme," as well as commenting on the prevalence of open smoking and drinking. Police officers had visited this hall, too, to little apparent effect, although on November 8, 1913, police had come to the hall and closed it down or, at least, made all the dancers leave.[6]

Another dance hall, X36, had roughly fifty couples present when investigators made an October 1913 visit. The "crowd was largely made up of an older element, although there were some young people there of high school age." The younger people tended to do the tango and the one-step, the older people "dances of the old school." Patrons of some of the other, and most objectionable, halls were present, and the report concluded that "no attempt was made to stop extreme dancing. The air was laden with tobacco smoke and liquor fumes, and, with the stuffiness of the hall, the place was sickening."[7]

The other two dance halls investigated by the citizens' group were perhaps more closely related to the working-class dance industry than those cited above. Dance Hall X43 had dances put on by students of a Portland dancing school. It is unclear if the students danced for money for each individual dance, as did the taxi-dancers of the next decade, who were actually emerging in the 1910s, but the Portland "students" were clearly making money from the dance, as were the women who held dances at Dance Hall X37. Dance Hall X37, like X43, apparently had dance-school connections, with older women serving as "patronesses." "The tango and the one-step in all their variations were danced through-out the evening," the report noted of X37. Some of the dances "were done objectionably."[8] Clearly, even with older women present, or students or teachers of dance schools at hand, the dances performed did not meet with the approval of the Portland citizens' group. Most likely, at these two halls or establishments, the dances were not substantively different from those performed at other social venues. The partners may have held each other closer, and money or tickets for dances may have changed hands as they did in taxi-dancing, but once again, the principal fear was that such dancing led to immoral acts.

The Citizens' Committee of Portland clearly condemned condi-tions at some if not all of the public dance halls but had little recourse. Although the group's report stated that "there is no public resort for the youth in the city more likely to lead to bad habits of vice than the public dance halls, when improperly conducted or allowed to go unregulated and uncontrolled," it also recognized that "there is no license required in the city of Portland for public dance halls." Police could only enforce the local ordinance that allowed for "keepers of such resorts" to be penalized if they were found to "allow their places to be used or frequented by noisy or disorderly persons, or suffer disorderly persons upon the premises." The chief of police was actually "doing the best he can to improve the conditions of the dance halls."[9]

To address the issue, the committee recommended two things: one, that a municipal ordinance be enacted to require licensing for all dance halls, and two, that a "special licensing board, to be known as the Recreation Commission to be appointed by the Mayor from men and women connected with the social and philanthropic agencies of the city." The establishment of this commission was one of the goals of the Citizens' Committee of Portland, and the commission as envisioned would have the power to grant, refuse, and revoke said dance hall licenses, and to "draw up rules for the proper management of such halls."[10]

A police raid or intervention that the Portland Citizens' Committee mentioned as having occurred in November 1913 may not have made the papers, but one Saturday night event certainly did. November 8 was a Saturday, and on Monday, November 10, 1913, Portland's *Daily Advertiser and Express*, as the *Portland Evening Express* was then known, reported on a police raid at a fraternal organization. Following an arrest at the "Elk's Home on Free Street" that Saturday, Howard D. Ferris faced the Portland Municipal Court. The case was essentially "a nuisance complaint that resulted from a large quantity of assorted liquors." Ferris was ordered to pay $300 in bail and to appear at the court again on Wednesday.[11]

No serious consequences ensued, although a count by the Sheriff's Department of Cumberland County established that a total of 2,400 bottles of various types of liquor had been seized, both on Saturday night and into the afternoon on Sunday. After being counted and placed "under libel," the bottles were stored in a room at the "Elks Home" until such a time as the court might announce its decision. Until then, "this improvised rum room will be fastened with new locks and the keys held by the sheriff." The liquor remained on-site because bringing it to the courthouse would cause "overcrowding." The court was going to test the "club system," and determine its legality. After the initial Saturday night bust, eighty-five lockers were opened with the aid of a "club member" and enough liquor was seized from them to double the amount already seized.[12] Perhaps this was one of the busts mentioned by the Citizens' Committee.

Another site possibly examined by the Citizens' Committee might have been the Pavilion, which advertised in November that it was under new management. The cost for a woman for a dance night was fifteen cents, men paid twenty-five cents, and people wishing to observe or otherwise entertain themselves from the balcony needed to pay just ten cents. A separate advertisement, written and inserted in the paper's regular columns, stated that the establishment had undergone "a complete change in many ways from how it was conducted under the old management." Referring to the two new male managers, the advertisement stated that "long and successful dancing around Portland has fitted these young gentlemen so that they know just what the public wants and how to give it to them." The floor of the Pavilion, the piece asserted, had no match elsewhere in the area and the music was fine, as were the "crowds" who frequented the establishment. The advertisement ended: "Remember, the Pavilion is the place to have a real good time."[13] Just how good a time, the Citizens' Committee might have wished to know.

Another nightspot that might have been investigated was "Pitt Street." On Friday, November 7, 1913, the venue ran an advertisement in the *Portland Express and Advertiser*, with the letters printed in various size fonts. It read:

Special DANCE!
TONIGHT

PITT STREET　　　　The "TANGO"　　　　(Properly Executed)

Perhaps the bit about "properly executed" was to assure readers that nothing licentious was taking place at Pitt Street, perhaps it was a statement of quality, or perhaps it meant nothing.[14]

An advertisement for the dance hall printed on November 10, 1913, simply stated:

DANCE
TO-NIGHT   PITT ST.

The managers of Pitt Street apparently felt that no more detail was needed, or they needed to watch their advertising budget, or, like the managers of the Pavilion, they thought regular column space was a more effective use of their money.[15]

In a shorter advertisement than the Pavilion's, and one printed a column over on the same entertainment page, the managers of Pitt Street asserted that if one had enjoyed the offerings of the venue the previous Friday (when the tango exhibit or contest had occurred) and Monday evenings, then one would enjoy those forthcoming that night. "The crowds present at these Monday and Friday night assemblies consist of the finest dancers in the City of Portland," the column, like that of the Pavilion clearly marked as an "Advertisement," stated.[16] People who wished for dancing but in a different sort of place could also enjoy the dancing and pictures at the Casino Theater in Westbrook, or the dancing at the Majestic Rink on Peaks Island, which advertised that many young people enjoyed taking the ferry to the island and dancing and skating at the Majestic.[17]

The *Express* would later, like other city newspapers, use a more critical format in its entertainment reviews, with most overviews of local offerings covered by newspaper journalists. The Pavilion and Pitt Street may have been included in the 1914 report on the dance halls in Portland, but the exact identity of the investigated dance centers remains unknown.

However, while possible transgressions at the fairs of Maine seem to have been declining, and vaudeville continued to hold a respectable place in the state, dance halls remained a public concern. Drinking and possible immoral acts remained the problem in some people's eyes, and not just at dance halls but also in restaurants. For example, in Portland, on September 4, 1928, the *Express* covered a disturbance at a local establishment.

As the paper stated it, "Flask tipping by flaming youths of Portland who engage in drinking bouts in certain Congress Street restaurants during the wee sma' hours of the morning must cease. Judge Max L. Pinansky made this clear from the bench of the Municipal Court today." The judge was irate about reports of young women drinking openly in eating establishments—in spite of Maine Prohibition—and of intoxicated young men getting in fights "over some girl."[18]

The same day this article appeared, another one specifically regarding dance halls appeared. Indeed, although not noted as such, this article seems almost part of the other, as it too referred to the same judge speaking out in Municipal Court that morning. "We will have to clean up some of these dance halls if conditions don't improve," Pinansky had stated. Two men had been arrested at one of the local dance halls. The argument had started inside the dance hall when one man blew smoke in the other's face, then spilled outside after one of the men was thrown out of the hall. The two men got into a fistfight, were arrested, and the arresting officer smelled liquor on both men's breath. "I can't see why some men can't go to a dance without having some liquor," the judge stated. He fined the men $10 each.[19]

Dancing had changed since 1900 in terms of audience participation. As forms of dance presented on the stage evolved, many people began engaging in "participatory dance." They themselves got up to dance, and the newer dances were not necessarily welcomed by everyone, especially by the older generation, who had found even some waltzes a bit too free; however, some illustrations of "very close" waltzing with a man's legs essentially wrapped around his partner's does explain why in certain situations the waltz could indeed be a form of erotic dance. The tango, the Charleston, the fox-trot, and other dances seemed just too free, too loose, to many people. Add alcohol to that, and the complaints flew onto the pages of the press.

Dance halls continued to exert an appeal, and elicit dismay, on and by Mainers, as these newer dances made their appearance. Although the smaller night spots may not have advertised, places such as the Riverside, the Jack-O-Lantern, the Gray Road Inn, and Island Park in the Portland area, as well as the (Ocean) Pier and the Palace Ballroom in Old Orchard, continued to advertise dances into the 1920s. They provided a venue for new types of dances, and some of them would host dance contests. In Lewiston and Auburn, in Bangor, and in other places, public or open dances were also regularly advertised. Later, in Lewiston during 1933, The Egyptian regularly advertised its ballroom, often noting its "10¢ Adm. . . . For a Whole Evening's Fun!" Another local dance hall advertised the same rate for a night's fun.[20] Lewiston did not see the dance contests and marathons that became popular elsewhere during the 1920s initially, nor, with generally lengthier contests, in the early 1930s; keeping prices low in town may thus have helped keep some locals in the Lewiston area instead of traveling to see the dance shows, which some people clearly did.

Then, as dance halls continued to cause concern, and as live vaudeville and the film industries continued to bring more and more female dancers to the stage in Maine and elsewhere, one particular variety of dance hall came to the forefront, the taxi-dance hall. It would prove highly controversial where the public actually knew it existed; in many places, only the dancers and clientele were aware of what was actually transpiring.

Taxi-dancers were in some ways the descendants of the hurdy gurdy girls in that they were paid by the dance and they danced with their customers as opposed to dancing for them. The rates per dance actually seem to have been lower, but then much of their heyday—the 1920s–1940s—was during National Prohibition, which started on January 16, 1920, under the Eighteenth Amendment, and they were not expected to bring money into the venue by encouraging men to drink more alcohol. And in some places, taxi-dancers were supposed to push patrons to purchase sodas and other nonalcoholic beverages. However, speakeasies—the illegal drinking halls of Prohibition—often had entertainers, including dancers, perform for their clientele. Some of these dancers were deemed extremely immodest. The overlaps between types of dancing and venues were often convoluted during the early 1900s, and ascertaining exactly what dances women (and men) performed remains problematic.

In large cities, sometimes regular little taxi-dancing communities developed, with the women living and working together, and attracting regular clientele, who would line up for a chance to dance with their favorite dancers, while other dancers found themselves sitting on the sidelines for long periods waiting to be chosen, which of course meant their earnings were lower than they might have been. As with other working-class female dancers, concerns arose that the women were prostitutes or were otherwise compromising themselves. As noted, the halls or ballrooms were often raided by police or banned altogether as threats to community morality.

Sociologists studied the taxi-dance halls, with the most definitive coverage of the business being a study conducted from 1925 through 1932 by Paul G. Cressey, published in 1932, and titled *The Taxi-Dance Halls: A Sociological Analysis*. Cressey interviewed dancers and their patrons to understand why both were involved in the business and why the business operated. He studied one neighborhood in Chicago in detail.[21]

Earnest W. Burgess, in his introduction to *The Taxi-Dance Halls: A Sociological Analysis*, linked the endurance dance marathons and other dancing venues for women to taxi-dancing. He stated, "The construction of magnificent dance palaces in our large cities, the night club, and the road house, all unprecedented in American history [are] linked by being for individual gratification or stimulation" (instead of being focused on "family or neighborhood entertainment") and by the "commercialization of stimulation." He believed that jobs such as those performed by the women in the taxi-dance halls did not necessarily lead to vice (including prostitution), "but it opens the door either to vice or to exploitation, or to both." Moreover, he asserted, "The taxi-dance hall and public dance halls are organized to exploit for profit a situation of promiscuity." He defined promiscuity as "intimate behavior upon the basis of casual stimulation."[22]

Cressey himself noted that taxi-dance halls were relatively unknown to the general public, typically being "located inconspicuously in buildings near the business centers of many cities." Women were generally paid 50 percent of the take on dances, with the other 50 percent going to the dance hall proprietor to cover the cost of the hall, an orchestra, and other operating expenses. The dancer "is paid," Cressey stated, "in proportion to the time spent and services rendered," had to dance with any man who purchased a ticket to dance with her, and had to dance with him as long as he kept paying to dance with her. Although known by other names, the term "taxi-dancer" was readily grasped by the public, as she was for hire much like "the taxi-driver with his cab."[23]

Some women in the dime-a-dance halls found that in order to keep getting dances, they had to engage in "sensual dance," dancing closer and more provocatively than generally deemed acceptable in the more legitimate dance venues. Others dancers found that being the "new girl" was the most lucrative element, and would travel to other cities and states to find more lucrative work, at least in the short term, as one of the "new girls." The women generally learned about the jobs dancing for money at the "schools" through word of mouth, and more than one woman said in the 1920s that she could find similar work in every city of any size in any state. Some of the women were experienced dancers, even legitimate dance teachers, and others learned as they went along.[24]

The dance halls used for taxi-dancing or some version thereof often used the terms "dancing hall" or "dancing academy" in their names. There were several of each in the 1920s and 1930s in Maine, with "dancing academies" most numerous in Portland, although some did not last long. A venue could use the taxi-dance system totally, or in just one degree or another. Although a venue that served 100 percent as a taxi-dance hall generally did not admit women who were not paid dancers, some dance halls combined having women as patrons and hostesses who would dance with men who did not have dance partners. One senses that this is the model most easily adapted to Maine in the 1910s on, and indeed one or two of the dance halls examined in Portland in 1913 were quite likely to have done this.

Another model, which also likely existed in Maine, was one that developed in San Francisco and other places in California during the gold rush of 1849 and at other mining frontiers. In this model, the women were not paid by the dance but rather by how much liquor they could get a patron to buy. In the East, after 1900 such places were sometimes known as "concert hall saloons." On Munjoy Hill in 1849, dancers were paid perhaps by the dance, perhaps by getting the men to drink, and perhaps for engaging in sex with them after the dancing. And in some places, according to Cressey, the women worked in traveling carnivals, in the "'49 camps" much like the one that came to Maine with the Eastern Maine State Fair, and likely others in Maine, in the 1890s. This model, according to Cressey, was soon introduced to regular dance halls and dance "palaces," and then used by some legitimate dance schools to help them keep afloat.[25] This, too, quite likely happened in Maine.

Women often took on new names when they signed up with a taxi-dance hall, in order to help secure their privacy and avoid detection by family members. They also experienced fatigue from their sometimes nearly nonstop dancing. One woman stated, "Sometimes I felt just the opposite [exhausted] but I couldn't afford to show my real feelings or I wouldn't get the dance." Many of the working-class women discussed in these pages would have felt the same way, and in some cases said straight out that they felt that way but they needed the money, and so they danced on.

Taxi-dancers often developed a community of sorts as they sometimes lived and traveled with other taxi-dancers, and often lived in the same part of a city, generally near the dance halls. They formed friendships, but as one woman told Cressey, "I don't go to the hall to make friends. I go there to make money." And, for some of them, dancing cost them friends and family, as their work was generally not respected and they had to dance with whatever man was willing to pay to dance with them, which sometimes brought the women into close contact with men of other races, cultures, and ethnicities, which at the time was generally not accepted.[26]

In 1930, a popular song came out about the life of the taxi-dancer, called "Ten Cents a Dance." Some of the lines are:

I'm one of those lady teachers,
A beautiful hostess you know,
The kind that the Palace features
For only a dime a throw . . .

Ten cents a dance
That's what they pay me,
Gosh how they weigh me down . . .

Fighters and sailors and bowlegged tailors
Can pay for their ticket and rent me
Butchers and barbers and rats from the harbors
Are the sweethearts my good luck has sent me . . .[27]

The "Palace" referred to in the song may have referred to the Palace Theater of New York, the Palace Theater of Chicago or that of Cleveland, or to almost any large dance hall in America. In Old Orchard Beach, in Maine, there was also a Palace Ballroom. In Maine, taxi-dancing probably occurred in the larger ballrooms and dance halls, especially in the Portland region, but the evidence is scarce. It may well be that the taxi-dance existed but was not referred to by that name. In some parts of the nation, as noted by Cressey, a somewhat different system developed.

According to Laurie and Green, the taxi "system" developed on the West Coast in dance halls "colloquially known as 'creep joints.' The gimmick was the 'instructress' charging 10 cents a 'lesson' to legalize the enterprise." Dance halls that began springing up in 1919 across the country—Cressey thought it had happened earlier—offered as many as fifty "teachers" or hostesses each. The women received about four cents of each ten-cent dance, and customers also bought beverages at the establishments' soft-drink bars. This system could easily be adapted to prohibitionist Maine. Orchestras were added as the dance halls of this variety gained popularity, and many of these became the modern "ballrooms" in which patrons could dance with the hostess, watch exhibition dancing, or sit in the balconies and watch novelty acts, depending on the occasion. This type of ballroom definitely existed in Maine by the mid- to late 1920s. So, without even using the term *taxi-dancing*, the practice could have existed and then morphed into the various ball-rooms and dance pavilions of the era in Maine.[28] The two versions were not much different, and either way, at one stage or another, women were getting paid by the number of dances they performed, either as simple dancing partners or as "instructors."

One hint that taxi-dancing may have been developing in some form in Maine can be seen in dancing advertisements for dancing lessons at Wilson's at 519 Congress Street in Portland in 1908. The lessons were held in the evenings, and the fees were almost double the price for men than for women. Women could get a series of twelve lessons for $3.00 whereas for men the cost was $5.00.[29] The dance itself was something men were expected to enjoy more, or needed instruction in, or to need dance partners for (and these dance partners might be women paid to serve as their partners), or men were truly the targeted group. This was not the only dance school that charged higher rates for men.

In the 1910s, when the taxi-dance craze was getting underway, Port-land had a number of dance halls and dance schools, as it did in the 1920s and 1930s. By 1920, at least four dancing schools existed (one of them was run by, or named for, Joseph Craig, who had offered lessons earlier in the century), and by 1927 at least six places offered dancing lessons. By 1929, under the heading "Dance Halls and Pavilions," four were listed in the City Directory, one as a "dance hall," one as a "ballroom" (located at 616 Congress, the venue then known as the State Ballroom would catch on fire in 1934), and two as "pavilions"—which according to Earnest Burgess often represented the "cheapest" type of dance hall, as they were often seasonal and unheated, and generally employed local bands. Pavil-ions were also likely the most popular form of dance hall in rural Maine and on the edges of the cities in the 1920s to 1940s, and advertisements for dances at them appeared in newspapers across the state.[30] They would come under close scrutiny in the 1930s, after dancers came face to face with a major fire in one of them, and safety concerns were voiced about the hundreds of wooden dance pavilions in the state.

In the 1930s, the number of dance halls and pavilions grew in Portland as in some other communities. In 1933, eight were listed, as were four dancing schools or "academies." Some of these were well established; others came and went. By 1935, the number of dancing academies and teachers had increased further.[31] This does not mean that they utilized even part of the "dance-a-dime" system, but likely at least one or two of them did to some extent or another.

Then, too, the Citizens' Committee of Portland had found two dance halls that seemed to be offering dancing-school-sponsored public dances—or students and instructors dancing with patrons—in exchange for money in their 1913–1914 studies of Portland's dance halls. The wording of the report was vague, and so the exact arrangements remain unknown. Unfortunately also, the report did not identify the dance halls by name, and thus tracing their history over the next few years is near impossible.[32]

What did seem to be happening was that women could and did dance for money in a similar fashion as taxi-dancers elsewhere, but perhaps just as importantly, a woman trained in classic ballroom dance, especially the tango, the waltz, and the fox-trot, could regularly compete for cash prizes at all sorts of dance venues. The prize was sometimes in gold or silver. Maine dance hall owners advertised their various dances and dance contests, and promoters noted in the early 1900s that one could reach the pavilions in and around Old Orchard Beach "by train, trolley, or automobile." Inside or immediately outside of Portland, some dance hall owners provided transportation to their establishments. This was during Prohibition yet, and as with other concerns, people expressed concerns that alcohol was somehow making it to the dances, even the competitive ones.

Several examples exist of some of the early dance contests, which required that the women have at least some training or dance knowledge, in the 1900s to 1920s in the Portland region. And, some places, like the

Sunset Ballroom, also held "dance exhibitions" that provided a chance for women to make some money showing off their dancing skills.[33]

On August 15, 1928, the Wildwood Pavilion, located about twenty-two miles outside the city of Portland at Steep Falls, held a "Carnival Dance." Accompanied by the standard live orchestra, dancers could compete in a waltz contest. The award was a silver cup. Another such contest may have been held the next day (the actual date for the contest was not mentioned in the Wildwood advertisements), as well as at the Pier at Old Orchard, which held a waltz contest; although the prize was not advertised, most such contests of the era had gold or silver purses as the final award.[34] Several dances were going on in southern Maine that month, as well as vaudeville offerings at local venues, and an early marathon contest in Old Orchard. Many things were scheduled during the summer months at Old Orchard, including regular fireworks displays and free concerts in the 1920s into the 1930s.

The Old Orchard Pier apparently had done well with its dance contest a week earlier, and on Wednesday, August 21, 1928, held another waltz contest. It also held dance contests on Monday and Wednesday nights during part of its season in the early to late 1920s—offering awards—and noted in its advertisements that one could "Dance Over the Waves." The Wildwood held a dance contest again a few days after the Pier's, this time staging a fox-trot contest, a prize awarded but not advertised as to its specifics. The Wildwood held another fox-trot contest on September 1, 1928, again offering a prize but without stating what it was in their advertising. Several Labor Day dances were going on that weekend, including ones at the Gray Road Inn, a "Midnite Carnival Dance" at the Wildwood, one at the Old Orchard Pier, and a "Midnite Dance and Frolic" at the Oakdale Pavilion in Auburn.

If one wanted to go to a dance and to see a bit of vaudeville during the same evening, one could go to the Riverside Pavilion, where late August 1928 saw one of the actors on the B. F. Keith's circuit perform. The Palace Ballroom at Old Orchard, in its turn, held combined dance, dance exhibition, and band concerts on August 30 and on September 1 of 1928, both on Labor Day Weekend. Then, the first night the Grand Police concert and ball featured an appearance by "Beda and Theresa, Stars of 'The Matinee Girl'—Dancing the New York Whirl, Tango and Adagio." The next offering was that of Paul Whitman and his recording orchestra of thirty, with dancing for all. Meanwhile, one could see aerial acts, dancing dogs, and high-diving women in the Portland area also.[35]

A few venues, including the Riverside and Wildwood pavilions, held "Spot Dances" for prizes in the late 1920s.[36]

On September 5, 1928, the Riverside Dance Pavilion ran an advertisement in the *Portland Evening Express* for a waltz contest that read:

GOLD WALTZ CONTEST
THURSDAY NITE
RIVERSIDE
Portland Westbrook State Road
Finest Patronage—Pavilion—in Maine
FIVE DOLLARS IN GOLD TO WINNER!

An orchestra would be playing that night, and buses would be free from the downtown area. Another advertisement in the same paper noted that that night there would be a dance contest at the Wildwood, a "Spot Dance," with prizes awarded.

Ballroom dancing was hard work. Whether the contestants were waltzing, fox-trotting, or tango-ing, the women faced several challenges, and in taxi-style dancing, or at the various dance schools, one of the problems would have been less trained, or untrained, male partners. Although writing of the dances seen in popular films, one quip on the Portland entertainment pages in 1928 was telling. The short article went:

These ballroom scenes in the movies look like easy work on the screen, but a whole day of dancing under hot lights grows monotonous. What 40 women had to put up with in the ballroom scene of "Sins of the Fathers," however, was far worse than monotony. Their partners were all specially selected character types, middle-aged, and supposed to be clumsy on their feet. They were, not only on their own feet, but on those of the women, all day long.

The article was labeled simply, "Dancing Daughters."[37]

Dances were regular events in Maine, and southern Maine especially saw a variety of dance forms, including ballroom dancing, the type of dancing popular in taxi-dancing. Dance pavilions in the Portland region, as well as those in Old Orchard Beach and other tourist locations, saw regular advertisements for dance halls, big bands, and so forth.[38]

Dance halls and competitions also experienced a surge farther north in the 1920s. Competitions seem to have taken a bit longer to catch on in the Bangor region, but they would do so, and in the meantime the simple number of public dances and places to go to dance throughout the middle and northern portions of the state increased remarkably during the era.

By 1923, the large growth in the numbers of public dances at halls and pavilions was evident. And virtually all of them employed live bands and orchestras. By then, regular dances were held at the Riverside Pavilion in Milo, the Chateau Ballroom in Bangor, the Orrington Casino, the Long Lake Sporting Club, and the Indian Lake Pavilion near Machias. Soon thereafter, one could also dance at the Swan Lake Pavilion. People could likewise dance at the Paradise Dance Pavilion in Hampden. The Paradise held a "Grand Ball" in July 1923 with a special "exhibition dance." A decade later, it would host a much longer dance.[39]

In August 1925, the Roseland Pavilion at Camp Benson held an exhibition dance featuring the Charleston, with a professional dancer on stage to "present" the dance to the audience members, who could then dance also. In addition, one group that toured the state in 1923 was the "Chicago Pirates," billed as the—or part of the—"Dance Original Wizzards." The group staged exhibition dancing and vaudeville in Maine and was advertised as promoters of the National Dance Tournament. The group performed music and dance routines at the Oakdale

Pavilion in Lewiston–Auburn on July 4, and then moved on to the Elks Hall in Waterville, the Pine Tree Pavilion in Ellsworth, and to Camp Benson. The group purportedly added "something new on every appearance." Then, the Northern Maine Junction advertised a "Big Dance" near Hermon with music presented by the Chicago Pirates. They likely presented dancing numbers also, although that portion of the troupe might have returned home.[40]

In addition to these venues, one might dance at the East Eddington Grange Hall in summer 1925, as well as at similar rural venues. The Bangor State Fair and the Monson Fair likewise provided for public dancing, as did the Maine State Fair in Lewiston, which had also in recent years had acts presented by "Keith's Vaudeville," the national circuit, not the Portland venue. Moreover, the Twilight Pavilion in Hermon held a dance in August 1925 offering unspecified prizes.

Other dances for prizes followed. The casino at Bar Harbor held a "Cinderella Ball" in September 1925 with the prizes offered being a pair of gold slippers and a pair of silver slippers. These were actual slippers, however, and they had to fit, however roughly, the women who won them. The Chateau in Bangor soon presented a Mardi Gras night and offered a silver cup to its dance contest winner on August 26. Then, billed as "The Sensation of the Season," the Prairie Pavilion in Brownville held a "Grand Gift Dance." Its contest included three big prizes: a "Ford Touring Car, [a] $145 Edison Phonograph, [and a] Red Star Oil Stove."[41] For the time and the place, these were indeed grand prizes.

Mainers now had experience with exhibition dancing and with dance contests, and the dance contests for amateurs and professionals would soon morph into something much bigger. Meanwhile, while Mainers may or may not have had personal experience with taxi-dancing, they were clearly aware that taxi-dancing existed. On January 3, 1934, the *Portland Evening Express* ran a news report out of New York City regarding "Taxi Dancer Missing, Police Think She has Been 'Put on the Spot.'" No explanation as to what a taxi-dancer was or the risks she might run were offered; readers were expected to know all about them. The missing girl, Marie Lambert, had been only eighteen years old and was out on bond on a charge of "aiding the escape of Gerard Simonson from Toombs Prison." Her mother had called the police following the girl's disappearance and after receiving a call warning her that her daughter had "seen too much" and had talked to the police too much.[42]

By 1934, the general population had become aware of taxi-dancing, while the focus for dancers themselves seems to have shifted. In Maine, taxi-dancing may have come and almost gone by the time Marie Lambert of New York went missing. And, by the time the early dancing contests in Maine reached their peaks in the 1920s, Penobscot Molly Nelson had won her own contest in Bangor, had been awarded the $10 prize, and had expanded her career thereafter. She left high school for a time and, after working at a few other brief jobs, in Massachusetts she signed up with a small vaudeville troupe. She had danced in vaudeville by the time she was fifteen or sixteen, and an extant photograph shows her engaged in one native dance, her body not yet formed into its adult shape. She wore a native headdress, a simple bandeau-style top perhaps made of suede, a knee-length skirt with ornamentations including several inches of fringe at the bottom such that when she spun her thighs would have shown, and bells around her ankles and moccasins on her feet. The photograph was taken circa 1918. Unlike many vaudeville and other dancers, Molly left behind a series of diaries that shed insight not into just her own experiences but also into those of other dancers. As discussed in Bunny McBride's work, *Molly Spotted Elk: A Dancer in Paris*, the troupe that Molly worked with in 1920 would travel from town to town and the performers would often stay in cheap boardinghouses while at a particular location. Throughout her career, Molly would save money to send home to her family on Indian Island. Molly would return to high school briefly, then return to Boston for the stage. She was still working in vaudeville, and in 1922—in her first surviving diary—she wrote of a beach theater gig in Rhode Island: "Had to ballyhoo in my costume. So tiresome I could leave the company. They're making a regular monkey of me." (Interestingly, some taxi-dancers of the era were also known as "monkeys," and the term was likewise applied to chorus line dancers.[43] And Molly did sometimes dance in the chorus line.) In addition to dancing, as part of her "ballyhooing," Molly had to dress in native costume and walk the streets to bring in customers to the shows, and had to sell tickets at the admission window before many of the shows.[44]

At age eighteen, Molly had started working with an "Indian revue" troupe out of Boston managed by Milton Goodhue, not unlike Lucy Nicolar before her. Molly wrote in 1922 that in addition to all the ballyhooing, he had sent her and other performers on "a tin can circuit of small dumps." (Some of these appearances were in southern Maine.) She had to participate in exercise sessions every day, and she often had to dance in three to four shows per day—which was common in vaudeville. Even in Maine, vaudeville dancers generally had to go on stage three or four times a day, often working into the wee hours of the morning. Molly wrote that some of the stages she danced upon were just about "as large as a bed." Her pay was not enough to save money to send home, so she did laundry for other people on the side. She boarded in a rooming house, and one night wrote that she had "ate a tin can dinner" in her room. This does not seem to have been an isolated incidence. Molly had to make her own costumes, and by summer 1922 she had had enough. She quit, only to find that her manager did not pay for her room as promised, so she had no money to give to her family.[45] Molly loved to dance, but the jobs she landed, as was true for other female dancers, were neither as lucrative nor as glamorous as she might have hoped.

Molly returned to her home on Indian Island and her high school in Old Town, where Penobscot teenagers attended the regular public school system, there being no public high school education on the island. Racism was a problem for Molly Nelson in Old Town and elsewhere, but Molly continued to write—her other great passion in life—and to dance, and performed a Spanish dance at a show open to the general public—as were many shows and dances—on Indian Island in spring 1923. She was then recruited to serve as a counselor in an all-white camp near Georgetown, Maine, bringing her native allure and skills to the camp. Her experiences at the camp were less than satisfactory, as was high school, and after attending another session of high school in the fall, she left it for good. She would later take remedial courses elsewhere and study at the University of Pennsylvania. In the meantime, she went on a tour of several colleges performing native dances, and joined a show known as the "101 Ranch," started by three brothers in 1906 and based at their ranch in Oklahoma.[46]

At the 101 Ranch, and for their traveling circus or show, Molly performed primarily as a dancer. She was paid about $35 a month. One of her sisters, Aphid, also worked for the company, riding elephants and horses and doing some dancing. Molly was billed as "Princess Neeburban," a name Molly had been using for some time previously and which meant "Northern Lights" in Penobscot. (Interestingly, Lucy Nicolar, with whom Molly would soon work, had a sister by the same name but with a slightly different spelling.[47]) Molly was adopted into the Cheyenne tribe during her time with the 101 Ranch, and returned East with the stage name "Molly Spotted Elk," which she would perform under for the next decade and more. The name was likely taken from her time there, especially from her adoption into the Cheyenne in which she would have been given an adoption name, and "elk" was a common one. Moreover, elk are largely a creature of the West.[48]

In 1926, Molly went to New York City for the first time. She performed in various clubs there, including speakeasies, generally performing Native American dances, some from the Penobscot and Abanaki, others more based in popular culture. She also secured work as an artists' model and joined the renowned Foster Girls dance troupe, dancers known for their combined gymnastic and dancing numbers. The women in the troupe underwent extensive training, and then went out to perform at vaudeville and other venues. In 1926, Molly Spotted Elk performed at the Hippodrome Theater in New York City, one of the theaters and clubs on the Keith circuit.[49] It would not be Molly's only performance at a Keith's venue, and she would later perform for Keith's in Maine as well as elsewhere in the state.

Molly, ever on the move, as were many female dancers of the era, next traveled to San Antonio, Texas, for an eight-month engagement at the new Aztec Theater. A large theater for its day—holding 3,000 seats—Molly initially danced as part of the chorus line, but she soon became noticed and received her own billing at the theater. She began dancing solos as "Princess Spotted Elk."[50]

Returning from her Texas engagement, Molly continued to model and dance, and she gave some dancing lessons. She wanted to return to school and to send money home, so she did everything she could to increase her income. She joined the Princess Watawaso's Indian Troupe, started by fellow Penobscot Lucy Nicolar, and soon danced at the Montauk Theater in Passaic, New Jersey, one of the Keith-Albee theaters. Lucy Nicolar soon organized another Native American troupe, and Molly with five others undertook a two-month tour with the Albee-Orpheum Circuit. They performed in numerous places. Molly Nelson danced, Lucy Nicolar sang. After their last show in Buffalo, New York, Molly went back to New York City and looked for more work. More doors were open to her now, and she joined the Ziegfeld Follies, "follies" and "revues" often being rather glamorized or spicy versions of the regular vaudeville shows. She also danced with the Foster Girls and in New York Revues, often categorized as an "art dancer," which included several styles of dance such as "Oriental," Spanish, East Indian, and interpretive dance. Molly danced at numerous vaudeville venues, often as a featured dancer. She then started performing at cabarets—nightclubs that served food and drinks still, legally, not including alcohol.[51]

Molly Nelson had more opportunities now, but the life of a working-class dancer was still far from easy. She wrote in her journal, talking about the life of a showgirl, "Always running at random here and there to this agent and that one for something to do. This show business is a heartbreaking one full of promises, troubles, glamour, and rush." Stage-door Johnnies also pestered her for attention, as they did other female dancers, and presented another negative reality. But a few promising leads came Molly's way, including an opportunity to perform at the Casino in Paris, which fell through, and she landed a cover photograph on *Collier's* magazine for their April 1927 issue. Her sister Darby also came to New York, and Molly took her on the rounds trying to find her entertainment opportunities.[52]

Molly, at least, soon secured additional work. She met "Texas" (Mary Louise) Guinan, a former vaudeville and Western film star, who in the 1920s ran a line of high-class nightclubs. (Some of her acts were, however, considered highly scandalous—the most controversial of these being perhaps a nude dancer who performed a version of *Leda and the Swan* with an eight-foot boa constrictor. Texas was also known in the late 1920s and 1930s for going into dance marathons to find recruits for her clubs.[53]) Molly started to dance in Guinan's nightclubs in the late 1920s, and in 1928 Texas had her dressed in what would become her standard press release outfit: a head-to-toe eagle headdress, an ornate affair, with just a brief, almost skin-colored fringed top and bottom, the bottom consisting of a short, angled, fringed skirt or scarf around her hips. A 1928 photograph—one reproduced for some of her appearances and on the cover of her biography by McBride—shows Molly posed, her upper torso bent over, one leg raised and bent in front of her, toes pointed downward, with the other leg posed almost on toe, as though she were captured mid-dance. Her feet were bare, her legs clearly muscular.[54]

At Guinan's clubs, Molly Nelson met members of the New York social elite, and she was billed as a feature dancer. She met William Douglas Burden, who after seeing her dance cast her as the female lead for his upcoming film *Silent Enemy*. Molly traveled to the Canadian woods in winter to shoot the film, which told the story of a tribe facing winter starvation. She became sick on-site but still wrote for a publicity flyer for the film, stating that it had been "a great privilege" for her to play the leading female role. She wrote, "I was not acting, but merely living and feeling the part of an Indian girl of long ago." Molly often struggled to get authenticity accepted in her performances, and being part of the film made her feel that she was at last having an opportunity to portray native peoples in a realistic manner. Unfortunately, although the film received solid critical reviews, it did not do well at the box office. It was a silent film, and silent films were on their way out. During filming, Molly had earned a salary of $200 per week, enough money to purchase a large home for her family on Indian Island. The film also gave Molly new opportunities. However, money was soon an issue again.[55] She would seek out new opportunities.

By the late 1920s and the 1930s, Lucy Nicolar was beginning to look homeward, much as Molly Nelson would do throughout her career. Roughly twenty years Molly's senior, Lucy would retire back to Indian Island in the not-too-distant future and settle there, although she did not entirely give up show business. She opened Princess Watawaso's Teepee with her second husband, a Kiowa native and an accomplished performer. The couple hired basket makers to weave on-site and sold various novelties. Lucy worked on a number of Native American causes, as she had long before indicated that she wished to do, especially on the issues of education and suffrage. She helped persuade the state to build a bridge to Indian Island from Old Town, and when Maine granted Native Americans suffrage in 1955, Lucy Nicolar cast the first ballot on Indian Island. She would die at the age of eighty-seven in March 1969.[56] By that time, Molly too would be back on the island, but first, she had more dreams to follow in distant places.

During this time period, Molly Nelson expressed a sentiment no doubt shared by many female dancers. She wrote, "How I wish I could always have the proper atmosphere to do my work as it should be. . . . The more I dance, the more I want to interpret my emotions without hesitation, to create a freedom of primitiveness and abandon. If only one could dance solely for art! Maybe someday I will have the chance. If not in America, then in Europe."[57]

Molly would get her chance in Europe, after becoming even more popular in some sectors of America, even working with the famed mother of modern interpretive dance, Ruth St. Denis, with whom she studied for a short while. She danced with the Provincetown Players by the end of 1929, and performed that year in J. J. Schubert's road show

"Broadway Lights," starring her friend and employer Texas Guinan. The show included three dance troupes, one of them the Foster Girls. Molly performed solo in the show, and she danced with some of Guinan's other dancers. And then, after another period of struggle in which she sometimes performed up to six shows a day, Molly received her chance: She went to Paris to dance with the Indian Band as part of the United States' Exhibition at the 1931 Colonial Exposition in Paris. When the other members of the group returned to the United States, Molly Nelson stayed on, and brought the dancing talent of Molly Spotted Elk to another continent.[58] Meanwhile, the Great Depression started its reign in Europe and in America, where women and men entered new dance competitions—increasingly longer and more strenuous competitions. Some of these began before Molly left for Europe; the longest occurred while she was in Europe.

Chapter Four

And the Victrola Played On

The Early Marathons in Maine and the Start of the Large Dance Endurance Contests, 1923–1933

THE EVIDENCE FOR TAXI-DANCING IN MAINE IS ELUSIVE, THE EVIDENCE for marathon dancing much less so. The dance marathon craze was rather short lived in Maine, but it was in Maine that the dance met its doom—in the short run at one particular marathon travesty, and in the long run by helping bring about national condemnation and eventual prohibition.

Marathons had their 1920s start in England (although one or two American dance contests lasting several hours may have happened before this) when two dance teachers danced for seven hours straight in February 1923, and then, after a few other and gradually longer exhibitions in Europe, in England the record increased to almost twenty-five hours. However, a marathon of sorts had previously been held in California, in San Francisco in 1910, one that purportedly did not allow the dancers to leave the floor for *any* reason. Sid Gruaman staged a relatively short endurance contest at his dance hall or ballroom in 1910, and held another one a few weeks later that lasted fifteen hours. In America in the 1920s, the first person to take up the English challenge was a female dance instructor, thirty-two-year-old Alma Cummings, who danced with a succession of six younger male partners for twenty-seven hours, on March 30–31, 1923. She soon lost her record to a student in Europe, then regained her record, dancing for some fifty hours. Then four American women—a department store saleswoman, a beauty contest winner, a file clerk, and a restaurant waitress—challenged Cummings for the record. That these working-class women and other women performed so well early in the marathon craze brought questions and challenges regarding gender and endurance to the surface.[1] Certainly the women had shown a distinct competitive facet of their personalities, and other women would continue to do so in subsequent years.

According to one study, some 20,000 people worked in the marathon industry at the height of the marathon craze, as contestants or as employees of the companies that managed them. Frank Calabria, psychologist and ballroom dancer, called the marathons "the dog end of American show business, a bastard form of entertainment which borrowed from vaudeville, burlesque, night club acts and sport." Arnold Gingrich, a 1930s journalist, referred to the longer endurance contests as "The Innocent Jail," the innocents in the jail being the dance contestants, who remained confined to the building in which they danced for days, weeks, or even months.[2] But if 20,000 people found jobs in the industry, and hundreds of thousands of tickets were sold to the dances, then the "bastard" entertainment may have been a jail to some contestants, but so were many other working-class jobs and, at the height of the marathon endurance contests, jobs were often scarce.

The early marathons in Maine were of limited duration. By 1933, they would be long and grueling. Both provided contestants a chance to win prizes, and for audience members or spectators, cheap entertainment.

The first Maine marathon, of sorts, located to date, was that of a short marathon held in Old Orchard Beach in the early 1920s, fast on the heels of a movement that was only just then reaching America, including Boston and New York in the Northeast, purportedly inspired by dancers in Europe and by Alma Cummings in America. Competition soon took up the challenge to best their records with some of the liveliest contests held in New York and New England, some of them held inside, others outdoors; some public, some private. In this case, both women and men sought financial remuneration for their dance exhibitions (although some professional dancers also engaged in marathons for publicity reasons). Both genders—especially as the years went by and the contests became longer and longer—were condemned, and both faced sometimes grueling work conditions, as the dances became increasingly commercial.

On July 17, 1923, couples in a marathon in Old Orchard danced the fox-trot and other dances to such tunes as "Little White Lies" and "Swinging in the Hammock" on a raised wooden platform on the beach. Music blaring, the sounds during the competition were described as "one of the weirdest cacophonies of sound ever to torment the human ear. From the dancing platform poured the raspy notes of a phonograph. Nearby a Salvation Army contingent set up headquarters hoping to drown the ways and sounds of sin to a soothing bath of prayers and hymns." But the phonograph played on, the couples danced on, and, according to the same account, "the louder the hymns, the more fervent the prayers, the harder the thrill seekers danced."[3]

The *Portland Evening Express* briefly covered the marathon, or "endurance contest," as the paper described the competition at Old Orchard Beach the day after it transpired. In a "special" to the *Express*, dispatched from Old Orchard the previous evening, the paper identified the July 17 event as being the "first marathon dance ever held at Old Orchard Beach." The Old Orchard Board of Trade had organized the contest and had offered the winning couple a prize of $50. To win the $50, the couple was supposed to dance from 2:00 p.m. until midnight, but the contest did not start until 5:30.[4] Perhaps the delay had something to do with the confusion on the beach that day and evening.

Once the contest began, four couples danced through until 10:00 p.m., at which time "a boy and girl were stopped . . . and given $5. At midnight, the three other couples were still dancing as lively as when the contest opened," the paper reported, "and the $45 remaining from the $50 prize was divided among them." The Victrola that had supplied the music for the temporary stage then fell silent, at least for the night of that contest.[5] Over the next few years, however, a number of such "endurance" contests were held, with those in the 1920s generally lasting hours, not days, in duration.

For example, on August 18, 1928, two couples, clad in just their bathing suits, fox-trotted for five miles, in a dance-race, from the First Congregational Church in Saco to the Palace Ballroom in Old Orchard, accompanied by trucks blaring out music from phonographs. After reaching Old Orchard, the contestants danced ten laps around the large dance hall, giving spectators time to catch up and watch the finale. The contest started at 7:30 p.m. and lasted until about 9:00, leaving the dance hall free for further fun that night. The winners, Irene Legere of Old Orchard and Arthur Lambert of Biddeford, completed the five-mile course in one hour and eleven minutes.[6]

The Saco to Old Orchard Beach marathon of August 1928 was advertised in Portland in advance. A small advertisement published on August 15 had simply stated that there would be dancing that night at the Palace in Old Orchard Beach, and **"Marathon Dance, Saturday Night**." The next day a small block advertisement stated that the marathon dance on Saturday night would be "FROM SACO TO OLD ORCHARD BEACH."[7] Entrants and spectators now had a better idea of what the contest was to be.

Two additional small advertisements for the event were printed on the entertainment "page" on the day before and the day of the event in the *Portland Evening Express*. There were no photographs or drawings in the advertisements, just the simple wording—in various fonts and on different lines:

The first read:

Dancing Tonight
Palace Old Orchard
Tomorrow Night
Marathon Dance
Saco—to Old Orchard
Send in Entry Blanks at Once

The advertisement on the day of the marathon was slightly larger, and stated:

PALACE BALLROOM
OLD ORCHARD
—TONIGHT—
MARATHON DANCE
SACO TO OLD ORCHARD
Contestants Leave Saco 7:30 and arrive
in the Palace Ballroom about 9:00 P.M.

One further line announced that Paul Whitman would be appearing on Saturday, September 1. August 18 was a Saturday, and an advertisement one column over from that for the dance marathon on the 18th advertised the "Old Orchard Excursions" being held throughout August, with the Boston & Maine Railroad offering a round-trip ticket for fifty cents. The tickets could be used "on all regular trains to and from Portland," and travelers were encouraged to "enjoy a fine outing by train and avoid motoring on congested highways." A rough pen-and-ink drawing that showed people enjoying the beach area headed the advertisement.[8]

Seven other dance halls advertised in the same Portland paper that they would hold dances the night of the marathon, and other trips in Maine and into New Hampshire were also advertised.[9] Mainers were on the move, and dancing was included in the entertainment for many Mainers, some as dancers and contestants, some as audience members.

A "Special Dispatch" also went out of Saco on August 18 about the marathon that night. The *Evening Express* carried the "Special" as well as the above advertising. The dispatch noted that the road dance would start at "the parish house on Beech Street at 7:30 o'clock." Already, "several couples have entered the contest and will dance over the highway to Old Orchard to music on phonographs on auto trucks which will precede the dancers. Upon reaching Orchard, 10 laps will be danced by contestants about a big hall, the total distance being about five miles."[10]

In case the distance seemed daunting to any would-be contestants, the *Express* also carried an article from Boston on August 18 that covered a twenty-six-mile marathon road dance. It had started, as had an earlier one, at the R. & A. clubhouse in Ashland at 6:00 a.m., and possibly ended on Commonwealth Avenue in Boston. This road dance, however, was not actually a contest. Rather it was one professional male dancer "and his four girl partners," at least a couple of whom made the entire course in a car, accompanied by the man's sponsor, himself a former dancer and a stage manager.[11]

Maine's Saco to Old Orchard marathon road dance was a true contest. It took place without major problems. However, dance in general was still an issue with some people, and the earlier concerns over dance halls and drinking or immorality continued. And just two days after the August 18 contest, the *Express* ran an article titled "Easy to Get Liquor at Dance Places, Court is Informed." Its lead-in read, "Certain dance halls in Cumberland County are apparently the easiest places in the world to secure liquor." The observation came from testimony from a man charged with "loitering with liquor in his pocket." Maine was still a dry state, as was the nation now, and the offender told the court that he had just entered the doorway of a dance hall at or near the Gray Road Inn, and had jokingly stated that he would love to have some wine, and a man had then quickly gone and brought him a bottle and sold it to him for $1.50. The assistant attorney general for the county supported what the offender relayed through his own attorney, characterizing "the situation about some of the dance halls as bad." He wanted to proceed with the case at hand and hold some other related trials in order to "get the entire picture of this situation." The judge wanted to get the situation under control and force the bootleggers out of business.[12]

Within a week of the road dance that ended in Old Orchard Beach at the Palace Ballroom—and within days of the above article about liquor and dance halls appearing—a regular marathon, or rather a modified one, was on, held at the Palace Ballroom. This time there were more contestants than there had been on August 18. The promoters had a larger hand in the affair and stressed that they were holding an indoor contest to avoid the dangers inherent in holding an endurance contest along the roadways. The *Portland Evening Express* carried small advertisements for the marathon, ones that made it clear that this was not to be one of the longer contests that would evolve over the next years, but instead be one limited in scope and duration.[13]

At least two advertisements ran for the newest marathon. On August 22, 1928, the *Portland Evening Express*, after advertising the musical offerings of that coming evening, stated:

Tomorrow Night
ENDURANCE CONTEST.
STATE CHAMPIONSHIP CHALLENGE

A lengthier advertisement in the paper the following day, Thursday, August 23, 1928, included a sketch of a couple dancing, the man rather debonair in sleek dark slacks and top and the woman wearing a light fitted blouse, a dark skirt, and a scarf flying out from around her neck. The sketch was printed alongside the prose. The wording read:

Tonight
Palace
Ballroom
OLD ORCHARD
Endurance Contest
STARTING AT 6 P.M.
FINISHING AT 11:30 P.M.
Mr. "Red" Ledger and Sister
Challenge All Comers

The marathon was clearly limited in time, as later ones would not be, and its "challenge" aspect was also somewhat unique to the Maine dance world.[14]

The Palace Ballroom was more suited and safe for marathons than were some of the other Maine venues. Popular during the Big Band Era in Maine in the 1930s, although enjoying some major local and national talent in the 1920s also, it was a sizable structure, and in the 1920s was home to uncountable large public dances in addition to the endurance contests of shorter duration. In the 1924 season alone, purportedly, "sixty thousand persons tripped the light fantastic on this dance floor," according to a contemporary source. The dance floor was constructed of bird's-eye maple, and covered "11,830 [square] feet. This was laid by first class workmen. . . . Its smoothness gives it elasticity, spring and life to the dancer," the source continued. The author extolled the various features of the dance hall, known at the time as the New Palace Ballroom, and reported that the dance floor "is always kept in the pink of condition for it is in charge of an expert."[15] Clearly, a floor that had some spring to it would have aided a marathon dancer who was on her feet—or his—for hours, and later days and weeks at a time, with only brief breaks allowed during the longer contests.

According to the same source, published in the mid-1920s, and critically important as seen in a later Maine marathon held in the autumn and winter months outside Bangor, the New Palace Ballroom "is fireproof and meets with the right requirements of the insurance underwriters." Not as critical for the more northern marathon dance in the 1930s but fantastic for the shorter one in 1928, the author of the "New Palace Ballroom" stated of the building, "Its location is ideal for it is on the famous Beach where the cool sea breezes sweep [through] the magnificent New Ballroom." The building also sported "ample parking space."[16]

"No expense was spared that it might please the aesthetic taste and give the greatest enjoyment to its patrons," the highly laudatory article continued. The building had "a spacious and beautiful lobby, the walls adorned with French Plate Mirrors, hardwood floors laid with the latest floor covering and a booth for the ticket seller that it is a gem of beauty." The dance hall, if it may be called that in light of its apparently high-class accoutrements, also had "broad stairs of gradual ascent" that led on both sides "into the ballroom that is unexcelled for beauty and convenience." The building contained some 140 windows with 52 of them overlooking the beach and the ocean. Sea breezes cooled the building, which even without the ocean breeze was well ventilated, and had "pure air."[17]

In some ways, the Palace Ballroom may have proved too fancy or expensive for the longer marathons, which would have required closing the building for days, weeks, and months to other uses, and would no doubt have cost the promoters of the long endurance contests too much, as it would the many people who came to watch them, some who came every day or every few days to check on their favorite dancers, as well as to enjoy some otherwise inexpensive entertainment during the harshest days of the Great Depression of the 1930s.[18] The direction of the marathons would move to the indoors over future months and years, but the road dances were not yet over.

Portland opted to have an "open road" contest in September 1928 over a five-mile route from City Hall to the Riverside Dance Pavilion in Riverton. Purportedly 3,000 people came as onlookers, arriving at City Hall's plaza to watch four couples start the dance-race on the evening of September 4, a Tuesday. Many of the spectators followed the dancers on foot, on bicycle, and in a motorcade of sorts some four cars wide and about two miles long. A mobile band—a complete dance band on a raised platform—followed along to provide music. "Trainers" also accompanied the dancers to provide aid and water and aspirin. A few dancers succumbed to fatigue and foot injuries. Water was thrown in dancers' faces to revive them, and bottles of aspirin passed around. Spectators cheered on their favorite dancers, and at the end, eighteen-year-old Gertrude W. Stairs of Spring Street, Portland, and Leon "Joe" Michaud, age twenty-one, of Cumberland Avenue were declared the winners, completing the five-mile course in forty-seven minutes. They won $15 in gold, while the dancers-up, Helen Scribner and James DeRoche, also both of Portland, won $5 or $10 in gold and completed the course in a little over forty-eight minutes. A third couple—M. G. Ludden and Ann McDermitt—purportedly dropped out due to "traffic interference," while a fourth couple—Doris Cleaves and George Arsenault—almost made it to the finish line in a timely manner but "were compelled to abandon the race when a pain developed in the girl's side."[19]

The number of spectators present to watch and follow the contestants may have been due in part to an advertisement for the event paid for by the Riverside Pavilion. The Riverside first advertised the event in the *Express* on August 31, 1928, as part of a larger advertisement. After introducing its ongoing bands and dancing nights, it noted: "Coming—Fox Trot Marathon—3 Gold Prizes—City Hall to Riverside—Enter Your Name Now." The Riverside next ran an advertisement for a spot dance contest with prizes for September 1, and included with it, "Marathon Dance, Tuesday Night, City Hall to Riverside. $20 in Gold—6 couples already registered—Leave City Hall at 7 P.M."[20]

Then, a decent-sized advertisement for the event appeared on September 4, stating:

TONITE
MARATHON DANCE
Starts from City Hall 7 P.M. via Forest Ave. to Woodfords, to
RIVERSIDE
On Portland Westbrook State Road.
Free Busses will follow the dancers —
Come early to get your seat—
6 Couples entered—$20 in GOLD—
DANCING STARTS AT RIVERSIDE
[on] Arrival of Marathon dancers—FREE BUSSES
From Oak & Congress 6:30 to 9:30
Free Parking 500 cars in the grove.

Clearly Riverside was willing to profit from the marathon in various ways, and advertised the free transportation and details necessary to get the population out not just to see the contest but also to dance at the pavilion that night after the contest. Several other dances scheduled for that night in the Portland area were also advertised in the newspapers.[21]

Similar contests were held over the next four years in various parts of Maine, and in 1933 three major and final marathons, each considered a "real" marathon, took place in the state: two in Old Orchard Beach and one in Hampden. The one in Hampden would result in disaster, and in a set of records revealing details of the life of a marathon dancer found nowhere else.

The other two marathons were underway by the time the one in Hampden started. The first of 1933's major marathons, held in Old Orchard Beach, started on June 28 at the Old Orchard Arcade and featured twenty-one couples, or forty-two competitors. There may also have been a few "solo" contestants who might or might not become part of a couple at some time. As with the other two major marathons, some contestants came from far away, from as great a distance as California and Florida, the perhaps most obvious lure—to subsequent generations—being a $1,000 prize. In addition, prizes of $300 and $200 were offered to the second- and third-prize winners respectively.[22]

Not just the cash final prizes motivated the women and men, however. It might be argued, and as evidence from the Hampden and other marathons indicates, marathon dancers also performed and worked in exchange for a place to stay and eat during the Great Depression. If one could stay on one's toes according to contest rules, one would be neither foodless nor homeless, and might also win various prizes, often cash, along the way, and as with the other dance forms discussed herein, money was sometimes thrown at the dancers' feet for their individual performances. For the audiences, as the Great Depression advanced, the longer marathons offered a cheap type of entertainment that they could go to day after day, especially if they found themselves among the large number of the unemployed.

The final contestants at the Old Orchard Arcade marathon danced for seventy-seven days, or almost three months, the contest ending on September 12. The rules of the marathon were straightforward and quite standard: For every forty-five minutes of dancing, a dancer would be allowed to rest for fifteen minutes. Two couples made it all the way to the end. Viola and Harold Hedlund of Minneapolis won the big $1,000 cash prize, with two other dancers dropping out, or rather dropping over with exhaustion, just moments before the final winners were declared. Catherine LaRose of Portland and Kenneth McCaye of Los Angeles, her dance partner, failed to make one final lap around the room, in what apparently was one of the specific "games" or activities staged during the marathon. As a report noted, during the days of the marathon—which were hot summer ones—"survivors perspired, grew dizzy, sometimes fainted. Young girls whimpered from discomfort and just plain fatigue. Somehow a few managed to keep going."[23] Yet keep going many of the dancers had, in a quest for the large award quite likely, but they also had *work* for those thirty or forty or sixty or seventy-seven days, or for however long they could stay on their feet, and the local population took note of their work, finding it a source of entertainment to watch them. And, of course, the marathon provided close to three months of employment for other people as well as the dancers, as the dancers needed to be housed and fed, their medical needs attended, music provided, and so forth. Generally, live musicians performed during peak hours of audience attendance.

It was this type of dance marathon, one that went on week after week, month after month, that inspired Horace McCoy's 1935 novel, *They Shoot Horses, Don't They?* that three decades later became a film of the same title starring Jane Fonda. McCoy had been a marathon bouncer in California and thus had direct experience with marathons, but some recent sources have suggested that he skimmed over the depth of what was actually happening at the long endurance contests in his quest to make a name for himself as a writer. In his version of the marathons, a totally dispirited, degraded female dancer asks her partner to shoot her in the head, for, in circumstances where there is no hope, "They shoot horses, don't they?" Her partner shoots her. There was more than one death in the novel, and there would be more than one death in Maine's marathons.[24]

Before death came to a Maine marathon, Mable "Bubbles" Everand and her partner, Ransom McNally, came in fourth place in the seventy-seven-day endurance contest at the Marathon Arena. This would have meant that they were competing well into the contest. "Bubbles" had a picture postcard made of her, reprinted in Daniel E. Blaney's *Old Orchard Beach, Postcard History Series*. The photograph shows an attractive young woman with large dark eyes and dark hair, cut and waved in the style of the era. She wore a light-colored blouse or dress, as well as a beaded necklace. She signed the front of the card "Sincerely Yours, Bubbles, #4."[25] This may indicate that she and her partner indeed came in fourth place or that they were team #4. If she had been a solo dancer, or, depending on the contest rules, #4 could have been just her number. Generally, the larger marathons gave each team or soloist a number.

Just after the seventy-seven-day marathon ended, the last of the dancers agreed to appear together again, in Portland. The dancers were to appear in a show at the Portland auditorium on September 14. However, so many people showed up for the Thursday event, reportedly "from places as remote as Farmington," that the result was "a near riot at the auditorium." According to the chief engineer of the Portland Fire Department, "Myrtle Street was filled to overflowing, women fainted, and strong men had to exert all their power to 'muscle into' the show." Firemen were pressed into service until officers of the law could arrive for crowd-control duty, and by the time they arrived the crowd had grown even larger. "Policemen were called from bed, and in some instances brought to the scene by the patrol cars," the *Express* reported. Even when police arrived, firefighters and police together were deemed "too few to cope with the constantly augmenting crowd that had trekked to into the City." Eventually the area was cleared and the show proceeded, described as "an exhibition of the 'Marathoners' who had danced the longest during the summer months at Old Orchard Beach." Sales of tickets had to stop before everyone who wanted to do so could secure a ticket. Everyone wanted to see the dancers who had managed to survive months of grueling dancing. Perhaps tellingly, the *Portland Evening Express* used the header "Near Riot at City Hall Victory Ball" on its continued page of coverage.[26] In this case rioting was averted, unlike during the events of 1849 or during a case of "revenge rioting" during the early 1940s.

Within a few weeks of the first Old Orchard indoor long-term marathon ending, and after the ruckus in Portland, another endurance marathon began. It started on October 27, 1933, and, perhaps importantly, it was held at the Golden Slipper Dance Hall. (This has also been called the Marathon Arena, as has been the location of the Arcade.[27]) The marathon would last for over four months, until March 4, 1934, ending at 7:30 p.m. By the time it ended, the winners had danced for 3,068 hours and 28 minutes. The winners both came from Massachusetts: Mildred Snow of Roxbury and Conrad Daoust of Bradford. During the marathon, two dancing couples had been married, and the justice of peace who performed the vows danced during the ceremony, as did the best men and bridesmaids and other members of the bridal parties.[28] This type of "performance" was not uncommon at marathons, and such marriages frequently ended in divorce after a given contest. Other elements of dance marathons were also purportedly staged to increase audience attendance.

One of the women in—or otherwise involved with—one of the Old Orchard marathons left behind her small, now faded, red leather autograph book. Held by the Old Orchard Historical Society into the twenty-first century, the small memento of the dance had once been owned by Evelyn Middleton, thought to have competed in one of the local marathons, but internal evidence suggests that she was an audience member and fan of the dancing, or possibly that she worked for the marathon. The first entry in Evelyn's book was signed by Ernie Steele, one of the judges, or at least that is what he wrote after his signature. Apparently Evelyn passed her book around toward the end of the contest, as Steele wrote to her: "Evelyn, Just a few lines wishing you loads of luck and best wishes until we meet again."[29] It may be that if he were the judge he had nothing more personal to write, or that he did not think it fitting to write anything more personal.

The second person to sign Evelyn's book left her with a poem. The writer, Jackie Collins, wrote:

Remember well
And bear in mind
A good true friend
Is hard to find
And when you find
One good and true
Give not the old one
For the new.

Jackie added a short salutation after her name. The ink is a bit old and smeared, but it seems to read, "Your City Person."[30]

The next signer also left a bit of a poem. The male dancer wrote,

You ask me to write
What shall it be?
Just two words
Remember me.

He signed his ditty, "Joe Perrinelli, Onion Song Kid, #31." His last name is difficult to decipher, but not his dance marathon number. (Another dancer, from "Team 7," signed her name Connie, and wrote much as Joe had, including the "two words, remember me" bit, and called herself Evelyn's "Marathon Pal."[31]

The next dancer to sign the book was dancer #1, and he dated his note October 27, 1933, indicating that the dance was possibly the marathon that started on June 28 at the Old Orchard Arcade but, judging by the number of couples in that marathon (twenty-one), and the fact that one of the books signers signed in as dancer #96, it was quite likely the long marathon that started on October 27, 1933, at the Golden Slipper Dance Hall, with him using that date to serve as a reminder of the opening of the marathon. Joey Kitchie (perhaps Ritchie) wrote, "To Evelyn, A cute thing and marathon sister, from Just A Dancing Fool?" followed by his name and dance number, with "His [or "Hrs."] 675 Old Orchard Beach Marathon Dance."[32] The number would seem to indicate the hour, not that he had been in 675 marathons. Another signer of the book wrote that he was signing the book at the 674th hour, so quite likely Joey signed it at hour 675. Evidence from a later Maine dance marathon indicates that the hour of the dance was generally noted on a bulletin board or via other signage.

The next signer dedicated her entry "To an Ardent Fan." The dancer, #96, wrote that she and Evelyn had "met at a marathon," and went on to say that she or they depended "largely on your support for our victory and success. I am Sincerely Yours, Thelma Kimel [or Kemel], #96."[33] Again, the signature is difficult to read, but the entry certainly seems to have been signed by a Thelma Kimel.

One dancer who signed the book wrote, "To Evelyn, As nice a girl as one could ever wish to meet. May you have all the luck and happiness that any one person can have. Best wishes till we meet again." The signee gave his full name and his town, and his entry would seem—unless she had people sign her book well after the June 28 marathon had ended—that it was indeed the October 27, 1933, marathon for which Evelyn had sought signatures. The signee was Larry J. Homes of Brookfield, Massachusetts, and he asked Evelyn to "please write." He signed the day as "Nov. 25, 1933, 674 hours, 30 days, Old Orchard Beach Marathon."[34] This last statement, with other internal evidence, would indicate that it was indeed the Golden Slipper Marathon that had started on October 27 and that would continue into December.

Another male dancer who asked Evelyn to write was "John Schmidt, Swiss Yodeler." He wrote to Evelyn that he wished her "happiness and good luck at all times," and after his signature stated that he was "Still Lonesome and Blue."[35]

Two final male dancers signed Evelyn's autograph book. One was Everett "Red" Lyer, "The Dancing Cop." "The Dancing Cop" wrote to her that he had danced 674 hours before losing his partner that night and would pick another one within twenty-four hours.[36]

Dancer #11, Loyde Judd of Freeport, Maine, wrote Evelyn a poem, and noted that he hoped to see her again at what appears to have been a "hayride." He wrote,

When the golden sun is sinking
And your mind from troubles flee
While of others you are thinking
Will you sometimes think of me?

He signed his name, number, town, and "Sincerely Yours."[37]

The last entry in Evelyn's book was signed "Flora & Harry, P [A]itchburg, Mass, Dec. 4th, 1933." The signee simply wrote, "hope you will always be nice and smart just like the first day I met you."[38]

Meanwhile, as the Old Orchard contestants danced through the winter, with or without Evelyn Middleton dancing, a dance marathon started at the Paradise Dance Pavilion or Hall in Hampden. This marathon would have tragic consequences and lasting repercussions for the dance marathons in Maine and elsewhere in America. And one of the signees of Evelyn's book, Loyde or Lloyd Judd from the Old Orchard marathon, would turn up at another marathon the following year, although that endurance contest was not identified as a marathon. Not all of the dance endurance contests were called marathons. Indeed, as the dances became larger and lasted for longer and longer periods of time, they encountered more scorn as some people considered the dancers unskilled, or not truly dancing; as the dancers became increasingly weary as days and weeks passed, their technique may have understandably deteriorated, and terms such as "walkathon" reflected the fact that the weary dancers sometimes simply shuffled or stumbled or almost walked around, as the days dragged on and on. On the reverse side, some of the dances, especially the earlier ones, were called "speed derbies," and that term was close to the one later used in Maine after the Hampden marathon ended, the dance in which Lloyd Judd would compete. But that was a hellfire away in mid-1933.

CHAPTER FIVE

Dancing in Paradise, Burning in Hell

The Paradise Dance Pavilion Fire of 1933 and the End of the Endurance Dance Era

ON HALLOWEEN, OCTOBER 31, 1933, SIXTY-SIX PEOPLE—COUPLES, plus a few solo dancers—started the Hampden dance marathon, "owned," as the person in charge called it, by Sidney Curtis of Revere, Massachusetts, and affiliated with the Golden Slipper Producing Company of Boston, a dance marathon promotion company that had a near monopoly in the larger marathons in the Northeast. By the time the marathon ended, national Prohibition, in terms of alcohol, had also ended. There were an estimated thirty-five to forty marathons of some variety being held in the United States at any given time in the early 1930s, including those in Maine. Promoters had to secure satisfactory shelters in which to house their contests, shelters that provided sufficient interior space to accommodate dancers, musicians, audiences, eating and resting facilities, and so forth, and provided adequate room for automobile parking. To meet these various needs, major promoters used existing, often centrally located, sports arenas or roller-skating rinks, set up large tents, or found structures they deemed suitable on the outskirts of towns. All this would soon change.

The Hampden dance was held in an old barn-like building, located not far from where Riverside Park had earlier helped introduce vaudeville to the region, built primarily for summer use—not for the chill of a Maine winter. Sidney Curtis leased the building for the marathon. He had sought to locate the dance in Bangor, but local ordinances did not allow for the type of marathon he proposed. As it was a controversial endurance event proposed, one local paper, the *Bangor Daily Commercial* (*BDC*) gave it coverage from the beginning, or near beginning, and ran event advertisements. Another local paper, the *Bangor Daily News* (*BDN*), would cover events later as they developed during the course of the dance—especially its end.

On Saturday, October 28, 1933, the *BDN* ran a short article about the dance marathon stating that—although there had been talk of revoking a permit given by the Hampden selectmen—the permit would not be revoked. One of the selectmen had sought legal counsel and been advised that "there are no laws in Maine to prohibit exhibitions of the sort planned and for which the permit was granted." The selectman, William G. Kimball, thereby issued a statement to the effect that "the selectmen have been unable to learn that the proposed exhibition in any way contemplated a violation of the laws of the state, and believe that the management and those who participate in the event are acting entirely within their legal rights."[1] So the show went on, but first, other complaints came in.

The *BDC*, also on October 28, 1933, reported on protests against the dance. It too quoted Selectman Kimballs's statement regarding the legality of the marathon, which the paper referred to in its headline as a "Marathon Ball." The paper also quoted "Mrs. Hatt, wife of Rev. T. B. Hatt," stating that, regarding the protest, "considerable opposition to the project had developed, with much of the opposition to the project being based on the injurious effect of continuous dancing on the health of young people." Reverend Shattuck had also had concerns expressed to him regarding the threat to health that marathon dancing posed. The *BDN* summed up the "tremendous opposition" to the marathon in "Hampden and the surrounding cities and towns. Situated as it is within a short distance from the Bangor city line," the paper stated, "those who oppose the proposed exhibition claim that the long continued physical exertion will lead to great body fatigue, keeping contestants from the relaxation and rest necessary for keeping body and mind in a healthy condition."[2] The dancers in Hampden would indeed suffer from a lack of rest and relaxation over the upcoming weeks.

The *Commercial* carried an article about the marathon the day it started. The header ran, "Golden Slipper Marathon to Begin Tonight; 40 Entries to Date; Contestants Fed on Specially Prepared Foods."[3] The number of contestants grew to at least sixty-six by that night, if it had not already done so, and as would be seen in more detail later, the contestants did indeed have a special diet, of sorts, or, one could say, at least they had their food prepared for them.[4]

The *Commercial* also stated that officials in charge of the show estimated that forty or fifty couples were expected to sign up before the endurance contest started at eight o'clock that night. A gun would be fired to mark the beginning of the dance, and National Marathon Dance Association rules would be followed. Judges assigned to the Hampden dance would make certain that the rules were followed. To remain in the contest dancers had to dance twenty-four hours per day, minus the short breaks they were given. Their "special diet" involved their being fed eight times per day.[5]

The paper also carried information about changes made to the building and grounds, as would also be augmented by later information. The marathon sponsors had had "the building completely renovated and converted into a[n] arena. A heating plant has been installed, and the road leading to the pavilion has been lighted and resurfaced."[6]

Joe McCormack, "well known stage and radio entertainer," would serve as the contest's master of ceremonies. For opening night—Halloween—he had arranged special "games, favors, and all other things that go with a celebration of this kind."[7]

A relatively large advertisement for the marathon also appeared in the *BDC* on October 31. It read:

CELEBRATE HALLOWEEN TONIGHT
At the Opening of The Golden Slipper
MARATHON DANCE
Paradise Pavilion, Hampden, on Route 1
Favors, Games, Souvenirs and Other Entertaining Features

SEE: The start of this contest
How they sleep
How they keep going

24 HOURS A DAY—THEY NEVER STOP
Admission Every Day From Now On

From 6:00 a.m. until 6:00 p.m., admission cost fifteen cents. From 6:00 p.m. to 6:00 a.m., admission cost forty cents.[8]

The *Commercial* sent a reporter to opening night. The headline the following day ran, "VIVIDLY PICTURESQUE SCENES AS COUPLES AT MARATHON GRIND ON HOUR AFTER HOUR; Dancers Sleep in Each Others' Arms as the Remarkable Contest, First Ever Known in Vicinity, Goes Forward; Nurses and Doctor Keep Watch."[9]

At least sixty-six people entered the Paradise Dance Pavilion marathon on October 31. They had signed up for a competition anticipated to last for months, but a few of these contestants did not even make it through the first night and day of the competition.

The *Commercial* reported that sixty people remained in the competition as of noon on Wednesday, November 1. Of those who remained in the dance competition, at least ten were from Maine: Edward Ashford, Connie Healy, Edward Burley, and Ann Faulkingham of Bangor; Dick Thomas, Russell Beck (later identified as "Ginger" Beck, "well known Portland boxer"), Helen Smith, and Mitzie Lyman of Portland; Emile Pelletier of Waterville; and Edward Larabee of West Bath. The other dancers came primarily from the Northeast—especially New York, Massachusetts, and New Jersey—although some came from Pennsylvania and others from Washington, DC; Chicago; and Kokomo, Indiana. One dancer, Dick Martin, came from San Francisco, California.[10] A few contestants would later testify to other places of residence.

By noon on Wednesday, some of the dancers were solo dancers, even if they had not signed up as such. This was the case for Edward Ashford of Bangor, for example, and for one or two other dancers. Others would experience the "solo" status as time progressed, as under dance rules a person whose partner had left the competition could remain a solo dancer, although some (if not most) of the solos would then be rematched to form part of another "couple."[11]

Four "couples" left the dance during the first twelve hours of the competition. One of the couples dropped out after just three hours, and the others dropped out over the balance of Tuesday night and Wednesday morning. However, both members of the four couples did not opt out; instead, just three of the male participants and one female elected to quit. The remaining person in each couple chose to dance on and was anticipated to later be part of a newly formed "couple." Women were already demonstrating an edge in staying power. The one young man left alone after the breakups of the first twenty-four hours decided he would dance with his dog, keeping his white canine on a leash. The *Commercial* reporter observed that "the animal seemed to be withstanding the grind a great deal better than its master." Another solo male dancer took it upon himself to sing to his fellow contestants during the early morning hours, when there apparently was no music of any other sort playing. He also spent much time making "caustic remarks" to the dancers to help keep them going. Another dancer strummed on a ukulele, with no attempt to keep in tune, "simply banging away dreamily."[12]

The "grind" was described in some detail in the newspaper. The reporter stated that early on Wednesday morning there were twenty-nine couples on the floor "swaying and shuffling along to the tune of a vocalist, who incidentally was a contestant." The reporter also wrote of how:

"Baby-faced" girls seemingly barely out of their teens struggled with sleep that apparently insisted on coming. They were fighting against nerves that were crying for rest. Their male partners sought to give a brief respite from the awful grind and all but carried them along the floor.

In one striking case, the man was actually carrying his partner and she slept in his arms. Feeling the strain of her weight, he tried to awaken her but she slumbered on. A short time later, however, when her partner appeared to be weakening, she roused herself and together they continued on the monotonous shuffle, the crisis pas[sed].

At 8:20 o'clock, a girl incapable of going further "threw up the sponge" and a few minutes later left the building sleepy-eyed. Probably the thought uppermost in her mind was home and a bed. Those on the floor watched her go and offered words of consolation as she passed. Her partner, relieved of her weight, continued on as a soloist.[13]

Other dancers seemed weary too, and one other girl, the reporter suspected, would soon drop out. She seemed to be one of the youngest dancers and wore "a boy's cap at a rakish angle." Her partner was dragging her about the floor, suspended in his arms as the reporter prepared to make his exit. Fatigue seemed to take its toll in another way too: At the outset of the competition, many of the contestants smoked frequently, but by the next morning, "with the exception of one youth who puffed a large cigar, they seemed too listless to bother."[14]

Floor shows—scheduled for 2:30 p.m. to 5:00 p.m., and another for 8:00 p.m. until "the wee hours of the morning"—might help rouse the more sluggish dancers who made it into the afternoon hours. An orchestra would also play throughout the afternoon and into the evening for the dancers, including providing music for those who participated in the floor shows.[15] The floor shows proved more and more grueling as the days passed.

However, some dancers and couples appeared to be holding up just fine, seemingly unaffected by their first "night of continual dancing." The reporter stated, "One couple in particular seemed particularly fresh, and from time to time put on a short exhibition of classical and acrobatic dancing." This couple was "small proportioned," and the reporter noted that there were few people of larger stature among the dancers. He consulted an official at the dance, who said that at marathons everywhere the participants generally were of smaller stature, and that those individuals of larger stature who did enter marathons did not "endure the grind for any length of time."[16]

A Mr. Al Kay introduced himself to the *Commercial* reporter as being an experienced vaudeville player and the "conductor" of the "Silver Slipper Dance Marathon at the Paradise Pavilion in Hampden." He stated that he had been in charge of some twenty-two other "such events," and in his experience, "The first 500 hours are the hardest." He said that once those first strenuous 500 hours had passed, "the human constitution . . . can thereafter function almost indefinitely." This was only his opinion, however, based on his work in promoting "such events." The implication was that "such events" were marathons, but they may also have included his work in vaudeville. When asked what long-term effects such endurance contests might have on the human body, he responded that in his experience no one had suffered any long-term damage. He backed his statement up by referring to a New York State Department of Health report that showed that statistically those who entered and completed such dance marathons "gained weight and were in better physical condition at the finish than at the start."[17]

For the audience members—although there were none when the reporter first arrived—"there is not a single dull moment . . . the scene presenting ever-changing novelties. It is interesting to sit and study the various participants and observe their respective ways of withstanding the sustained grind." The manager, Kay, had told the reporter that the pavilion doors were never closed, and that despite some popular belief that the dancers could stop dancing, anyone standing still for over five seconds would be disqualified. "A keen-eyed judge maintains watchful vigilance over the floor." So too, was there a "nurse" on duty, and a doctor on call to monitor other aspects of the dance.[18] The "picturesque scenes" that greeted the reporter when he stepped into the pavilion overlooking the Penobscot River apparently did have some dangers lurking, dangers that would come to light only after the last remaining participants had endured the first 500 hours and more of the marathon.

Before the marathoners reached their 500th hour in Hampden, however, police came to close the place down. On Sunday, November 5, at hour 121, members of the Penobscot County Sheriff's Department, the Maine Highway Police (later known as the Maine State Police), and the Bangor Police Department, under the direction of Sheriff John K. Farrar, raided the dance hall and arrested twenty-one people. The Bangor police apparently held back at the Bangor city line while the other officers entered the pavilion at 11:15 p.m. and "broke up the party." Sixteen couples remained in the contest at that point, just about half the number who had started the contest the previous Tuesday evening. Of those arrested, nineteen were men and two were women. The two women arrested were Kay Wise, reported in the press as being from Worcester, Massachusetts, and Margie Lyka of Philadelphia.[19]

Authorities raided the Paradise Dance Pavilion and made the arrests for violations of Section 39 of Chapter 135 of the "Revised Statutes of Maine." The law as then written included the passage that:

> *Whoever on the Lord's Day keeps open his workshop, workhouse, warehouse, place of business, travels or does any work, labor or business on that day except work of necessity or charity; uses any sport, game or recreation, or who is present at any dancing, public diversion or show encouraging the same shall be liable to a fine of $10.*[20]

Ironically, although the fine might be set at $10, bail was set for each person arrested at $100, a steep sum at the time. And, of course, the law could have been brought to bear at the Old Orchard marathons or at other dances in the state that ran into Sunday mornings if not the day, or similar types of entertainment, but by and large the law was already antiquated and seldom used in such situations.

An estimated 1,000 people were at the marathon as audience members when the authorities entered. The number of arrests could have been much higher. The officers worked quietly, and, it was reported, "so orderly and well organized was the raid that very few of the nearly 1,000 people in the hall knew what was happening until after one patrol wagon load had been taken to Bangor and the officers ordered the building cleared of spectators." Officers cleared the dance hall quickly by making the announcement that "all those not wishing to ride to Bangor in the police cars are asked to leave the hall."[21]

Most of those arrested were not dancers but rather employees of the marathon company including the "manager, assistants, and people working about the building." Also among those arrested were five orchestra members. They were taken to the Penobscot County Jail in Bangor, and either held overnight or released upon furnishing bail. Both women posted bail. All contestants still in the competition, in addition, were summoned to appear in court the following morning at 9:00 a.m. as witnesses, where the question of preferring charges against them would be determined. In addition, authorities, according to the press, were considering bringing further charges against some of the marathon workers or managers.[22]

According to the *Bangor Daily News*, Bangor had turned down a request for "a similar show," and Hampden's selectman Kimball had stated that as complaints from the Hampden residents had arrived only after a permit had been granted to the Golden Slipper Company for its marathon, nothing could be done to stop it. However, on Sunday, numerous complaints had come in, and when he learned of them the sheriff had decided to take action. The Bangor police had apparently driven to the city line and brought some of the prisoners back to the city rather than make arrests themselves, as the dance hall was outside of the city.[23]

The marathon managers had taken some measures to try to avoid being cited for blue law violations. The *BDN* had a reporter on hand at the pavilion on the night of arrest. Purportedly, the "husky door keeper" at the door had asked visitors to "Put your donations in there," into a box marked for "charity," as "hundreds of people went down to see the Marathon. 'Supposing there isn't a donation,' dared a man acquainted with the law prohibiting taking of admissions at amusement places on Sunday. 'Well I suppose it's O.K,' the doorman answered, 'but I call that a dirty mean trick.'"[24]

Also according to the paper, "It was a sad looking group that walked around the ring the early part of the night, but not as bad as the one seen after midnight Saturday when several men and women were being dragged about by their partners, sleeping on each other's shoulders, or falling against the railing only to be awakened by a partner passing by." Once the orchestra arrived on Sunday, however, at about 8:30 p.m., things began to liven up. Jazz music was played with live singers, the master of ceremonies told jokes and introduced the couples, and then he "pleaded for 'the only money the contestants receive, that which is thrown onto the dance floor by the audience.'"[25]

After the raid, the contestants tried to keep moving, as required by contest rules. However, they seemed to have stopped, or at least moved out of sight to do their dancing, "when police warned them that unless they went to their sleeping quarters in adjoining rooms they would be taken to the jail." A doctor also entered the women's quarters to check on the welfare of a young woman who had dropped out of the contest a few hours previously.[26]

The show, however, went on. After the raid, the managers barred spectators from the ongoing dancing from midnight Saturday until midnight on Sundays. According to the *Commercial*, regarding the court hearings, "Immediately after dismissal of the charges [against the dancers], the troop went back to Paradise and took up where they left off. According to officials at the time, the raid proved valuable advertising. Attendance jumped." Soon thereafter local ministers banded together to denounce the marathon, one group involved being the Bangor-Brewer Ministerial Association.[27] Seeming unconcerned with such activity, the marathon dancers continued their endeavors into late autumn. A few individuals and couples dropped out over the following weeks, while others stayed in the endurance contest as winter prepared to set in and a major storm reached the region in early December.

Winter's unofficial arrival notwithstanding, twenty-five of the more than sixty people who had started the contest on October 31, 1933, including one solo dancer and two males in a separate contest, would survive the endurance contest for over forty days, and then four of them would fail to survive one particularly cold and stormy December night. On that stormy Sunday night, fire roared through the dance hall.

At approximately 11:20 p.m., Sunday, December 10, 1933, six weeks after beginning the marathon dance contest in Hampden with over sixty-six other people, nineteen-year-old Gertrude Sousa was roughly awoken from her brief allotment of sleep by her bed partner, Lee Wynne, to a scene of confusion and panic. The alarm had been given by three men—a cook, a furnace tender, and a contestant—that the Paradise Dance Pavilion was being rapidly consumed by fire. Ten of the women still involved in the contest, plus nine male contestants and the contest "nurse," Kay Wise (or Wice), had gathered in a small back room, some on their rest break and others standing around the heater, temporarily excused from the dance floor to try to warm themselves. Two contestants were in the kitchen getting coffee. Several of the men—also suffering from the cold—had joined the women in their room to try to get warm. The men generally took their breaks in their own room.[28]

Just after the alarm was raised, a few of the men occupied elsewhere in the flimsy building—a single-story wooden structure—and two female contestants who had gone to the kitchen for coffee, as well as a few other people gathered in the women's quarters, were able to reach the front door of the dance hall and escape before flames engulfed most of the building. Others were less fortunate.[29]

Some of the twenty-five dancers still in the contest were moving on the dance floor at 11:20 p.m. on December 10. There being no audience present that late on Sunday, as Maine sporadically tried to enforce its blue laws as evinced by the earlier raid on the pavilion, which among other things forbid dance halls from holding performances on Sundays, the dancers were either shuffling through their steps, basically just pacing the floor so as not to be disqualified, or working on painting their "kitty," or dancers' cashbox, to add a picture of Mickey Mouse. Others were on their fifteen-minute break and resting, and some huddled around a stove or furnace in the women's quarters, that heater being the most effective of the three heating the rather primitive wooden building. Some of the dancers had been temporarily excused from the dance floor as the temperature was excessively cold on the floor, forcing some of the dancers to wear their coats or other extra garments even as they danced. Only a few dancers—trying to catch their fifteen minutes of sleep—actually were indeed asleep. Although the pavilion in Hampden, used for other recreational purposes over the years, was closed to the public, it would open again at midnight, and Sidney Curtis and his employees anticipated that perhaps 1,000 people might show up in the following hours, according to the county attorney's preliminary hearing into the fire held in the following days. It was the end of the dancers' day of relative rest. Soon they would have to endure close public scrutiny as they did their regular, forty-five minutes on the floor, performed in special shows, performed vaudeville-style acts if they desired, and competed in periodic elimination sprints pitting couples against one another and geared toward instantly eliminating one or more couples from the competition.[30]

The dancers did not perform for the public on Sundays after the police raid, but they still had to remain on their feet and keep moving. One stated a few weeks later that they would sometimes sleep on the dance floor, resting their head against their partner as the partner assumed the responsibility for keeping them both moving. He explained, in reference to both sleeping and an earlier reported fire at the marathon and whether it had actually happened or if he had been aware of it, "You see, when you are sleeping you are sleeping on your partner's shoulder and you don't know what the devil is going on." He had no idea if there had indeed been a previous fire. Even on December 10 when fire broke out and contestants and employees screamed out, three dancers had to be forcefully awoken.[31] At that point, they had been competing for almost 1,000 hours.

As with the marathon currently ongoing in Old Orchard Beach, and apparently sponsored by the same company, the contestants had only fifteen minutes of each hour to sleep, plus bathroom breaks and medical time. Or, putting a spin he thought more positive on it, Curtis later testified, "They have to keep going forty-five minutes out of every hour, either walking or dancing, that means a total rest of six hours every day, but it is in snatches, because [they have] fifteen minutes every hour. On top of that, they are allowed half a[n] hour of hospital attention every twelve hours, which adds another hour on it, then there are other periods, like clean-up period, things like that, perhaps giving them a total of eight hours sleep out of twenty-four."[32]

Of course, the contestants might not necessarily be able to simply drop into sleep during their fifteen-minute breaks—and with the foot and muscle problems many developed, they might need the attention of the so-called nurse, who was not an actual nurse but a woman trained to function as one for the dances, during their hospital breaks—and contestants did indeed need to shower and attend to other hygienic needs during their clean-up periods.[33] And, as Curtis admitted, "Of course, they keep dropping off, you know, for various reasons—either they just get sick of it or tired, one thing and another, and the last remaining couple get the prize money that is awarded."[34]

But there was other money to be had. The reason some of the dancers had their "kitty," or cash box, out to paint it that night was because money thrown to the dancers as a group by the audience was kept in the kitty and later divided among the dancers. In addition, the marathon featured three "vaudeville" shows per day, as the owner called them, in which the dancers could perform by themselves, dancing, or if they could, singing or performing other talents. The audience would then throw money at the dancer's feet, and she or he (but it was mostly women who did this) would be able to keep the money for herself.

And so the men and women were dancing, or trying to get warm, or resting, or sleeping when the fire erupted and spread rapidly that cold night. Some contestants made it out the front door to safety; others did not. By the time Gertrude Sousa and Lee Wynne got out of their bed and put their shoes on, neither the distant front door nor the even further away fire exit remained an option. Harold McCoy broke the nearby small window that he and another man tried but were unable to open any other way, and the people left trapped in the women's quarters had to try to struggle to escape through the twelve-inch by twenty-two-inch window.[35]

Smoke filled the air and the lights went out. Lee Wynne woke up Helen Francis Emery and started to go over to Helen's bunk. Gertrude Sousa, or "Gertie" as the others called her, told Lee to get out through the window right away. Lee did so, with Gertie's help, Gertie giving Lee a helping push. Lee knocked her head on a rock as she fell through the window, and later thought that she had lost consciousness temporarily. She thought that she had grabbed Gertie and yanked her through the window, and that Gertie had landed on top of her, but this was not the case. Other people also thought that Gertie had made it out of the inferno. The next day, however, searchers would find Gertie's body crouched below the window, still inside what remained of the building, her hands covering her face as if to shield it from the flames that had rapidly leveled the structure.[36]

From the evidence taken at the county attorney's preliminary hearing into the fire in the following days, it seems likely that Gertrude had stayed in the room, hopefully voluntarily, while two other women, Kay Wise and Helen Emery, and perhaps one or two men, exited through the window. Kay Wise insisted that she herself had been the last one out. Perhaps she was mistaken due to the confusion and the thick smoke.[37]

Helen Emery made it out of the building, perhaps aided by Gertie, but sustained severe burns to her body from the waist down. Two sisters, local women, found Helen wandering around in the snow, dazed and suffering from the cold and her injuries. They led her to the nearby Dickson's Filling Station, from where she was transported to the Eastern Maine

General Hospital in Bangor. She died on December 12. She was just twenty years old. Her death certificate, under the name Helen Francis Emery, remains on file with the State of Maine Archives.[38]

Two men also perished as a result of the conflagration. Firemen found the bodies of Emile Pelletier (age twenty-five) and John Ryan (age thirty-six) in the ruins of the building, identifiable only by the relative sizes of their bones and the absence of the two men from the list of survivors.[39]

Witnesses had last seen John Ryan in the men's quarters where he had gone to rest. Conjecture had it that he was not asleep and had wasted time trying to get his money or trunk out. Emile Pelletier had escaped from the men's quarters and then returned for his coat, against the advice of comrades who managed to escape the inferno, some with, some without, personal possessions.[40]

In addition to the gruesome deaths of the four young contestants, several of those associated with the marathon dance suffered severe injuries in the fire. These included burns received from struggling through the fire to exit the building, and from burning objects falling on them. Lacerations, hysteria, a back injury, frostbite, and exposure to zero-degree temperatures outside the pavilion also took their toll, and Eleanor Ryan, wife of "Johnnie," remained hospitalized in critical condition and unaware of her husband's death for some time.[41]

Eight dancers total were known to have entered local hospitals following the conflagration. These included Helen Emery of Malden, Massachusetts, receiving severe burns on her legs and torso, as well as—one Lewiston paper reported—"frozen legs." These injuries from the start had her listed as in critical condition and would prove fatal. Kay Wise, initially identified as being from Worcester, Massachusetts (but reported in one paper as being from Chicago and suffering from exposure[42]), sustained burns and a back injury and her situation was considered likely to prove serious. Marjorie Lyka of Philadelphia "was overcome with hysteria." Dorothy Wilson (possibly an employee of the marathon) of Chicago sustained less severe injuries and was soon released from the hospital.

Captain Harold McCoy of Kokomo, Indiana, sustained burns and lacerations. Russell "Ginger" Beck, the Portland boxer, was burned on his face and hands. Thomas Garry Jr. of Dorchester, Massachusetts, was treated for exposure and frozen feet and left the hospital on December 11.[43]

The temperature that night had been close to zero degrees. The wind was strong. It had been snowing for close to thirty hours. The drifts had piled up.[44] Both inside and outside the Paradise Dance Pavilion, it was Hell.

An examination of the marathon in Hampden, the hearings that followed, and the reactions of the local and state populations reveal attitudes toward the dances and the people engaged in them, including the conditions under which the women and men worked, performed, and lived. Although in general the public responded with shock and sympathy to the fire and its casualties, a lack of understanding and a moral displeasure also surfaced.

Hearings into the fire began immediately. The day after the dance hall burned, local authorities began a four-day, preliminary investigation into the fire and the conditions at the Paradise Dance Pavilion. They tried to examine every facet of the marathon that might relate to the fire, including such details as to what the female contestants used to absorb their menstrual flow (Kotex), to where the promoters kept it (a medicine chest in the "hospital" room), to what other purposes the product might have been used (padding for the dancers' shoes). The resulting 178-page transcript of the hearing indicated that officials sought to determine the possible negligence of the proprietor of the dance, Sidney Curtis, on various levels and issues.[45] This, and other aspects of the dances in Maine and the fire at the Paradise, reveal valuable information on such subjects as labor history, protective legislation, hazardous working conditions, responses to the 1920s and the Great Depression, social values, and—as with the other forms of dance studied herein—the entertainment value of the marathons. The events at the Paradise Dance Pavilion show, as do—to some extent but in less detail as less is known about them—the other Maine marathons, the reactions of the local population to the dances, the structure of the marathon industry, and the conditions under which the women and men in the contests lived, worked, and sometimes died.

Curtis had rented the dance pavilion in the autumn of 1933 and had signed a lease on the building that was to expire in March 1934. Before opening the marathon, he made various changes in the building. He had installed two furnaces at opposite ends of the building, which burned coke for fuel and had air funnels extending fourteen to twenty-four feet toward the center of the building. These two furnaces became a focal point of the hearings.[46]

Various witnesses testified that during the week previous to the conflagration one of the furnaces had had a small backfire or other type of misfire or flare-up, possibly caused by a fire attendant purportedly inclined to throw kerosene into the furnaces to get them going at full capacity as quickly as possible. The possibility that harsh winds had caused a chimney malfunction was also suggested. Other witnesses denied knowing anything about the incident or insisted that it was of no consequence whatsoever.[47]

The exact condition or safety of the heating arrangements remained unknown. The question of whether the contestants themselves sometimes manned the furnaces was never satisfactorily settled one way or the other. Asbestos tiles supposedly surrounded the pipes near the ceiling, and the building had a slate roof—which one might think a deterrent to a fire, but the entire roof had quickly caved in. Both furnaces had been running full-blast on the day and night of the fire, as were small oil stoves in the contestants' quarters. A portable heater was used on the coldest days on the dance floor itself, and this also seems to have been in use when the fire erupted, or had been in previous hours. The portable heater, however, was supposedly used against Curtis's wishes, as dancers had been known to catch their clothes on fire when dancing too close to it. Yet, except for the heat sources in the women's quarters, the stoves did little good and much harm. On the night of the fire, and on at least a few occasions before then, the contestants had had to dance laden down with extra sweaters and coats and still felt the cold. The hearings into the conflagration did establish that in all probability the fire of December 11 originated at the furnace at the rear of the building.[48]

Other "improvements" that Curtis made in the wooden structure included the addition of a men's "rest room" along with a "rebuilt" women's restroom. Although Curtis did have running water installed in the building, he decided that a three-seater, old-fashioned privy for the women, and one single privy plus a urinal for the men, would suffice for the sixty-six original contestants, the approximate twenty-six employees, and the general public who came to watch the marathon. Although there was some question about how clean the facilities were kept (no one seemed to argue about how cold the add-on to the building was), Curtis insisted that an employee tended to the restrooms two or three times each day. "I made it my business to check that," he stated, "because I felt I wanted it clean enough so that I could use it myself, and I like to be fairly fussy about where I sit."[49] At least Curtis did have a choice about where and when to sit, and how long he might do so.

Curtis had also added a fire exit to the dance hall. Unfortunately, the exit was situated such that no one used it during the fire. The two small windows Curtis had also had installed—one in the men's quarters and one in the women's—did save at least a few lives on December 10. The hearing did not establish that anyone had exited through the men's window, although one contestant testified that he thought he had heard John Ryan break its glass, presumably so that he could try to climb out. Testimony did not clarify how high off the ground the windows had been placed; some witnesses established their height at about six feet above the ground outside, while Curtis stated the height to be closer to three feet.[50]

By the time the fire erupted on December 10, those contestants not yet eliminated from the competition had confined themselves to Curtis's building for more than forty days in exchange for their room and board, and in hopes of winning the $1,000 prize. As stated, contest rules required that the dancers remain on their feet for at least forty-five minutes out of every hour, dancing or walking or occasionally standing still. They participated in special shows at scheduled times, put on vaude-ville-style acts three times per day, and collected the money audiences threw at their feet, an estimated $3.00 or more per day. This was in addition to any monies thrown at the dancers when they put on indi-vidual performances and that they could keep themselves, and was to be split among the remaining dancers once the 1,000-hour mark had been reached. In addition to the allotted fifteen minutes of rest each hour, they received thirty minutes of hospital time every twelve hours. They occa-sionally received other short breaks to attend to their hygienic needs. The eleven couples, one solo dancer, and two men in a separate category had followed this schedule for almost 1,000 hours previous to the disastrous Sunday night. Exhaustion had inevitably taken its toll on the dancers, and, as noted, at least two or three of them had to be forcefully awakened when the alarm was given.[51]

A local physician examined the contestants each day, and Kay Wise saw to some of their needs. Other marathon workers kept records of con-testants' trips to the toilets, and "trainers" gave the dancers leg and foot massages and oil rubdowns as needed.[52]

Sidney Curtis employed about twenty-six people to attend the danc-ers' needs and to keep the hall operating: six male orchestra members, a master of ceremonies, two judges, five ticket sellers, two doormen, two "deputy sheriffs" or bouncers, two men to tend to the furnaces, and one errand runner, as well as two male attendants and three "matrons" to supervise the dancers. These people worked in shifts and generally lived or boarded in the surrounding area. Curtis contracted out the feeding of the contestants. One Frank Crandall fed the contestants for free in return for the privilege of selling food to the marathon employees and to the general public who attended the shows. The food given the contestants was generally considered adequate and fairly generous in quantity, and a doctor who examined the contestants about once a week said that he had found the dancers "in good physical condition," and that those who did not remain in good health "were disqualified by the management." Some dancers, the doctor asserted, "had actually put on weight" during the contest. They did at least have adequate food to eat, and eating in moderation likely helped keep them awake.[53]

Although amateur local persons participated in the marathon at the Paradise Dance Pavilion both as contestants and as employees, a fair number of the dancers and the workers possessed previous experience in the marathon business. Sidney Curtis, the proprietor of the marathon, as stated, was associated with the Golden Slipper Producing Company of Boston, as was Myer Kurtz, an employee who handled some of Curtis's business matters. According to Kurtz, most people who wanted to get a job with the marathon signed up with the Golden Slipper Company, a company that booked people for various dance contests. In addition to Kurtz, the Golden Slipper had sent Joseph McCormick, a contest judge from New York City, and Bernie Marr, who had traveled throughout the United States and had recently signed on with the company. The second judge (William Waltz of Baltimore), a trainer, and the nurse also came from out of state and had had previous experience in the dance industry.[54]

The nurse—whom trial transcripts identify as Kay Wice and the local press referred to as Kay Wise, may well have been the Kay Wise credited with winning the longest endurance dance contest ever, a nine-month marathon in Chicago in the early 1930s. Kay Wise had received her training in the business and was not a licensed nurse.[55] As she was from Chicago, odds are that Wise was indeed the noted marathon dancer.

Because the fire occurred at a time when the dance hall was essentially closed to the public, the majority of Curtis's and the company's employees were not present at the tragedy and did not testify at the hearings, so their home addresses remain unknown. However, those workers involved with unskilled jobs appear to have been native to the region.[56]

Although Mainers participated in the Hampden marathon as contestants, workers, and audiences, women and men alike had come from across the nation to compete in Hampden. Of the twenty-five regular contestants still participating on December 10, 1933, twenty-two came from out of state and had participated in previous marathons. The majority of these came from the Northeast and the Southeast, although one came from San Francisco, three came from Chicago, and one from Indiana. In addition, Kay Wise, the so-called nurse, was a seasoned dancer and was also from out of state. When asked at the hearing, Wise had no idea what her legal address was, and after looking at her notes, identified Oklahoma City as her address. (Wise had also been identified as being from Chicago in the press.[57]) Both of the women who died from the fire, Gertrude Sousa and Helen Emery, were from the Northeast, from Massachusetts.[58] The women who danced in the marathon were generally young women in their teens or twenties who had moved several times in their lives, at least in part to work in the dance industry, and this was also the case for many of the other working-class female dancers in Maine.

All four of the dancers who died due to the Paradise fire had participated in other dance marathons before coming to Hampden. The *Bangor Daily News* reported in the days after the fire that John Ryan and his wife, Eleanor, "were well known entertainers, having appeared together on many stages in New England," and the *Bangor Daily Commercial* stated that John Ryan was a "professional marathon dancer, having competed several times with his wife." Gertrude Sousa, although quite young, was described as being a "pretty" girl and the "outstanding dancer entered in the marathon." She had been in a marathon dance in Lawrence, Massachusetts, and with her last partner, the deceased Emile Pelletier of Waterville, Maine, had entered a marathon in Somerville, Massachusetts, in which she or they won a trophy. According to the *Commercial*, "because of her beauty and dancing ability she was induced to enter the Hampden contest. She had danced under the name 'Songia.'" Gertie's partner in Hampden and in at least one other marathon, Pelletier had been in other marathons too, in addition to the one in Hampden and Somerville. Helen Emery was only twenty years old but also had some previous marathon experience.[59]

One of the male contestants, Stan West, stated to the author several years ago that he had completed approximately forty marathons during his career, had married one of his dance partners—Margie Bright, whom he met at a marathon in Avon, Massachusetts—and had won twelve first-place prizes. The first was with Margie Bright, and they had danced for some ninety-four days to win the prize. Before he came to Maine, West had been a street dancer of sorts, and had entered his first dance marathon in 1932 in Manchester, New Hampshire. A clog tap-dancer as well as a singer (he and his partner in Hampden sang for the crowds), he did not stay in his first marathon for any great length of time and was disappointed that he did not really get to showcase his dancing skills.[60]

In Maine, just before he went on to Massachusetts, West had been resting on his cot when the trainer told him that the building was burning and he had to get moving, fast. He could not find his dance partner, Peggy Worth, as he escaped the building after the lights went out. He eventually learned that she was all right. He was taken in by a couple living near the dance hall, slept there for about a day and a half, then stopped and looked at where the Paradise had stood—there was nothing left of it but the ruins on the ground. He picked up a twisted piece of metal for a "souvenir."[61]

Of the two male dancers who died in the fire, Emile Pelletier had lived in Maine and was from Waterville; John Ryan, the other male fatality, had resided in New York.

The deceased dancers had been in other marathons besides that at the Paradise Pavilion, and it seems had performed in other dance venues also. For them, quite likely, Hampden was just another job. They had been housed and fed for forty days, might have anticipated winning the grand prize, and would at least have expected to receive their share of the kitty—both what it contained on December 10 and, after that initial distribution, whatever additional monies they might collect before March, should the contest go on so long, which if the first forty days had been a guide, might have netted them an additional $500 to $600, although how many ways additional monies would have been split, and when, is unknown. In addition, throughout the course of the marathon, from the first day on, the women and men who put on individual performances could keep the money the audiences threw on the dance floor in appreciation of their dancing or just of the dancers themselves. Young women like Gertrude

Sousa could expect to earn both part of the kitty and a bit of extra cash from their individual performances, whether doing a hootchie-cootchie solo or a vaudeville routine—with or without their marathon partner.

Clearly, marathon dances had become a big business, with both management and dancers traveling from state to state, and monetary rewards being most likely to fall to those with experience in the trade. In Maine, this seemingly remained the case, but in terms of its population base, Maine saw more marathons and longer lasting marathons than did many other similar-sized states. Maine was already a tourist destination, and holding marathons in Maine made financial sense, although the larger, indoor ones were as likely to cover the colder months as well as the warmer ones. However, Curtis had booked the Paradise Pavilion into March 1934, the other large marathon currently running in the state lasted into that March, and either contest could have lasted into the summer tourist season, as at least one American dance marathon—in Chicago—had lasted nine months.

Working the marathons had become a steady form of work for the dancers, as was also true for employees of the marathon. For some of the contestants, the marathons had also become something of a family business as well: At least six of the final contestants had immediate relatives—spouses or siblings—as co-contestants, including a pair of sisters, brother and sister Lee and Everett Winn of Massachusetts, and at least a few married couples, including John and Eleanor Ryan of New York City. Three of the other dancers, two of them married, Ray "Pistol Pete" Wilson of Michigan City, Indiana, and his wife Dorothy, along with Tommy Garry of Chicago (who, along with "Pistol Pete," had served as a comedian as well as a dancer in the Hampden marathon), left for Miami a few days after the fire to sign up for another marathon to be held in Florida. Two sisters, Rita and Pauline Williams, left for Boston, as did night manager Al Ross. Sidney Curtis also left Maine, for Revere, Massachusetts, just after the hearing.[62]

The marathon at the Paradise had had at least some appeal for the local population. People had come to watch the dancers even in the slower hours, they had come to watch the special shows and acts, and they had thrown money at their favorite dancers' feet. The reporter from the *Commercial* had reported that there was always something intriguing to look at when he visited the show just after it opened. However, such appeal apparently quickly disappeared after the conflagration. The local press followed the events as they unfolded, referred to the fire as "the holocaust," and both the *BDC* and the *BDN* featured photographs of the dancers, the ruins of the dance hall, and a dinner held in the dancers' honor on December 14 at the Chateau Ballroom.[63]

The *BDC* printed a photograph of Eleanor and John Ryan wearing matching sweaters, hers reading "Eleanor 30" and his "John 30," 30 apparently their dance number at the Hampden dance or at another contest, and the *BDN* printed pictures of John Ryan's Boston bull-terrier puppy. The *BDC* printed several photographs of contestants on December 11, including one of an attractive couple with the caption: "Emile Pelletier of Waterville, Me. And Gertrude Sousa of Lowell, Mass., both of whom were burned to death." Gertie wore a fancy dress in the photograph, Emile a black suit and a light or white shirt with a light-colored tie or ascot. Helen Emery was photographed with Arthur Pathe, seemingly her partner at the dance. The deceased Helen wore a short-sleeved, patterned dress with a wide dark belt, her partner a dark suit in the photograph.[64] All the couples photographed seem to have had dark hair, although red hair also looks dark in black-and-white photography. Newspapers in Portland, Lewiston, Bath, and other Maine cities and towns also covered the fire, generally printing Associated Press articles from Bangor, as did newspapers located outside of the state.

The *Lewiston Daily Sun* was one of the Maine papers that covered the fire and its aftermath. The AP article sent from Hampden essentially covered the same news as the Bangor papers, but stated, "At least three marathon dancers were burned to death and many others injured in a fire which destroyed the Paradise dance hall here tonight at the height of a fierce northeast blizzard." "Three bodies," the paper noted in its December 11 morning edition, "were found in the wooden structure." The next day the paper reported that a theory of arson had been discredited after the all-day questioning by county officials into the fire. The high winds might have caused the chimney to collapse, thereby setting the roof and a wall on fire, and the fire, whatever its initial cause, had spread too rapidly for a fire hose to be employed.[65]

The *Portland Evening Express* (*PEE*) reported that the only water the firemen could secure was from "an ice-bound brook." They could do little to "quench the flames." The *PEE* also reported on the controversy surrounding the marathon and the police raid on it, and stated that opponents had already asked that a special session of the Maine State Legislature, in session the week of the fire, declare marathon dances illegal in Maine.[66]

The Penobscot County medical examiner, Herbert Scribner, and the county attorney, James Maxwell, met together in the morning immediately after the fire and scheduled the lengthy hearing held that week. The Bangor City Council, moreover, immediately proposed stricter ordinances governing dances in Bangor, although the marathon dance had been held just a few miles outside of Bangor, and thus any such dance held at the site in the future would not be subject to any such laws.[67] Local ministers, like those in other parts of the state, condemned the marathon dance industry.

The general public may have gone to the marathon to watch the dancers and shower their favorites with what small amount of change they might have, but some sectors of the general public had also denounced the marathons. Even after the Hampden location was selected, local ministers and others, including some local police, protested the opening, citing their concerns for the health of the dancers. However, Hampden had no ordinances regarding licensing "places of entertainment," so Curtis had simply rented the building and made a few changes. Bangor did have ordinances governing dance halls in general, and in the days after the conflagration several such establishments were identified as having potentially hazardous conditions.[68] Women danced in those halls also, sometimes for the entertainment of the public, and they too were at risk should a fire erupt, as were men who attended the dances.

Hampden, however, was subject to state law even if it did remain free of restrictive local ordinances. The Hampden town health officer, the Bangor health officer (even if he did not hold jurisdiction), and the state district health officer from Waterville had visited the Paradise premises only the day before the fire and pronounced the building "an absolute fire trap." Unfortunately, they waited a bit too long to make their inspection, and any changes they would have requested had had no time to be made. The Bangor fire chief also made a belated statement about conditions at the Hampden dance hall, although he had not visited it himself, and stated that it "could never have happened in Bangor." However, subsequent investigations over the following month showed that it could, indeed, have happened in Bangor.[69]

On December 12, the press reported that the Bangor Fire Department chief, W. S. Mason, had stated that it was his belief that the fire was a result of arson. However, this theory was soon put to rest during the investigation.[70]

The Bangor police chief and the city inspector, along with the city health officer, concluded, after inspections of local dance halls, that:

Many of the dance halls of the city are not properly equipped with emergency exits, have no red lights at existing exits, [have] doors opening inward, windows opening on fire escapes fixed so that they will not open, fire escapes blocked with snow and ice, flammable decorations creating fire hazards, and booths made of flammable materials.[71]

The associated report cited twelve Bangor dance halls and stated that no licenses for dances would be issued until improvements had been made.[72]

As far as other complaints might go, as noted, the Hampden marathon was raided by police one Sunday soon after the marathon started, on a charge of violating Maine's blue laws, or the "Sunday law," and twenty-one people were arrested. Yet the state law only called for a $10 fine for each, and, in total the management paid $250 in fines. In addition, according to one source, a Hampden minister had earlier charged into the pavilion shouting, "This is a sin against God." Other local ministers denounced the dance world after the fire and urged tougher ordinances.[73]

Initially, the Sunday raid and perhaps a few other inspections and denunciations had increased business for the marathon. According to the *Commercial*, during the days following the first—and possibly other—raids, public attendance at the marathon increased markedly. Moreover, "the more recent attacks of the Bangor-Brewer Ministerial Association caused the building to be crowded every night. On two evenings last week, it was necessary to close the doors to new comers so crowded was the structure." The paper also speculated that it was indeed fortunate that the fire occurred on a Sunday evening when the public was not present, as "had there been an average attendance at the time, the result would doubtless have been one of the most ghastly tragedies in the history of Maine."[74]

A letter to the editor reached the pages of the *Commercial* on December 14. It questioned if there were any laws governing the running of dance halls in rural areas, and if not, why not? The writer stated, "The terrible tragedy at the Paradise Dance Hall in Hampden is certainly one that should cause a considerable thought as to the laws governing the running of such places." In cities, periodical inspections were made of buildings that might be put to such use, but in the country there apparently was not. Rural dance pavilions, the writer asserted, were often large wooden fire hazards—there were hundreds of such dance halls in Maine—and the danger posed by holding such large public events in these places was increased by the paper decorations often used, and by the continual smoking by people inside the pavilions. Most rural pavilions only had one door in the event of danger—the one people entered to attend the dance—and, where there was more than one exit, the other exits were often locked to prevent people from entering for free. "The ticket taker sees to it [that] if there are other doors they are locked," the writer asserted.[75]

The male writer questioned if anyone had ever seen a fire extinguisher in such a country dance hall and argued that the events of December 10 demonstrated that inspections by fire departments were needed in "rural districts." If there were no existing laws to that effect (and if there were, they were not being enforced), "then why with this terrible tragedy fresh in their minds don't our state legislator[s] start legislation to avert a recurrence of what has happened or that even worse tragedy that would have happened had the hall been full?"[76]

Public sentiment ran hot, and after the preliminary hearing into the fire concluded that Sidney Curtis held possible criminal responsibility for the tragic blaze, Sheriff John K. Farrar arrested Curtis on four counts of involuntary manslaughter on a warrant dated December 12. In "a courtroom crowded to the door with spectators," Judge John T. Quinn in the Bangor Municipal Court set Curtis's bail at $5,000 and ordered him held for trial at the January term of the Penobscot Superior Court, in Bangor, on four counts of manslaughter. James D. Maxwell argued the state's case that Curtis had failed to provide adequate exits and heating apparatus, and that the tragedy had occurred because of his negligence. Curtis's attorney, Michael Pilot, argued that Curtis had "equipped the building to the best of his knowledge and that the exits were adequate under ordinary conditions." He had also paid for the funerals and was paying food and lodging for the survivors of the fire. Curtis made bail. However, after investigations were complete, in early 1934, the grand jury failed to indict Curtis. No explanations were specified.[77]

Quite likely, the lack of specific regulations regarding dance contest halls in the town of Hampden comprised a major factor in the court's decision. As revealed at the preliminary hearing just after the fire, and as reported by the press before the marathon started, Hampden had no regulations for dance halls, and although Curtis had insisted on securing a license for his dance, that license had no true legal status. Curtis had testified in December that he did not feel at all negligent in his duties, and that he had set up the dance pavilion in accordance with the State of Massachusetts, as he had no knowledge of what—if any—the State of Maine required. Curtis had shown himself willing to make the changes deemed necessary by local officials. Then, too, the seating of the jury coming at the same time that Bangor officials reported on similar fire hazards at that city's dance halls perhaps influenced the jury to be lenient in deciding Sidney Curtis's culpability in the Paradise fire. A noticeable reluctance of certain dancers to testify against Curtis may also have aided his case. Eleanor Ryan, Russell Beck, and Harold "Captain" McCoy failed to appear at the trial although the county attorney had summoned them to appear. They seemingly just ignored their subpoenas. McCoy was from Kokomo, Indiana, Beck was from Portland, and Ryan from New York (Brooklyn).[78] They perhaps simply went home, wishing to put the nightmare behind them, especially Eleanor Ryan, who had just lost her husband.

In the end, besides any personal property losses he may have sustained due to the fire—the building itself was insured—the economic cost of the tragedy for Curtis appears to have been limited to the cost of new outfits for some of the survivors, possibly a few bus or train tickets, and the $100 he voluntarily paid to the relatives of each of the four deceased to help cover funeral expenses.[79] And some of these expenses may have been reimbursed by the Golden Slipper Company.

The dancers' "kitty"—the money the audience had thrown at their feet—did not go to the surviving dancers. The 1,000-hour mark had not yet been reached when the fire erupted—although the dance had gone on for roughly 960 hours—hence, a couple of days remained before the contents of the metal box were to be distributed.

The *Bangor Daily Commercial* reported the day after the fire, on December 11, that part of the kitty had been found near the ruins, broken open, the money stolen by "ghouls" who had descended on the site soon after firefighters extinguished the blaze. The box was estimated to have held between $200 and $300 in cash. Another cash box, used in the office by staff and containing about $100, was also plundered.[80]

Some of the kitty was found in the ruins, however. The *Commercial* reported on December 13 that some of the money thrown to the contestants had indeed been discovered. Coins found included pennies, nickels, dimes, and a few quarters and fifty-cent pieces. In a weird twist, the newspapers said, "Monday morning several of the members of the contest went to Hampden to look over the ruins and salvaged eight quarts" of the coins. Asher Brown of New Jersey discovered a cross of sorts created by coins fused during the conflagration. The kitty was to have been opened five days before Christmas and distributed among the dancers still competing. Instead, much of the kitty was lost; some of the found coinage included the three-plus by four-plus-inch cross, would be displayed at Quality Cleansers, who had had "an exclusive contract with the Marathon Association during its stay in this vicinity."[81]

In another peculiar twist, New Jersey police had sought a man they believed to have entered in the Hampden marathon. Police in Hackensack had sent a deputy sheriff—who was also Hampden's police officer—a photograph of a man believed to "be competing in a dance marathon held at the Golden Slipper in your city." The sheriff, after investigating the possibility, responded that the photograph did closely resemble one of the dancers, but the dancer was shorter than the communication had stated, and so, Sheriff Farrar stated, "I am convinced the man wanted in New Jersey is not among our marathon survivors." The fugitive had jumped bail on grand larceny charges.[82]

Some of the surviving marathon dancers did appear in public in Maine one last time. On December 14, the Bangor region saw an evening of entertainment featuring some of the participants in the Paradise Dance Marathon. Very large font, bold letters declared "**MARATHON**" and in smaller print, "Contestants will appear in person as guests of" and again in a large, but different, font: "**Chateau Ballroom, Tonight.**" The public was encouraged to:

Come and Greet Your Favorite Team
SNAPPY FLOOR SHOW with **BERNIE MARR,**
Master of Ceremonies. Plenty of Entertainment.
PERLEY REYNOLDS' COMMANDERS
Dancing 8:30 to 1   **Admission 40¢**

It was this evening of entertainment that the local press covered. The *BDC* noted, in its coverage of the fire's aftermath, that Edward Nickerson, manager of the Chateau, was hosting the dinner, and that the marathon dancers were to give a floor show "identical to those put on while the marathon was in progress." Those scheduled to appear were "Dick Giblin, Frank Sharabba, Helen Kelley, Herbert Lewis, Ashur Brown, Steve Serenko, and others." In terms of the local region, Perley Reynolds would continue to entertain people in the region in following years with his "New Commanders" orchestra or band, playing for various public dances.[83]

In spite of the last money-making homage of sorts to the endurance dancers, the trend was toward condemning the marathons, in Bangor and elsewhere. Marathons would survive for a time but came under increasing scrutiny.

In addition to local concerns, which were substantial, during the week of the Hampden fire, a consortium of ministers in the southern part of the state met to denounce marathons in general, as well as to urge the rejection of a state lottery and the impending appeal of the 26th Amendment to the Maine Constitution pertaining to the importation of liquor into the state as well as its manufacture and sale. Fifteen members of the Ministers' Union of Portland and Vicinity met at the Portland YMCA, and Dr. John E. Schroeder of the Blain Street Congregational Church addressed the group. Those assembled then empowered their secretary, Reverend A. W. Wentworth, to transmit to the superintendent of the Christian Civic League of Maine, Reverend Frederick W. Smith of Waterville, resolutions pertaining to their support of the league's position on the above matters. They also appointed Reverend Benjamin Brewster, bishop of Maine, to represent the union at an upcoming committee hearing on the lottery bill and to denounce it.[84] The *Portland Press Harold* ran the headline: "Clerics Stand Against Rum, Lottery, Dance." The meeting took place that day, December 11, the day after the Hampden fire.

While the Bangor City Council immediately after the fire proposed stricter ordinances governing dances in the city, the Maine State Legislature acted as well. Prior to that December, state legislation simply provided that municipal authorities were "authorized to make reasonable regulations for the licensing and conducting of dance halls, and to provide suitable penalties for violations thereof."[85]

On December 15 and 16, the Maine State Legislature introduced and passed amendments to the state law code that restricted anyone from competing in marathon dances, walkathons, or similar competitions for more than six hours in any one day, or from entering such competitions within twenty-four hours of having entered or competed in another such contest. Violations of said provisions were punishable by fines of up to $500 per violation. Furthermore, even with the changes, no such competitions could be held in any Maine town or city without prior municipal voter sanction. Maine governor Louis J. Brann signed the bill on December 17. Further legislation passed in the 1940s provided for stricter licensing and specific fire codes. However, it is worth noting that the bill as it passed was an amendment to an earlier one that would have placed restrictions *only* on minors and women participating in marathons.[86] Following the events in Maine, other states soon placed harsh restrictions on marathons as well, and the contests largely ended.

It would not be until 1976 that the Maine State Legislature would vote to legalize marathon dancing again, and with it walkathons in Maine. They approved the measure in light of a dance marathon in Lewiston planned by the Maine Chapter of the Epilepsy Foundation of America, Inc., whose supporters promised, "We are not administering a grueling test of endurance." The dance would include thirty-minute breaks for the dancers, plus nap breaks, and times for showers and meals.[87] This would not be like the marathon that claimed the lives of four people from the Hampden fire of 1933.

However, some dance promoters did seek to circumvent the new legislation restricting marathons after the Hampden fire. In Old Orchard Beach, the most popular site for marathons previously, no doubt because of the people who continued to visit the state even during the Depression as well as its location in the more heavily populated section of the state, which allowed for both locals and people from areas like Portland and Lewiston–Auburn to travel there without too much difficulty, at least one dance hall decided to test the limits of the new legislation.

In 1934, the Palace Ballroom served as the location of a "Speeda-thon," purportedly much like the previous marathons, although it would seem, from the continued other events held there that year, that it was much more limited in duration than the long 1933 contests and was probably more like the marathon dances of the 1920s and early 1930s. In addition, according to one study, "speed derbies" came out of the marathons and were more directly athletic. Contestants generally wore helmets and shorts, and "performed athletic stunts in a circular fashion on a floor set up with pylons." The contestants danced, too, but as Carol Martin posited, "These shows were the cousins of the dance marathon," but they were very different in tone and appearance. They eliminated contestants "faster" than the longer dance marathons, and some argue they were more "brutal" and "less complex." A printed "List of Contes-tants" for the 1934 "Speedathon Circus" listed eighteen teams, the names of the contestants (although some were clearly dance names, not given names), and the state or town they "represented."[88]

One person from the 1933 marathon that had started on October 27, 1933, was Loyde—as he signed his name—or Lloyd—the more common and printed first name on the list—Judd. Judd had signed Evelyn Middle-ton's autograph book in 1933, and in 1934 the list of contestants for the Speedathon included his name as part of team #13, with Irene Milliard listed as his partner. They represented Biddeford in the contest.[89]

Other teams represented Canada, New Hampshire, Rhode Island, New York, Massachusetts, Vermont, and Connecticut, while in-state teams represented Old Orchard Beach and Saco, Portland, South Portland, Westbrook, Lewiston, Sanford, Brunswick and Freeport, Augusta and Gardiner, and one solo dancer (at least he was solo at the time the list was printed), Al Pliant, who represented Waterville. The couple representing Westbrook, team #11, was identified as "Minnie Mouse, Mickey Mouse."[90] Seemingly no one on the list had participated in the Paradise Dance Pavilion Marathon of 1933; the tragic events in Hampden had kept at least those dancers away from the Speedathon.

One dancer at the Hampden dance marathon, however, Stan West, eventually began to participate in the roller derbies of the late 1930s and 1940s that also had dance components. A professional marathon dancer, the new contests in skating presented another challenge and money-making opportunity for West, as did derbies and speedathons or speed derbies for other dancers elsewhere. Women, too, participated in the new contests, and not only in Old Orchard Beach.[91]

Closer to Bangor and the ruins of the devastating fire, the Chateau near Bangor continued to hold public dances, and some of them offered purses, of a sort. For example, in addition to hosting the marathon dancers' good-bye party in December 1933, and the Thanksgiving time dance in 1938 wherein a ten-pound live turkey served as a prize, it held a roller-skating "elimination race" just for women the same week as the Paradise Dance Pavilion fire. Women could gain entrance to the hall and rent skates for ten cents; it cost men twenty-five cents. It appears that the racing was dancing, or held dance elements, and that the Chateau served as a skating rink of sorts on nights when regular dancing was not on the agenda. Just as importantly, and showing the new direction female exhibition dancing would increasingly take, the same week that the Chateau held the marathon dancers' dinner, "The New Bijou" theater ran a large advertisement, with pen-and-ink sketches, for "**BIG TIME VAUDEVILLE**."[92]

While on the Bijou screen Ginger Rogers would appear with Joel McCrea in *Chance at Heaven*, on the stage Bangorites could see "**5 Acts**" of vaudeville, billed as "**ALL BIG ACTS**." Judging by the sketches, the attendees could expect to see a male singing group, a blackface routine, and two female acts: one of them featuring a woman in a black halter top, the other act approaching the burlesque, a dancing woman wearing a marching hat and cane, and either a necklace with pasties or a tiny bikini serving as a top. The sketch closely resembles one of Keith's sketches published in Portland and may actually have been for the same act. The acts at the Bijou would appear for "**3 BIG DAYS!**"[93] Risqué vaudeville or burlesque would become increasingly popular in Maine as the marathon dance craze was essentially legislated away.

CHAPTER SIX

The Dance Didn't Go On, and They Really Weren't Strippers

The Shipyard Workers' Riot of 1943, Another Dance Hall Fire, and the New Vaudeville, Burlesque, and Movie Dancers in Maine

ALMOST EXACTLY A MONTH AFTER THE DEADLY CONFLAGRATION AT Hampden, another Maine dance hall caught fire. On January 9, 1934, fire erupted at the State Ballroom in Portland, located in the "Recreation Building" at 616 Congress Street.[1]

The fire began in the back room of the State Ballroom, located on the third floor of the downtown building, and spread rapidly. Flames shot through the front windows of the building and toward the roof of the adjacent Sears & Roebuck Building, and prompted witnesses to sound the alarm at 10:30 a.m., by which time the top portion of the building was described as "a mass of flames and smoke."[2]

Congress Street, a major city thoroughfare, was shut down for blocks as firemen from several stations descended on the area. Policemen arrived as well, and both automobile and trolley car traffic was rerouted. At one point, four firemen were blown through a third-floor doorway by an immense back draft. The fire was under control by noon.[3]

The State Ballroom sustained the most damage, as might be expected, but fortunately the hall was closed to the public at the time of the fire, and unlike the situation during the Hampden and other marathons, dancers did not live on the premises; thus they were not there to sustain injuries or worse. Two on-site workers were feared missing for a short time, but both were eventually located unharmed. A bowling alley located in the building's basement sustained extensive damage, ending up as it did with two feet of water on its floors, and a pool room on the first door was also damaged, primarily by water. Smoke damaged other businesses. The slate roof on the Recreation Building helped contain the fire, and that on the Sears & Roebuck Building helped protect that building from catching fire.[4]

The dance hall's owner, Leon P. Gorman, had workers start cleaning up almost immediately after the fire was extinguished. He anticipated having the ballroom open for business that very night. He said he had no idea how the fire might have started, as there had not been a dance there since Saturday night, and that there had not been anyone in the back room when it started. He did not have insurance, and losses were estimated for the building at about $28,000.[5]

Portland's Recreation Building was a much more substantial one than the Hampden Dance Pavilion had been. A three-story brick or masonry building, it had been remodeled for "recreation purposes" in 1923. The ballroom was seventy feet by sixty feet in size and had been "built" to hold some 900 people. Elsewhere in the building, the basement held twelve bowling lanes for the public plus two private ones, and the billiard rooms had thirty-six tables. The building had once served as the home of the First Free Baptist Church.[6] There may never have been a marathon there or even a burlesque show, but this and other "ballrooms" and large dance halls attested to the popularity of dance in the state, and this is also the type of establishment most likely to see some version of taxi-dancing during the era. The ballroom reopened once the management made the necessary repairs.

The void possibly left in entertainment by the now-banned dance marathons would not last long into the 1930s. Within three weeks of the Hampden fire, Keith's theater in Portland had something new to advertise, primarily to its male audiences. On January 1, 1934, it ran a large advertisement for its new "Big Stage and Screen Show"—one that it defined as vaudeville but portions of which seemed to be, quite frankly, burlesque. The advertisement billed the show "By Candlelight" and featured the film *The Screen Test* and the "Big Time Vaudeville Act" of the "Fantastic Revue—A Song and Dance Spectacle" as well as the Radio Haymakers in "A Barnyard Musical Comedy." Although the advertisement included a small illustration of two couples dancing or embracing with just their heads and shoulders shown, the most prominent feature of the entire advertisement was a sketch of a woman dancing and kicking her legs up Rockette-style in just high heels, star-shaped pasties, and seemingly a thong or other brief bottom held up by three strings or straps, and holding a clock on whose face it read, instead of the numbers, "Happy New Year."[7]

The dancing girl was gone from Keith's next advertisement, and never would such a risqué drawing or photograph grace the ongoing advertising of the following weeks. The advertisement that appeared on January 2 started with Keith's "Big Vaudeville Show!" on stage, followed by its "Barnyard Musical," its "Revue Fantastic" presented by Louis Modena, still billed as "A Song and Dance Spectacle," and its movie *The Screen Test*. A few titles had reversed their wording, a few key descriptive words added, but no dancers of any variety were shown.[8] Public backlash may have explained the change.

Dancers did appear the following day in Keith's advertisement. There were three of them, relatively quite small along one border of the block advertisement, almost shown floating above a sketch of an orchestra. Although their backs seemed to be bare, the sketches were much less suggestive than that of two days previously; they were side views, and the dancers seemed to be wearing small shorts or short skirts.[9] Yet the picture still conveyed the impression that one might expect to see scantily dressed dancing women at the theater.

Keith's found itself needing a change of policy. It shut its doors briefly in order to make the changes. On January 4, the *Portland Evening Express* ran an article about the upcoming changes at Keith's. Apparently the vaudeville "burlesque" was proving quite popular, and the theater was changing its policies such that it would hold three shows daily except on Saturdays, when it would run four shows. The shows would now present one feature film and seven vaudeville acts. The program would change twice a week and accompany "a drastic downward revision of prices" made in order "to bring vaudeville to Portland at prices below those prevailing before the war" (World War I). As advertised by the theater in upcoming days, prices for the shows were ten cents, twenty cents, and thirty cents for matinees, and fifteen cents, thirty cents, and forty cents for night shows. *The Fog*, a romantic mystery thriller, would be the first film featured in the new setup. The Carson and Kams Revue was the first act specifically billed as a dance routine.[10]

Its new programming underway, Keith's management seemingly decided it was time to entice an audience once again with a more risqué advertisement. On January 9, the theater used an illustration of a clearly topless woman, although in this instance the scantily clothed dancer was not as centrally placed in the advertisement. The woman carried a cane and was straddling or riding a segment of a large circle or hoop, with further advertisement information in the hoop. The woman wore only high heels, a top hat, gloves, and low cut short-shorts. One largely exposed breast was covered somewhat by a strategically placed arm. Directly behind the woman was a clown who wore a rather demented or leering grin, depending upon one's interpretation. The Dorothy Martin Revue, "A Moonlight Fantasy" dance troupe, had top billing of the vaudeville acts, with shows starting at 2:30, 5:40, and 8:35 p.m.[11]

The following day, a stylized Little Egypt appeared in Keith's advertisement. She was clad in a belly dance bra-type top, her midriff bare, and wearing a short chiffon or silk looking skirt with a headdress and arm cuffs. The advertisement did not say if the featured dancers were doing Eastern or Oriental dance, but the inference that some element of belly dancing was there was apparent. The connotations seem particularly evident when one glances at an adjacent advertisement, one for the State Theater, whose current feature film was *Dancing Lady*, and the lady in the accompanying photograph was wearing a very similar outfit to that of Keith's Little Egypt dancer with just the addition of what seems to be a feather boa. The illustrated woman may also have gone with the other film being shown, *Girl without a Room*, who was further described as being "Without a Room and Board"—the allusion could have been to belly dancing or to some form of prostitution, or both.[12]

The mixing of vaudeville and burlesque with suggestive film advertising had started somewhat before the tragedy in Hampden and continued for some time. During the week of the fatal fire in Hampden, and just before the conflagration in Portland, the State Theater in Portland advertised its current main film, *Hoopla*. The star of *Hoopla* was Clara Bow, and she was advertised to be "giving the most [soulful] performance of her career." She was also pictured in a belly-dancer's outfit with a skimpy top, a coin necklace streaming down her bare belly to meet an open front skirt and short undergarment. She had her hands positioned behind her head, and wore bracelets and anklets.[13]

Separate coverage of *Hoopla* was also printed on December 15, 1933. A review published in the *Portland Evening Express* that day called Clara Bow the "original 'It' girl." The film had been adopted from the play *The Barker* and—with just a change to the original ending to update it, remained the same story of carnival life, with new emphasis on Clara instead of on the carnival barker. Clara had "shimmied her way into prominence," the shimmy being a classic belly dance movement and seen in some other dances of the era. Clara was asked to deceive young Richard Cromwell, the carnival barker played by Preston Foster, but finds herself in love with him instead. He was the first man to ever treat her decently. He defends her from the crowds when she dances for the men. The two marry, and the barker, son of a wealthy man, returns to the study of law, while Clara earns the couple's bread and butter and becomes "the drawing card of the Chicago Fair midway." This may have been the Chicago fair at which the first Little Egypts appeared in 1895.[14] Either way, the young woman's talent is seen as such, not as just a bawdy dance, and the barker's family comes to accept her.

The same week Bow's film was running, Ricker Gardens held a charity dance. Two live orchestras played that Thursday night, and "Vaudeville and Dancing Acts" were featured. Admission was higher than that for some places, at fifty cents, but the money went to the Santa Claus fund of the Acacia Club and the American Legion. The State Ballroom announced that it would not be having a dance the night of the benefit, December 14, 1933, so as not to compete with the benefit.[15] Just three weeks later, the State Ballroom caught fire.

Vaudeville performances had regularly been presented in Maine cities since the turn of the century. They became more risqué as time passed, and by 1934 were offering more burlesque than they were other forms of dance. Film advertisements also followed that trend for a number of years. Off to the side, in the "seedier" establishments, women were taking off more clothing, but these places did not advertise in the major papers. However, since the early 1910s, some Portland citizens had complained of immorality occurring in Maine's dance halls and recommended stricter ordinances and licensing for all dance halls.[16] Such concerns continued in the 1930s.

Theaters advertised vaudeville performances in Bangor, the Lewiston–Auburn area, and other locations during the time the larger marathons were ongoing or ending, as they did films featuring dancing women or actresses portrayed as such, although in general Keith's Portland advertisements slipped into the burlesque style most often. Still, it was not alone in being suggestive in its advertisements.

In Bangor, the aforementioned vaudeville at the Bijou Theater had run the same week as the fire at the Paradise Dance Pavilion, and in November 1933 the Opera House had shown the *Footlight Parade*, the house's offering limited to the "100 girls!" in the movie billed as "The Mightiest Musical of All Time!! Music-Girls-Romance." (The same show, featuring James Cagney, advertised with a dancer shown wearing just shoes and flowers, appeared at one Portland theater the following March, and had also run in Portland the previous October—when three scantily clad dancers illustrated the advertisement at the State Theater;

that advertisement added to the regular cast list "and 300 cute girls!") Other vaudeville acts had been staged at the Bangor Bijou during the previous few months, and the New Bijou advertised that one "Bangor boy" was appearing in a vaudeville bill there in late October, and that more would be staged in coming months and years.

In some cases, vaudeville acts that appeared in the Bangor region had also appeared at Keith's in Portland. A new, direct link to the Keith's entertainment appeared in July 1941, when George McKay's Criterion Theater advertised, along with a midnight show and a matinee as part of its "Big 4th of July Celebration," "5 ACTS OF VAUDEVILLE DIRECT FROM KEITH'S RKO, BOSTON," the Boston location being the home base for the Portland venue.[17] Bangor had not been totally cut off from the Keith's circuit after its disastrous fire of two decades earlier. It did not, however, have the same presence in the vaudeville and burlesque world as Portland did, nor did any other city or town in the state.

Other media images of female dancers continued to reach Mainers wherever they might live in the state. For example, in 1935 the makers of Chesterfield cigarettes, the Ligget & Myers Tobacco Company, ran an advertisement in the *New York Times* and other venues that reached Maine readers featuring a supposedly Turkish—or possibly Greek—belly dancer. The smiling woman wore a headband, a midriff top with short sleeves and beads or coins, a coin and beaded belt, and a long gauzy skirt with the same trim as on her top. Instead of the more traditional Turkish bare feet, she wore dark shoes, of the type common to ballroom danc-ing. In one hand she held a pack of Chesterfield cigarettes, in the other a number of tobacco leaves, both arms in a traditional dance pose with hands lifted, elbows down. Just behind her hand holding the leaves was an enlarged pack of the cigarettes, with the branding apparent, and behind her also a crescent-shape cutout featured sun-drying tobacco leaves hung on drying poles. The lead-in read, in large script, "The aromatic Turkish tobaccos used in Chesterfield give them a more pleasing aroma and taste. . . . Every year we import thousands of pounds from Turkey and Greece." Following script noted again that importing the tobacco was expensive but blended "with our mild, ripe home-grown tobaccos helps give Chesterfields more aroma, helps to give them a pleasing taste."[18] The woman pictured seemed pleased enough.

Cigarettes at the time might have seemed harmless enough, even with a female dancer accompanying an advertisement for them, yet places like Keith's and the smaller remaining houses continued to test the parameters of public and governmental censure. For some periods after 1934 Keith's had very innocuous advertisements in terms of being risqué, even though the theater's offerings may have still highlighted females, and, in particular, female dancers. Sometimes such advertisements had no illustrations at all or just sketches; at other times, they showed fairly well-covered women. Other changes were also apparent in local papers. However, overall, the acts billed promised that a certain amount of skin and erotic dance would be up for viewing.

In early 1937, for example, in May, Keith's advertised its "Black and White Revue." The show featured "Betty Babette, French Nudist," and "Lovely Lane, Sepia Nudist." Lane, the "sepia nudist," was perhaps the sole "black" portion of the Black and White Revue, but other performers may also have been African American. The dance trio of "Tom, Dick, and Mary," appeared, as did a novelty act, a radio personality, and "'Egg-Head and Shell,' Harlem's Duo," as well as the "Three Inkspots, Dancing Demons." The advertisement for the show published in the *Portland Evening Express* featured a pen-and-ink drawing of two women in fairly modest one-piece dance apparel, rather like one-piece bathing suits.[19]

But in case anyone missed what the show had to offer, the next day the same newspaper ran another advertisement, this one also featuring a pen-and-ink drawing, but this one was clearly of a blonde dancing girl, her legs spread in a high kick, her top seemingly just a set of pasties. The front of her lower costume was unseen behind her high-kicking leg, but a flouncy skirt covered at least her backside. She also wore a smile and a headband. In this advertisement, "Lovely Lane" was billed specifically as a "Colored Nudist," and "Tom, Dick, and Mary" as the "Fastest Tap Trio in Vaudeville." Two films were also part of the show, one starring

James Cagney, the other Jane Withers. A third advertisement, also done in pen and ink, pictured a blonde woman in a one-piece body suit with strategically placed cutouts, and with feathers (or wings) peeping out from the back, and identified as another one of the acts, "Bob and Kitty," an acrobatic routine.[20]

The *Express* ran a brief review of the "Black and White" show. The review identified a few of the other acts in the "variety revue" and provided a bit more information about the dancers. According to the *Express*, "Featured are Lovely Lane, colored nudist, whose dance is breathtaking, and Betty Babette, whose scarf dance is graceful and daring." The tap dancing in the show was "clever."[21] Although Lovely Lane was identified as a "nudist," judging from another "nudist" featured later in 1937, it is doubtful that she appeared in Maine entirely nude, but may well have appeared elsewhere in the buff, or topless, or wearing pasties and a G-string.

In early 1937, public dances were still extremely popular throughout Maine, but the dance contests of the 1920s and early 1930s were no longer in evidence. Big bands, however, were regular offerings at local dance halls. Louie Armstrong and his orchestra made an appearance at the Old Orchard Pier on July 3 and 4, for the Pier's "grand opening" for the summer season. Local film advertising was fairly subdued, although the movies carried some big-name actors such as Mickey Rooney, Spencer Tracy, Jane Withers, and Bette Davis. Keith's, the most racy of the theaters to feature dance routines as part of its vaudeville acts, advertised its "Follies Begere [*sic*]." The new show featured "**30** Beautiful Girls—Girls **30**" in "Dances, Song, and Comedy," while on Sunday, July 4, a "Gala Midnight Show" would feature "Uncle Ezra Stebbens and His Radio Barn Dance Follies." The *Evening Express* published a brief review of the "Follies" show, noting the various types of dance, comedy, and magic performed, and noted that "eight pulchritudinous girls form the dancing line which also appears in a showy number."[22] Beautiful women were always a plus.

The following day after the review appeared, July 3, the newspaper's headlines proclaimed the disappearance of Amelia Earhart and her navigator, but stated that they were safe somewhere "In the Middle of the Pacific," and that an S.O.S. had been received. Just below the main article about Earhart on the front page, Keith's ran a small block advertisement touting its midnight show on July 4. A large advertisement was pasted on the stage and screen section of the paper, however, with no burlesque-type sketches except perhaps where a line of chorus girls disappeared behind another section of the drawing, their clothes seemingly disappearing along with the upper portion of their bodies.[23]

On July 6, Earhart's missing plane had not yet been found, and the *Evening Express* declared her "Still Adrift in Mid-Atlantic." The reports were still positive as to her eventually being found alive. Keith's projected as positive a portrayal of its show in its advertisement of the day, and on July 9 the newspaper declared there was truly a "Dancing Treat in Stage Show at Keith's." Dancing was the main feature of the newest show, and of such variety that the report said it "does not prove tiresome," and that the dances and dancers were "each outstanding of its type." All in all, the show was "one of the most talented ... seen in Portland in many months." There was tap dancing, acrobatic and contortionist dancing, an "adagio number," and dancing on roller skates.[24]

Rudy Vallee came to the region a few days later, playing first at the Old Orchard Pier on July 30, and later, on September 25, at the American Legion Hall in Westbrook, adjacent to the city of Portland proper, this being his "home-town Legion Post." Duke Ellington played at Ricker Gardens in Portland on October 9, and a few days later he and his orchestra played at Ricker Gardens with Ella Fitzgerald appearing also. Meanwhile, Keith's ran rather subdued newspaper advertisements for its shows, which featured basic vaudeville acts as well as films, with dancing that included some rumba, baton swinging, and "kick-waltzing." Reviewers sometimes noted such things as "solo and specialty dances," in addition to any traditional dances, including ballet and the new tap dancing that had become popular of late. These "specialty" dances might have been just about anything, within limits.[25]

Then, in October 1937, after a period of having advertisements with no or very modest imaging, Keith's decided to become more blatant. While the city's Ricker Gardens advertised on October 7 that Duke Ellington and his orchestra would appear on October 9, a Saturday night, and Chick Webb the following Wednesday, Keith's ran a large block advertisement, after having had no such advertising for some time, featuring a *photograph* of a young woman, apparently naked except for a star-spangled banner a few inches wide covering her breasts and part of her hips, the woman being shown from a side view in a sitting position but with her face turned outward and wearing a large smile. The theater was putting on a "Special Show Monday Nite" [*sic*]. "It's Daring," the advertisement announced, and would feature Earl Taylor's "Glorified Revue" with "30 girls, 14 scenes, 15 B'way Stars." There would also be a showing of the film *The Prince and the Pauper* staring Errol Flynn and the Mauch twins, and of *Secret Valley*. The newspaper ran this advertisement on Friday and Saturday, and noted that Thursday night, before the new show started, was "Ladies Night" for both the matinee and evening lineups. Prices before the new show ranged from fifteen cents before 1:00 p.m., fifteen cents and twenty-five cents for shows between 1:00 and 6:00 p.m., and twenty-five cents and thirty-five cents for the night shows.[26]

On Saturday, the theater ran another blatant ad, one more so than that of the previous two days. The new enticement showed another photographed naked woman, this one more of a woman and not a young girl as the previous one had seemed, leaning on a pillar-type seat, her hands clutching her breasts and a thin scarf or veil that traveled from her hands down to cover her genitalia. At her feet was a small sketch of a dancer with Keith's popular star-clad bits of fabric, and on the opposite side of the large advertisement was a sketch of a dancer shown face-on and wearing just a bikini-type bottom piece and a blindfold. Her breasts were sketched sans nipples, but the sketched woman, as well as the photographed one, were clearly topless, and the photographed woman clearly naked. The ad said that the "Revue Glorified" would open at a special midnight holiday show on Monday, and added to its list of dazzling features, including now "30 glorified girls," "1069 eye-dazzling costumes," and an "Added Attraction!" This added attraction was billed as being "Dress and Undress" and featured "The Stage's Most Intimate Scenes. Actually Taking You into the Showgirl's Dressing Room."[27]

As if all that were not enough, patrons had another unique offering to enjoy. They could look at a girl "In the Fish Bowl in Our Lobby." No further details were given on this; perhaps the woman was dressed as a fish or mermaid, perhaps not. This scene was billed as their "Extra! Extra!" The price for all this was to be thirty-five cents for all seats, and the doors opened at 11:30 p.m. There were two films being shown also, but their billing was quite insignificant.[28]

The *Portland Evening Express* ran a photograph on its entertainment page featuring one of the dancers from the "Glorified Revue" in its Saturday edition. Connie Cella was described as "one of the attractive girls" in the show, which would run for four days. Cella was shown in a peignoir type of gown opened at the front, sitting, with her bare legs crossed. There was no mention of nudity.[29]

As Keith's was presenting its new lineup, Chick Webb made his appearance and brought with him both his orchestra and Ella Fitzgerald. Glenn Miller played in mid-December at Ricker Gardens. Maine clearly brought in some big acts during the 1930s and would continue to do so in the future, especially during the tourist seasons.[30]

Keith's came out with a new advertisement when its gala show opened. This time it featured mirror-image women, arms up holding an "on stage" and an "in person" orb respectively, clad in just angle-strap shoes and some filmy material barely covering over their torsos. At first glance they appeared to be nude. The advertising used basically the same words as the Monday before, with the revised lure of "See for the First Time Intimate Scenes of a Show Girl's Dressing Room." The following day just one of the women would be included in the theater's advertisement, with the reminder that "It's Different! It's Daring! 30 Glorified Beauties, See them Dress and Undress!" They also told patrons, "Don't

Miss It!" Advertised just below Keith's ad was one for the film *Damaged Lives* being shown at the Colonial Theater, which would soon enough make headlines for its own risqué tendencies. The film was billed as being "the picture they said could not be shown. . . . Tears aside the veil of secrecy!" In a small box, the theater advertisement stated, "We suggest you do not bring children under 16." The show had been running for several days. Perhaps Keith's and the Colonial were chafing under the constrictions of the era of Hayes censorship.[31]

"SEE THEM DRESS AND UNDRESS!" Keith's advertisements stated that October. Five years later, a mob would spill into the streets in Portland following a vaudeville show in which the men wanted and demanded to see the women undress. In the meantime, the four-day show at Keith's and its "attractive girls" entertained numerous Portland theatergoers. On one night of the show, Keith's promised "free cash prizes," whether to the dancers or the audience was not clear, but probably to the audience.[32]

The *Portland Evening Express* reviewed the new stage show. It called the show "a mixture of comedy, music, and dancing, backed by a line of attractive girls and moving at a rapid tempo." Comedians of both genders appeared, and Mark Lea played "the burlesque judge." Some people may have called the act "vaudeville" still, but the word "burlesque" had again made it into the newspaper. Connie Cella was noted as the featured dancer. There was also a team of "fast-stepping male dancers" and, as the paper described it, "the twelve Taylorettes and Girdellers Models back up the numerous acts."[33] The paper did not give the show any type of rating or age or audience suggestions; perhaps the show was not as risqué as the advertisements had suggested. The paper did note that this was to be the first in a new set of shows changing weekly at the theater.

Keith's continued to advertise the "Revue Glorified" over the next couple of days, using a different model, a woman who seemed to be wearing a bathing suit, in a photograph accompanied with text one day, and on another day one accompanied by a sketch of a woman wearing what seemed to be a skirt with suspenders only as high up as her nipples, or perhaps they were spaghetti dress straps pulled down to just cover her nipples. Either way, she was essentially topless.[34]

The next show in the offering was the "Jimmy Hodges Revue" featuring "girls, girls, girls." Prizes were being offered on some nights, as they had one night during the Glorified Revue, as well as films and on some nights a "Blue Dinner Service." The illustration for the new show was less risqué but rather more odd, as the sketched female featured seemed to be some combination of fish or bird and woman. She was wearing some sort of body suit with wings spreading up off her breasts, and fins or some such attached to the bottom of the suit, with a matching belt and hat combination pulling the peculiar ensemble together. She also had a rather demented grin on her face. The next advertisement for the show featured a perhaps even more peculiar woman, this one photographed in a little-girl-style dress and a massive sunhat. In case one missed whatever message she was meant to convey, in the lower right portion of the advertisement, a sketch of a line of six chorus girls showed them kicking their left legs up high, a smile on their faces, and perhaps nothing covering their breasts.[35]

After this latest show, sketches and photographs of women—clothed or not, demented looking or not—disappeared from Keith's advertising once again. Meanwhile, the State Theater was showing what it billed as "Actual Motion Pictures of Brady-Shaffer, Gangsters in Bangor." The two men, Al Brady being at the time Public Enemy No. 1, had just been gunned down in the streets of Bangor by the FBI. Meanwhile, along Portland's Elm Street a roller-skating rink was proving a local attraction; orchestras, local and from away, played throughout the region.[36]

During this time, Keith's regularly held "News of the Nation" shows in which the theater would run newsreels produced by Fox Movietone News. The newsreels changed every Wednesday and Saturday, and were presented in "cooperation with" the *Portland Press Herald* (*PPH*) and the *Portland Evening Express*. It also began offering a dinner service for customers with a "card."[37]

Keith's ran the news clips throughout the year and advertised its Harry Berry "Sunkist Vanities" as being a "show of radiant joy" on October 23 and 25, once again using a live model. This time the photographed woman was clearly wearing clothes. She had on a body or bathing suit with what appeared to be fishnet covering her belly and middle back. On the 23rd, the dancer's head and upper torso were visible, while on the 25th her entire body was shown. She was photographed up on her toes on one foot, with the other leg kicked back and her arms bent in, palms out to frame her smiling face. A third advertisement for the show featured a photograph of three women lined up wearing low-cut marching-band-type uniforms, the women wearing top hats and apparently part of the show's "California Girl Band."[38]

The next offering from Keith's was the mythology-based "Leda and the Swan" featuring "Miss Helene." This was part of the upcoming "French Follies," which also included the dancer Conchita doing a "jungle dance." Either Conchita or Miss Helene was performing burlesque, as a sketch of one of the dancers showed her wearing a bikini, leaning back in a seated, casual pose. Furthermore, the *Express* in its review of the show ran the headline "Burlesque Bits Pep Up Show," and also noted an "unusual" lion act. The burlesque in the local shows was finally being recognized as burlesque. Although the lion act was described as "the climax and piece de resistance of the revue," Conchita, "a svelte Mexican senorita," the review stated, "gives her interpretation of a primitive jungle dance and does it with considerable abandon"— and Helene "puts into sensuous grace the classical myth of the beautiful maiden who fell in love with her swan." Helene "typified" the "graceful exotic" in her dancing and may well have been using some of the more sinuous moves used in belly dancing, as well as in other forms of dance. Other women also danced during the show, and films as usual accompanied the live stage performances.[39]

The next show to appear at Keith's featured the "Manhattan Merry-Go-Round" with a sketched, lingerie-clad woman in its advertisements, seated with her legs kicking down and up, accompanied by, on film, Shirley Temple in *Wee Willie Winkie*. (The film had played at another theater a couple of weeks earlier.) Following days would reveal more details, along with a top-hatted, fishnet-stockinged, strapless-dressed dancer possibly used as an image for Francis Renault in "Slave of Fashion," although the image may have been for Zorita in her "Danses a la Moderne." It was announced, in words and highlighted by a photograph, that Francis Renault was a female impersonator. She would appear in various shows over the next few days, including in a few special midnight shows. The entire show was billed as "Big Time Vaudeville." Fifi Dorsey, whom the local paper interviewed, would appear late in the month, along with "Girls-Girls-Girls" on the stage, otherwise called "OO LA LA PARIE," and later billed as "A Spicy, Daring, Satire, with fourteen beautiful women."[40]

Keith's was not the only theater to turn to the risqué to pull in customers. A sketch of Mae West appeared in an advertisement for the State Theater at the close of October 1937, that portion of her body visible clothed in a classic belly dancing outfit with a fringed bra top, exposed stomach, and a low and angled skirt. She had bangles on the arm shown, hoop-earrings, and seemed to be doing a shoulder shimmy. The title of the movie was *I'm No Angel*. Little Egypt was back, even if fleetingly.[41]

The Strand also had some vaudeville presentations during the period. In late November 1937, for example, it held a special midnight show, with both film and stage offerings. Katherine Hepburn and Ginger Rogers starred in *Stage Door*, a dance musical, while the "Lady Godiva Revue" with "Dazzling Artist Models, Comedians, Dancers, Singers, and Exponents of Beauty" appeared live on Thanksgiving Eve. There were several dances being held in the area that night as well, some with door prizes, including two turkeys being given out at the Driftwood.[42]

The year 1937 also saw Maine's most celebrated dancer performing at Keith's in Portland. Molly Spotted Elk, née Molly Alice Nelson, appeared on Keith's stage for a few nights. Molly Nelson had been living in France from 1931 on, staying there after performing at the Colonial

Exposition in Paris. She had fallen in love and would eventually marry a French man with whom she had one child, a daughter, in 1934. In France, she had achieved perhaps more celebrity than in America, although not as great a one as Josephine Baker, the African American dancer who rose to fame in the 1920s and whose time overlapped with that of Nelson in France. Molly Nelson, also started work on a novel.[43]

Molly's daughter arrived two months early, before Molly had a chance to return to her beloved Indian Island in the face of increased political unrest and economic strife in France. However, by autumn she and her daughter, Jean, arrived in Maine. They stayed at the home Molly had bought for her family. By winter, Molly felt a need to return to work, both to support her daughter and to resume her art. She was now thirty-one years old and had not danced professionally for a year. In early January 1935, she received an invitation to perform with a dance ensemble in a Native American–based opera, *Minnehahah*. She left for New York, leaving her daughter in the care of her mother. Unfortunately funding for the opera soon fell through, so Molly started knocking on doors again. She secured work once more as an artist's model. News of her arrival soon reached the press and the *New York Post* ran a short piece about her. Shortly thereafter, Molly found a job dancing in a Greenwich Village club. In May, however, she returned to Maine. She missed her daughter Jean and her soon-to-be husband, also named Jean. In August 1935, she received an invitation for a one-day appearance at the Abbe Indian Museum in Bar Harbor. She accepted, and later wrote that she "sang and danced on the green, the audience sat under some trees."[44]

Molly also danced in Bangor that year. In August, she performed at the Atlantic Casino at 169 Exchange Street. The Atlantic Sea Grill, part of the overall Atlantic Casino, had been created in the late 1920s and survived into the 1940s. Molly Spotted Elk initially accepted a week's engagement at the casino, a week that her biographer reported turned into three. The Atlantic Casino, which billed itself as "The Only Night-club in Maine," did advertise its acts during this time but not daily, and it also apparently ran overlapping acts. So although the casino did advertise Molly's appearances, it did not do so consistently.[45]

Tickets for the floor show at the Atlantic Casino cost fifty cents in 1935, the same price as charged for a full-course dinner. On Saturdays, from noon until 2:00 p.m., one could enjoy both a floor show and a luncheon for fifty cents. On Sundays, one could purchase a "special dinner" up to midnight. On other nights, dinner service ended at 8:00. "Club Suppers" cost seventy-five cents, and seemed to be charged when special floor shows were held. Dancing for the audience members from 6:00 p.m. until 2:00 a.m. was also a feature of the club, and the casino had its own orchestra for the enjoyment of its patrons and that sometimes accompanied various dancers and singers.[46]

Other acts that appeared during the month of October at the Atlantic Casino included a "Sensational All Colored Revue, Direct from Harlem," which was to appear for a week. There was no special cover charge for this show, but dinner cost seventy-five cents that week. Earlier in the month, the casino had held a "Brand New Floor Show" as well as an "Amateur Night, Don't Miss It!" Amateur nights allowed aspiring dancers and others to test their stuff on a public stage, and it had been at such a contest that Molly had won her $10 prize as a teenager. A "Club Supper" that week cost seventy-five cents, so apparently two levels of dinner or supper meals were indeed served at the casino.[47]

At the outset of October, one act at the club involved a former marathon dancer of sorts. Jeff Roland, who had won "the recent New England professional endurance contest, in which he danced 68 consecutive hours in wooden shoes," appeared at the casino. The contest was most likely not in Maine, as even sixty-eight hours of continuous dancing in contests was no longer allowed in the state, although adding the term "professional" may have allowed the contest to sneak in somewhere. At the casino, when Roland danced in his heavy clogs with "frenzied agility," his last dance "brought half of those at the tables up standing—an unusual personal triumph," according to a review in the *Bangor Daily News*. In addition to Roland, a female singer appeared that week, as did a magician and a dance team from Providence. The dance team performed "a modern version of the waltz and a fox trot rumba, European style."[48]

In case anyone might wonder why watching or dancing a waltz could still be a big deal, images of waltzing in earlier years included ones in which the man had almost "captured" a woman's legs between his, leaning her backwards at the same time as he held her thighs between his. One article published in Maine called the waltz, done European style, "the waltz which came before the world was ready for it." This had been published a decade earlier, so maybe the world was ready for it. In the 1910s it was not, nor had been many places in the 1920s.[49]

During the third week of October 1935, the *BDN* ran another article or review of the casino, stating in its title, "Prominent Dance Team to Head the Casino Program." The featured dancers had, like Molly Nelson, performed on the Keith's circuit. The two dancers were "O'Hanlon and Zanbuni, the best known dance team that the Casino has ever engaged." The two had come to America in 1921 under contract to the Shuberts, had starred in a number of the Shubert shows, and then went on the vaudeville circuit for Keith's, dancing at some of the circuit's most prominent venues. They had toured on other well-known circuits as well, and appeared in British films before coming to the United States. A blues singer and a tap dancer would also perform during the show. The *BDN* stated that it was anticipated that the show, opening on October 21, would prove "the best show of the season—a show booked with the idea of pleasing 6000 teachers who will be in Bangor this week."[50]

The *Bangor Daily Commercial* saw less advertising by the casino. However, in terms of advertising for Molly Nelson, it ran a wonderful November advertisement. On October 31, during which time Molly had started her run at the casino, the *BDC* carried an advertisement featuring two black cats (who may have been smoking or blowing noisemakers) and stated that there would be a dance that night at the casino, with "Noisemakers, Favors, and a Lot of Fun!" at the "New Atlantic Garden Club."[51] This may have been a recent addition to the club, one allowing other performers, such as Molly Nelson, to appear on the main stage and dance floor. The *BDN* also carried an advertisement of the same sort for the casino on October 31, this one featuring a witch in black silhouette, flying in front of the moon on her broom, a black cat left behind on the ground.[52]

Then, on November 2, the *BDC* printed a fairly large photograph of Molly Nelson, seemingly a photograph of her taken circa 1930 when she was twenty-seven. This was a less commonly reproduced photograph of her than the headshot of her taken in New York in 1930, which showed Nelson straight on, her fingers grazing the sides of her face, her eyes large and her face smooth and radiant with a trace of makeup on, and wearing a Native American beaded band around her forehead, and her native attire clothing her more thoroughly than the scanty outfit of the more famous 1928 portrait featuring her ankle-length eagle headdress. The photograph printed in the *BDC* featured the same headband and upper-body garment as the 1930 one but showed Nelson at more of a three-quarter angle, with one of her hands grazing one side of her lower face and her makeup and expression much the same as in the other portrait. Quite likely, it was another photograph by the same artist taken the same day. At any rate, it clearly showed Molly dressed in attire she preferred more than the scanty garments she was often asked to wear for performances, and looking radiant in Native American dress. The text accompanying the photograph stated simply: "LAST APPEARANCE TONIGHT, PRINCESS SPOTTED ELK, AT THE ATLANTIC CASINO" and, perhaps showing the size of the nightclub, its address was given as "161–169 Exchange St., Bangor."[53]

The *Bangor Daily News* also took note of Molly Spotted Elk's appearance, and not just in paid advertising. On October 29, it ran an article about her, and, to a lesser extent, about the casino. It noted that the casino's manager had hired several "American dancers" since opening its doors, but that "last night his program was headed by a real American dancer, one whose people roamed the trackless forests of the Penobscot," before Columbus ever sailed to the Americas. The article stated that Molly Spotted Elk "has been really prominent" and that "last night she appeared in a rumba rhythm dance followed by an Indian dance typical of her people. She is lithe, sinuous, and graceful." Starting that night, October 29, she would "present a new and sensational Nautch dance in addition to the two she gave yesterday." On October 2, the *BDN* carried an advertisement for Molly's show. Again, like the *BDC*'s, it noted that "Last Time Tonight For Another **Grand Show**, at the Atlantic **Casino . . . PRINCESS SPOTTED ELK, Great Indian Dancer**." The Club Casino Orchestra would provide music for customer dancing, and dinner would be available up to 8:00 p.m. for fifty cents, and suppers for seventy-five cents up to 2:00 a.m. The advertisement did not include a photograph of Molly Nelson.[54]

Interestingly, her Bangor appearance was the first time Molly Spotted Elk's sister Eunice saw Molly dance professionally. She later stated that "when Molly performed at the Bangor Casino, everyone was silent." She said that her sister's dance "inspired awe," and its strength and truth was evident. When Molly finished, she said, tears ran down her own cheeks. "It just stirred me. I can't explain. It struck me as something so honest, so down to earth, primitive, pure."[55]

Molly soon had to move on again, however, leaving her daughter once more with her mother, Philomene, on Indian Island. She landed gigs with the Wahaletka Indian Revue, with a New York nightclub, and then with a Philadelphia revue for $75 a week, a salary that would allow her to save money to take herself and her daughter back to France. First, however, she went home again, then headed to California to work as a film extra as well as landing a few somewhat bigger parts in a few major movies, including *Ramona* and *The Last of the Mohicans*. She continued to correspond with her daughter's father, Jean Archambaud, a politically oriented journalist who found himself in increasingly dire straits as the decade marched on and the Germans posed a real threat to his country. He would have preferred to move to the United States to be with Molly and their daughter, but it did not work out that way. Molly Spotted Elk returned to New York in October 1937, found a few small jobs including a secretarial one in the dance industry, then in

November she came to Maine, returned to New York City again, and in May 1937 appeared at Keith's in Portland.[56]

Keith's would emphasize Molly's more "scandalous" aspects in its advertising. In New York during her last stay, in the early spring of 1937, Molly—who had declined to do so in Paris—had agreed to dance topless, writing in her journal, "Dislike it, but if it brings money then money it will be." Moreover, she had modeled nude for various artists over the years, including in 1937, and Keith's would bill her as an "Indian Nudist." On May 3, while Mainers and tourists alike had the opportunity to see Benny Goodman and his orchestra at the Old Orchard Pier, and Count Basie at the Pier on May 8, or attend a "ball" at Portland's City Hall that offered such prizes as an RCA radio, a General Electric refrigerator, and a two-door Terraplane sedan, at Keith's one could see its "**Cavalcade of Stars**" at three shows a day. Keith's billed the show as "The Season's Smartest Show," with the "Lowest Stage Show Prices in History." A sketch of a smiling woman in a hat, high heels, and what appears to be a strapless bikini top and a very short skirt or shorts accompanied the text. At the show, there would be "**20 PEOPLE ON THE STAGE**."[57]

On Tuesday, May 18, Keith's announced that starting that Thursday a new show would begin. The show, "International Scandals," would feature "**Princess Spotted Elk**, INDIAN NUDIST," as well as stars from France, Germany, Italy, Spain, Japan, Ireland, and Africa. With World War II looming on the horizon, this was not a show one might expect to see a few years later. The show would have eight "Big Acts."[58]

The following day, May 19, the *Portland Evening Express* included a photograph of Molly Nelson on its regular entertainment page. Like the one printed earlier in the *Bangor Daily Commercial*, the photograph seemed to be another photograph taken by the same photographer at the same time as the more frequently printed portrait of Molly. It showed her dancing in her floor-to-toe eagle headdress taken circa 1928 when she was roughly twenty-five. In this photograph, instead of being pictured with her torso bent forward, she was standing upright, one leg again shown raised and bent to the front, toes pointed downward, feet bare, with one arm held at a ninety-degree angle to the front and bent at the elbow such that its forearm was raised toward the sky, hand fisted, the other arm similarly posed but bent at the elbow to the back and its hand fisted downward. The caption simply stated, "Princess Spotted Elk, noted Indian dancer and native of Old Town, will be the featured dancer with the International Scandals show opening Thursday at Keith's."[59]

That same day, and placed lower on the same page, Keith's ran an advertisement for the new show. It noted that the eight vaudeville acts would include the feature dancer, "Princess Spotted Elk, Indian Nudist," plus "Nina Lartique, French Star, Yukie, Japanese Hula-Hula [Dancer], Gerard & Marco, Italian Ambassadors of Joy, Reed & Ryan, Irish Comedians, and Siegfried & Co., German Jugglers, AND MANY OTHERS." Tickets for the show cost ten cents, twenty cents, or thirty cents, depending on the show, with the thirty-cent shows being those performed after 6:00 p.m. The floor shows were held for Molly Nelson at 12:40, 4:40, and 8:30 p.m.[60]

A similar advertisement appeared the next day, and on May 21 another advertisement included "Graner & Wilson, Harlem Dancers & Comedians" as well as the "Dancing Carrs." On the screen, Will Rogers was playing in *David Harum*, along with Carole Lombard and Fred MacMurray starring in *The Princess Comes Across*.[61]

On May 22, Molly's run at Keith's ended. The venue advertised the same, stating, "Last Day on Stage, Indian Nudist, Princess Spotted Elk." It did not include the other stage acts in this final notice of Molly Nelson's appearance.[62]

The *Portland Press Herald* and the *Portland Evening Express* both featured news of Molly's appearance in Portland. In addition to the photograph and notice posted in the *PEE*, the *PPH* included an interview about Molly's future plans, most notably her hopes to return to France. She did not give her reasons, but her reasons were largely centered on reuniting with her child's father. In June 1938, she returned with her daughter to Paris where she married and had a book accepted for publication on Indian legends. However, the publication fell through due to political and then military events in Europe. The Germans invaded France, her husband accepted a role to help settle and otherwise aid refugees, and with the Nazi's nearing her doorstep—which had changed numerous times by numerous miles—Molly and little Jean were forced to leave France. Jean Archambaud could not leave, and Molly never saw him again.[63]

Jean Archambaud tried to leave France, but was unable to do so. He fell ill and died in October 1941 while aiding refugees. Molly never married again, and she never found dancing opportunities again like she had when younger. In her forties, few people wanted to hire her for the type of dancing she did in the venues in which she had performed in the past. The nightclubs, cabarets, and vaudeville houses were largely a young woman's territory. Molly suffered a mental breakdown and was hospitalized in the Bangor State Mental Hospital for a year, having been returned from California in a straightjacket. Molly Spotted Elk died of a fall in the family home at age seventy-three. Her beloved mother had died two weeks earlier, leaving Molly alone to wander the home she had bought with her dancing earnings so many years before.[64] A Maine legend had passed. As time went by, people increasingly realized that Molly was indeed a legendary figure. She had wanted to publish a book of native legends; instead, she became one.

Molly was still alive and dancing and writing as 1937 drew to a close, however, and her daughter Jean would one day donate Molly's numerous writings to the Maine Folklore Center. Meanwhile, in 1937, the Portland and Old Orchard area finished the year much as it had the previous few months. People could go to various dances and see live acts and film shows, and in mid-December they could also dance to Glenn Miller and his band at Ricker Gardens or to Artie Shaw on Christmas night. Keith's offered the only real vaudeville show in the region on New Year's Eve, although there were dances throughout the city area and numerous special screenings held on New Year's Day. The same had been true for the preceding month and would continue into 1938. Keith's, in addition to its news offerings, throughout 1937 had continued with its practice of having Ladies' Night, and had had special dinner shows where it distributed free "blue dinnerware." The Depression was still on, and venues had to lure people into their establishments as best they could. However, Keith's in Portland would not survive Molly Spotted Elk's appearance for long. It closed in 1938.[65]

Burlesque made its own brief flash in advertising in Bangor at the same time. Molly Spotted Elk had performed at the Atlantic Casino in 1935, which continued to offer floor shows along with dining and dancing. Elsewhere on the entertainment list, generally more circumspect than the advertising in Portland, the *Bangor Daily News* in late October 1937 ran a large film advertisement featuring a woman in a peculiar bikini, made largely of leaves and flowers. The show was being held at the Bangor Opera House on Main Street and was billed as the *Footlight Parade*. The newspaper reviewed the musical and called it the "best show in years" to come to Bangor. The show was primarily a film of the same name and pulled large crowds into the theater. The *BDN* called the musical "a gorgeous spectacle of lovely singing, dancing, femininity, and with enough of a plot to make the sequence of events a matter of more than passing interest." Furthermore, according to the paper, "a large chorus . . . danced and sang its way into the hearts of the large audiences privileged to hear and see the big musical show on Monday." Offerings at other local theaters were not of the vaudeville/burlesque form, but rather one was *Ann Vickers* based on the novel by Sinclair Lewis, and the other offerings included a film set in England and a comedy that may have had a row of chorus girls kicking up their heels at some junctures. Interestingly, the following week *I'm No Angel* starring Cary Grant and Mae West would come to Bangor's Opera House, but their advertisement, unlike that of Portland's, would not show Mae West as a belly dancer, although the *BDN* in its announcements did state that West was "spread[ing] a new heat wave from shore to shore." It was the end of October, and there were women being portrayed as misbehaving, dancing scandalously, with some perhaps even doing the old hootchie-cootchie, but there was no dance marathon opening outside Bangor or elsewhere in Maine that

Halloween. There were no large endurance-type contests taking place, and the tenor overall was toned down in most advertising and theater productions. This would not last.[66]

That Mainers, even in the Bangor area and northward, were well aware of how far dancers might go in some venues is evident in an article ran in the *Bangor Daily News* out of New York City. The article appeared in the *BDN*'s November 1937 entertainment pages with the header: "**NO NUDES IS BAD NEWS TO GOTHAM CABARETS.**" The leading sentence, by George Ross, stated that "Censorial wrath again has been visited upon Broadway's nocturnal nudity." It seems that the son of a well-known judge had visited the International Casino, referred to also as a cabaret, "where the damosels [*sic*] are indifferent to the rest of the world's custom of wearing clothes." The young man soon told his father what he had seen, and his father contacted New York City mayor Fiorello LaGuardia. The mayor looked into the matter and informed those involved that they had to close down for one Sunday, sit around and consider their sinning ways, and that the dancing girls were to appear with at least some clothing in future shows. Another club was found to have similar nudity and entertainments, and was likewise chastised.[67]

The crackdown had already begun before the mayor's complaints, however. In May 1937, a National Entertainment Association had sounded the alarm, and both the Portland area and the Bangor region knew that censorship was making its way further into the dance industry—and not only in advertising, as seen throughout the year in Maine. Movements were afoot to shut down and/or reform burlesque houses and cabarets throughout the area. In New York, where nudity had been part of many dance acts at the trendier dance venues, on May 24, George Ross of New York declared, in an article that ran in Maine newspapers, that it "Looks As If It Will Soon Be Known As 'The Gay White-Washed Way.'" Ross discussed the tightening down on New York's entertainment center. The "municipal axe which recently cut down the city's burlesque houses dangles precariously over their [the cabaret owners'] heads and they are accordingly being prim and cagey," he wrote. He stated that risqué dances such as the fan dance, the striptease, and the bubble dance were "being consigned to a secretive place in the basement, and in Broadway floor shows the girls are putting on more clothes than they have ever worn since the G-string was invented."[68] Two of the dances Ross had mentioned had been created by Sally Rand, and the third, the striptease, also had its history in vaudeville and burlesque, in particular being associated with Gypsy Rose Lee and a couple of her contemporaries.

Ross stated that the reform movement overtaking New York City "was a more earnest striving for reform than the club owners have anticipated." One show had made its nude feature dancer into a comedienne, and another had changed its performances of striptease acts to the waltz. The big clubs of the Hollywood, the Paradise, and the French Casino had subdued their acts, and the correspondent stated, "Club impresarios blame the burlesque managers for their predicament. They plead innocence on the grounds that they never indulged in the vulgar ballyhoo that aroused the authorities to a war upon burlesque." This might be true for some cabarets, but Ross contended that for many this was laughable, as "cabarets for the last five years have been as hostile to the strip tease as the burlesque houses which spawned Ann Corio, Margi Hart, and Gypsy Rose Lee. Smut has been as prevalent around the ringside tables as it was in the sullied temples of burlesque."[69]

A bill in the New York State Legislature, if passed, Ross stated, would have put censorship essentially in the hands of one person—the "Commissioner of Licenses" would have the power to shut down "any show found unfit for the public eye and ear, without resorting to the courts." This bill was met with strong opposition, and the governor of New York ultimately vetoed the bill. "It was a close call," however, "and left Broadway pale, trembling, and weak with fright." Broadway producers were being careful but still proclaiming their right to artistic freedom. They purportedly had little sympathy for the plight of the burlesque houses. Nor did the cabaret houses. But everyone, from the clubs to the theater, was being careful. The article that ran in Portland was accompanied by a photograph of a scantily clad dancing girl from the Hollywood Club, as well as a headshot of a dancer from the French Casino.[70]

Mainers, including Bangorites and people farther north, could read of the issues surrounding the New York cabarets and nightclubs. Some Bangor acts came straight from those same venues. Its papers—whose circulation reached both the very northern tips of Maine as well as the midcoast regions and the interior of Maine—carried Associated Press articles on nudity at the cabarets. Later, burlesque houses would again be subject to the same scrutiny in New York, and they would be shut down entirely in the 1940s.

Meanwhile, the Atlantic Casino continued to pull in audiences to watch women dance, and Portland saw women dancing on several stages. In addition, Maine continued to see a variety of dances held in the 1940s and 1950s, with vaudeville/burlesque continuing to hold an appeal. Advertisements in some parts of the state were much less blatant than those at places like Keith's had been in the early to mid-1930s before censors cracked down on the film industry and public standards for other advertising became tighter. Yet women still clearly danced on Portland stages, and in the late 1930s the Colonial Theater advertised its "Big Amateur Show" that allowed local women another chance to perform, be it vaudeville or other dance forms.[71]

Although Keith's in Portland had closed, there was still sometimes a direct connection with the vaudeville seen in more northern parts of Maine with that of southern parts of the state, and with the general New England area. For example, in 1941 the George C. McKay Criterion Theater in Bar Harbor held a large Fourth of July celebration featuring "5 Acts of Vaudeville Direct from Keith's RKO, Boston," as well as a movie, *Bachelor Daddy*. Not just the Bar Harbor venue but also one from Bangor had seen acts sent from Keith's in Boston, as had Keith's in Portland in previous years.[72]

Elsewhere in the region that holiday, dances, although not necessarily ones featuring dancers as performers, were currently being held at the Crystal Ballroom in Dover–Foxcroft and in Frankfort and Winterport, the latter two featuring orchestras and catering to military members and their dates. Another dance was held at the Carmel Auto Rest Park on July 3, with two "big dances," one at 8 p.m. to midnight, the other from midnight to 4 a.m. A new large tent had recently been erected to stage shows and dancing events. There were to be prizes, and ladies would be admitted for free if they came with a soldier, sailor, or a marine in uniform, or any man showing military credentials. Although not part of the advertising, a few years earlier, Alfred James Brady ("Public Enemy No. 1"), Clarence Lee Shaffer Jr., and Rhuel James Dalhover, members of the infamous "Brady Gang," had stayed at the Auto Rest Park the night before two of them were shot down in the streets of Bangor by the FBI and the third arrested and held for extradition and later execution.[73]

Other dances were currently being held at the Bar L Ranch in Newport, at the New Gypsy in Bucksport, and the Pleasant Lake Pavilion in Stetson, and a few spots were holding roller-skating dances.[74] The year 1941 seemed a bit tamer than some previous ones, but dancing shows remained popular, as did regular public dances. By about 1943, however, advertising showed a decided decline regarding local dance venues, and less suggestive advertising in general for films and at places formerly advertising vaudeville or burlesque in both northern and southern Maine. The war years were generally quieter as more and more young men went to war, but this was not always the case. A Portland riot was one such exception.

The Colonial Theater in Portland offered both films and live acts in early 1943. For example, in late January, on the 25th, the theater advertised a couple of films, and stated that the following day it would have "Down Easters on Stage." On March 6, the theater advertised that it had "5 ACTS-VAUDEVILLE-5," and a new Sunday show. In some ways, the Colonial may have been trying to take advantage of the opening Keith's had left behind, but the Colonial had also offered some live entertainment in the past. Then, on March 15, 1943, the Colonial billed a new "vaudeville" show, seemingly one aimed at the great influx of men in Maine working primarily at the shipyards. The advertisement seemed to be more of a burlesque offering, however, and possibly more.[75] And it would have lasting repercussions.

On March 25, the Colonial Theater announced, in its block advertising:

COLONIAL
On the Stage
BLACK SATIN REVUE
On Screen
LURE OF THE ISLAND
MEXICAN SPITFIRE
MIDNITE SHOW TUES. NIGHT

It was this last offering, the midnight show, which along with the "Black Satin Revue" caused mayhem in the theater and in the streets, and illustrated some dangerous conditions women confronted on the Maine stages.[76]

On the night of March 15–16, some 750 men packed the Colonial Theater, pushing it beyond standing room only, with other men spilling out onto the streets. An estimated 1,500 men altogether were present inside the theater and on the street. Most were men living in Maine and working the shipyards, building boats for the war. The workers protested when the featured "colored stage show" dancers, as the local papers described the women, disappointed them by not performing a true striptease, which the men had apparently expected. The members of the "colored dance troupe" seemingly were not strippers but were instead more in the line of vaudeville/burlesque dancers, and they completed their show as scheduled. But the men wanted more; specifically, they wanted more skin. And they may indeed have been promised more skin, although the details remain a bit obscure. The manager of the Colonial Theater, Wyman Packard, said the next day that he had "rented the theater, moving pictures, and the regular colored stage show to a shipyard committee which sold tickets to the shipyard workers." Workers told reporters that they had paid $1.50 each for a ticket, and that they wanted to get their money's worth.[77] Other details would be forthcoming.

A "stag show" portion of the evening purportedly was to start at midnight and was supposedly halted when police were informed that it was "indecent." A few members of the police force were in the audience, according to early reports. The manager of the theater later, in the face of an immediate investigation, said that he had rented the theater for $100, that the "regular" show had been put on as planned (apparently not some special strip show), and that when the master of ceremonies had said, "That's all, boys" and started the motion picture part of the evening, the men got out of hand. Calls of "Take it off!" meaning "take it all off," and "Give us back our money!" had erupted from the audience.[78]

Not content with yelling, the men began smashing chairs, throwing beer bottles, and in general tried to destroy the place. As described by the *Portland Press Herald*, "Chairs by the score were smashed, windows were broken, a water fountain in the lobby was broken off with water spurting out, and other machines there were tossed to the ground."[79] A later article identified some of the machines and furnishings destroyed as having been "candy machines overturned," with other glass-panel fronts broken, as well as stating that "bottles were thrown on the stage, several seats were ripped from the floor, the upholstery on others was smashed and torn, a water fountain was snapped off allowing water to flood the building," and so on. Some rioters suggested that the place be torched.[80]

The *Portland Evening Express* reported on March 16 that the riot of "1500 shipyard workers and sympathizers left the downtown Colonial Theater a welter of damage and debris." It stated too that "all available police and Navy shore patrolmen were required to put a quietus on the roaring, shouting human throng whose destructive hands flung bottles and ripped away furnishings" when the stag show they had anticipated did not materialize. The paper printed a photograph of the interior of the theater showing some of the havoc wrought by the crowd inside the building.[81]

Still not content, even after trashing the interior of the Colonial, the riot spread outward as other people gathered and members of the audience went out onto Temple and Congress Streets. As it was reported, "A shouting mob, including many intoxicated men, battled the police, resisting arrest and hurling bottles through windows and signs of the theater and adjacent stores." Furthermore, "as scores of police officers, aided by Naval shore police ["sailors and officers alike"], attempted to quiet the [rioters] the crowd rapidly increased as word spread of the trouble."[82]

"The angry mob," the follow-up story continued, "worked its way to the street where it was swelled to about 1,500 persons as police sent in a riot call." In response, "all local police, Navy and Coast Guard shore patrols responded." By 2:00 a.m., the crowd had "overspread onto Congress Street, stopping traffic and bringing a flood of calls from adjacent apartment house dwellers." Traffic was halted for about an hour. In addition to calling out all the regular troops and "rushing bundles of large nightsticks to the scene" (for the police), the fire department was called in case hoses were needed to suppress the rioters, but actual fires elsewhere in the city prevented much of a response from that department, although two pumpers were brought in for crowd suppression should they be needed.[83]

Although there was no fire at the theater, the fire department and other officials did have a few things to say about conditions at the theater. Portland police captain Harold K. Maguire had brought the crowd under control after reminding them that "we are all Americans" and urging them to go home peacefully after promising to look into getting the men refunds. If justified, he had said he would meet with a committee of them in the morning and probe into the events at the Colonial. Maguire told the press that "the doors were closed and the front exits locked, that patrons filled every seat and overflowed into the aisles, that men were smoking, and [overall], conditions were terrible." He said that conditions were such that a fire at the theater might well have resulted "in another Cocoanut Grove disaster."[84]

Maguire was referring to the Cocoanut Grove fire the previous year, in which 492 people had lost their lives in a Boston nightclub. Had its regular audience of about 1,000 people been in attendance when the Hampden marathon dance fire of 1933 erupted, Maguire might well have referred to that disaster as well. As it was, once the case of the Cocoanut Grove fire went to court, the public heard testimony that the nightclub had been a "firetrap" with too few exits, locked doors, and "blind alleys." The owner, manager, and a wine steward were tried for manslaughter, and Mainers could read about the fire and the trials in their local newspapers.[85]

A number of men were arrested or ordered to appear in court in the hours following the Portland riot. Two men, apparently rioters, were arrested on warrants charging them with "glass throwing." They were each held on a $500 bail. Other incidences of rock and bottle throwing had occurred outside the theater by various parties, and police and some rioters had exchanged angry words while other rioters cheered on the arguments and the destruction.[86]

The manager of the theater, Wyman Packard, was quoted as stating that "the theater 'is wrecked and somebody will have to pay for it.'" He related how the riot had started, how he had not charged admission at the door but had instead rented out the venue. He stated that he had rented the theater, some motion pictures, and a stage show—apparently the female dancers—to a shipyard workers' committee. They were the ones who had sold tickets to a "stag affair" at the shipyards in South Portland. However, although he admitted no fault on his part, Packard was soon ordered into court for questioning.[87]

It came to light via the State Insurance Department that the theater did not have a state license as required in addition to its city license. And some members of the city council recommended suspending the city license. One councilman, George A. Harrison, said that "I don't believe we can be expected to furnish entertainment for a group of people who don't know how to behave themselves. . . . It looks to me as if the only thing to do is to stop the shows."[88] It was unclear whether he meant all such shows in the city or those just at the Colonial. However, in the days that followed, the manager and one of his workers faced prosecution and the Colonial Theater was effectively closed due to damages.

On March 17, according to the *Evening Express*, "City and State lumped four charges against Wyman U. Packard, manager and operator of the downtown Colonial Theater." The janitor, Edwin Libby, was charged with "permitting the doors to be locked." Packard's bail was set at $2,000 and Libby's at $50. The two men arrested on charges of throwing bottles outside the theater, both shipyard workers, were fined $50 each.[89]

The warrants against Packard were "allowing a pile of sand to be placed inside a door of the fire escape at the theater; permitting the aisles to be blocked; permitting the three main entrances of the theater to be locked; and using a moving picture machine without a license from the State insurance commissioner." Both the janitor and the manager pled not guilty. A maximum fine of $650 could be levied were the manager found guilty of all charges. According to the state inspector, the Colonial had never had a permit to show motion picture films, not since the law requiring them had gone into effect in June 1939.[90]

Women had danced at the theater previously, and men had been in attendance at both stage shows and film presentations; conditions at the theater were deemed a "death trap," in which disaster might have occurred at any time. Police who had been in the audience in plainclothes denied having ordered a striptease deleted from the show. A meeting of various parties had apparently decided on "the identity of the sponsor of the stag show," which was purportedly the first such show that officials knew of in Portland. The city manager acknowledged that he had heard rumors that some had been held outside the city limits.[91]

On March 18, the person now deemed responsible for the nonstaged stag show, shipyard worker Charles R. Decker, was arraigned. Both he and Wyman Packard were charged with "conspiring to stage an obscene show." With the fifth charge against him, local officials determined to recommend at a special city council later that day that Packard's theater license be revoked. Moreover, his legal status had been clarified somewhat. Packard had taken over the theater as a tenant at will in early January 1943, but the license held by the former operators, good until May 1, was seemingly not transferrable. He did not appear to have secured a new license. Investigation into this aspect of the case was ongoing. Meanwhile, he made bond on the previous $2,000 bail, but a new bail was fixed on both him and Decker. Other people were also being investigated in terms of the staging of the show on the night of the riot and the sale of tickets. The FBI had also expressed an interest in the case, in the possibility that a federal amusement tax might have been evaded on the $1.50 tickets sold to the men. In addition, in the event of future problems of this nature in the city, the Cumberland County Sheriff's Department had offered its department's aid.[92]

On Friday, March 19, the Portland Municipal Court indicted "Grand Jury consideration of circumstances resulting in a Tuesday morning riot." Judge Robert W. DeWolfe found probable cause to hold both Packard and Decker "on a joint charge of conspiring to stage an obscene performance." Both men pled not guilty, but as the two waived a hearing on the conspiracy charge, the press was disappointed to discover that details that might have come out in court that day did not emerge.[93] They would have to wait until the grand jury heard the case in May.

Packard was acquitted on the charge of causing the main entrances to the theater to be locked during a show, but was found guilty of the other charges and fined $175 for them. Edwin Libby, the janitor, was fined $50 for permitting the main doors of the theater to be locked during a show. He appealed, and his bail was set then at $500. He did admit to locking two of the main doors. The police captain testified that two of the theater's double doors had been locked when he arrived at the scene at 1:00 a.m. on the night and morning of the riot, and that one-half of the third double door was also locked. Libby said that he had locked them "on orders," but whose orders he had not said.[94]

As for the charge of having placed sand in front of the fire exit door, Attorney MacDonald asserted, "'Some of the audience would have died like rats' if there had been a catastrophe." So, too, although it apparently did not come up in court, would the women who had danced that night have been endangered, as well as any women who might actually have agreed to strip. The sand pile was purportedly about eighteen inches high and four square feet wide. In addition, the aisles were "plugged with men" when the rioting broke out and, the police captain stated, "everybody I could see was smoking." He later stated that one aisle was actually clear when he arrived, and that he had gone to the show after hearing that a striptease act was scheduled for after midnight. After he arrived, he sent the janitor to unlock all the doors. By then, however, the riot was on.[95]

A state license inspector testified that he had spoken to Packard about renewing the theater's license about two weeks before the riot, thinking that Packard represented the former operators, the Adelphia Corporation. He had then learned that the corporation had dissolved. Packard, on all charges, said that he was innocent, and his lawyer called him "an innocent victim of the shipyard hoodlums" who had wrecked the Colonial. His client, however, still faced the grand jury at its May 1943 session.[96]

But when the grand jury of the Cumberland County Superior Court met in early May, it did not indict Wyman U. Packard, as the manager at the time of the riot, nor did it indict Charles R. Decker, identified in the papers then simply as "a shipyard worker." The jury "quashed the bills" against the two men whom Municipal Court Judge DeWolfe had ordered held on bail and for "grand jury consideration" on the charge of conspiring to present an "immoral show" at the Colonial Theater.[97] The public thus never learned any more potentially scandalous details about the night of dancing at the Colonial, but after the black female troupe danced on March 15–16, 1943, no more shows of any type appear to have been presented at the Colonial in following months. Between the lack of a license and the damages sustained in the riot, the theater was effectively closed. It did not reappear in *Portland City Directories* or elsewhere.[98]

And, even though Prohibition had ended a decade earlier nationwide, this does not mean that some Mainers did not favor bringing it back to the state, even if they could not control what happened throughout

America. Although it was not the first such attempt, on the heels of the 1943 riot—indeed, on the same day—prohibitionists saw a bill they had supported killed in the Maine State Legislature. The proposal, if passed, would have banned "all beer parlors and cocktail lounges in Maine, and give the State Liquor Commission complete control over all liquor sales." The Temperance Committee had introduced the bill, although not all of its members supported it. The State Senate first rejected the proposal, then on March 16 the House of Representatives followed suit.[99] Had some people been able to ban all risqué dance performances in 1943, they no doubt would have done so.

In general, theater offerings in Portland and elsewhere in the state became more subdued as World War II progressed. Workplace shortages were being experienced, as more and more men went to the war and more women moved into the places vacated by the male workers. A major exception in Maine, and the core of the riot of 1943, was the large number of men working in the shipyards, many of them from out of state, building vessels for the war effort. Women, too, participated in this type of work, and here as elsewhere, they could expect to earn more money than they generally might in the working-class dance industries. In Bath alone, some 1,067 women found jobs at the Bath Iron Works by March 16, the day of the 1943 Shipyard Workers Riot. Newspapers soon began to advertise for male workers on their front pages, so dire was their need, and even police and fire departments suffered from labor shortages.[100] As men seemingly made up a large share of the audience for female-based dance presentations in the vaudeville, burlesque, and film theaters, a decrease in such offerings is perhaps to be expected, especially with the national censorship then in place. After the war, the type of advertising seen in the 1930s did not reappear. Some of the same types of dancing shows may well have been staged—indeed, they probably were—but the advertisements for them simply did not suggest as risqué a content as they had previously. Public dances and dance halls, however, remained popular. And new dances and new dancers would soon appear in the Pine Tree State.

CHAPTER SEVEN

Bring Back the Hootchie-Cootchie

America and Maine Greet the New Eastern
Dancers of the 1950s and 1960s, Exotic and Erotic
Dancers Spread through the State, and a Little
"Supper Club" Showcases Female Dancers in the North

BURLESQUE WOULD BECOME ASSOCIATED WITH EARLY STRIPTEASE, A
term supposedly coined in 1937 but popular in the 1920s, which in its
turn would experience suppression. It reemerged in the 1960s and 1970s
in go-go dancing that became topless in some places, then full nudity
in others, and in many places would later come to combine elements of
earlier burlesque with a more explicitly sexual content. The new "striptease" reached northern Maine by the 1970s, with the *Bangor Daily News*
in 1975 running an article titled "Stripping, A Business Just Like any
Other." This business would cross the lines that taxi-dancers, hurdy gurdy
girls, marathon dancers, vaudeville, and even the more risqué burlesque
performers would not. And belly dancers would generally try to distance
themselves from the strippers with whom so many people had, or still
did, associate them.[1]

Belly dancing survived into the late twentieth and early twenty-first
centuries in a way the other forms did not. It evolved in some ways, yet
remained a form of dance treated with suspicion or derision for much
of the 1900s. Recent years have seen it become more mainstream and
accepted. Yet misconceptions persist, and in many places it continues to

be seen primarily as an erotic form of dance. Call it erotic dancing and it has certain connotations; call it folk dancing and it conjures up something altogether different.

Belly dancing (an American term) developed in the Middle East and in Europe over hundreds of years before it became well known in America. "Little Egypt" appeared at the Chicago World Fair in 1893, and it may be that one or more belly dancers had already performed at the Philadelphia Centennial in 1876. One undocumented reference attests to this. Another source documents that Egypt, Turkey, and Greece (also Tunis) sent delegations and exhibits to the Philadelphia Centennial, so there may indeed have been such a performance. Immigrants of various origins also likely practiced their old dance form in their new homeland. In particular, Turkish and Greek cafes and clubs had performers in the old world style for dance and music in the early 1900s, and this seemingly included Eastern or belly dancers. Several major American cities like Chicago and New York certainly did have Eastern dancers in these rather isolated venues in the early twentieth century.[2]

Images of belly dancers spilled over into the popular culture by the 1930s, if not earlier. They appeared in advertisements for vaudeville, burlesque, and film, in America and in Maine. The dancers were not always identified as belly dancers, but their costumes certainly indicated an association. In 1954, the Broadway show *Fannie* opened on November 4, featuring Turkish dancer Nejla Ates (with various spellings including Nedah Atesh or Najila Attash), who had been performing in the United States at clubs for at least a couple of years. This is credited with ushering in an era in which true belly dancers came to the attention of the general American population once more. More mainstream clubs, rather than just the ethnic ones, then started adding the newly exotic dance and music to their offerings, many of which relied on foreign dancers in the late 1950s and early 1960s. Egyptian film-star twins Lys and Lyn Gamal (again, with various spellings) came to the United States in the late 1950s and helped add to the demand for club performances.[3] However, images of belly dancers or women dressed as such had long been before the public eye, and one might argue that the new images had been brought to America long before *Fannie*.

Dancing in various forms remained popular in Maine in the late 1940s to the mid-1950s, even though advertising had changed and censorship had some impact on shows. Women still performed in public for money, films still hinted at burlesque and exotic dancing, and private venues continued to operate, sometimes on the edge of respectability, as did the ever-popular public dances in communities throughout the state. The popularity in general of dancing perhaps made it easier for Maine to remain open to the less respected forms of dance.

And dance did not always present itself in the most obvious of places. In northern Maine, in Old Town, one establishment in particular kept the lesser-known and borderline-acceptable dances before the public. While modern belly dancers sometimes point to the role of *Fannie* in bringing Eastern dance—as belly dancing was sometimes known—to popular attention in the 1950s, another film also appeared in Maine in 1954 that likely accomplished the same thing. By late spring, Mainers as far north as Orono and beyond could go to see the film *Veils of Bagdad* starring Victor Mature and Mari Blanchard. Advertising for the film clearly established belly dancing as central to the movie—if the title alone did not do so—with one woman dressed in a "modern" belly-dance costume leaning against the male protagonist, and another (or the same) woman shown to the side dancing in full frontal glory, her arms moving in a version of the traditional "snake arms" of Eastern dance and her hips swaying. She wore a bra-style top with a high-cut flowing skirt. She also had a dance or "hip scarf" wrapped around her hips with a separate bead or coin belt around her waist. Mari Blanchard, the object of the included photograph in the advertisement if not in the sketched portrait, would soon be identified as an "Oriental Dancer" and appear in film with another woman also identified as such and who indeed was a belly dancer.[4] The traditional "Dance of the Seven Veils" may or may not have been part of the show, a dance in which the performer slowly reveals her regular costume from under seven layers of veils, spinning and dancing without pause throughout the performance, a complicated and difficult dance to perform correctly.

Locals could watch *The Veils of Bagdad* at the Strand in Orono in June. And, not far away—indeed, just down the street in Old Town near the junction of Stillwater Avenue and Center Street—they could go to see a supposedly authentic Eastern dancer at the Anchorage Hotel.[5] The city of Orono is the home of the University of Maine, and both communities, which in essence overlap, are close to Bangor with its larger population base, including the then-new Dow Air Force Base, built to meet demands of World War II just as the southern Maine shipyards had expanded during the war years. The Anchorage Hotel was also easily accessible to regions farther north, and could, with an attractive offering, establish a large and solid clientele.

In the 1950s and beyond, the Anchorage offered customers both lodging and a restaurant and a bar. With the downstairs of the large building devoted to food and entertainment, the establishment essentially served as a "supper club"—what the era often called venues that offered food, alcohol, and live floor shows. Burlesque houses had been outlawed in some places, including New York City, one of the original homes of the burlesque nightclubs. The supper clubs in many ways filled some of the same needs and desires as the burlesque houses had, and seemingly presented some of the same dances, even in New York. The Anchorage regularly featured female dancers, including go-go girls in the 1960s, women who danced—in some places in cages—to popular music wearing things like very short miniskirts, tight or small tops, and "go-go boots," the now classic style being high, white, and shiny, although other styles existed.[6] Go-go dancers were generally paid by the night, but customers also threw money at them.

Before the go-go dancers arrived in the 1960s, however, the Anchorage brought in numerous dancers of several styles of dance, including Eastern dance, albeit initially under the name "Hindu dance." On June 1, 1954, the Anchorage ran an advertisement announcing that it was now presenting Neja—also identified as Niya—Sima, "The Golden Hindu and the Only Authentic Hindu Dancer in America." The advertisement included a photograph of Neja dancing or posing—a jewel or diadem on her forehead—wearing an ornate halter-bra top with a matching skirt as well as a fancy veil draped over one arm and shoulder and held thus out to that side, then continuing around her body and wrapped around the lower portion of her opposite arm, a now-classic veil position for belly dancers.[7] The veil, it should be noted, is considered an American or Western addition to the dance.

On June 2, the same advertisement appeared in the *Bangor Daily News*, this time juxtaposed with an advertisement for a ballet recital at the Bangor Opera House, a photograph of a featured ballet dancer showing her wearing a classic short tutu, tights, and toe shoes. One could choose the type of dance most suited to one's taste when deciding which venue to attend. Of course, with the ballet recital being a 3:45 p.m. matinee on June 3, and Neja dancing at two shows nightly that week, one could go to see both forms of dance performed. Or, in an odd twist, one could go see "Aunt Jemima in Person" at the Opera House, a portrait of her showing her smiling, with her iconic scarf over her hair. Aunt Jemima appeared as part of another show, and if one chose to go see Neja dance, one would also have the chance to see a comedian perform as part of that show.[8]

The Anchorage advertised that it served fine food and catered to wedding parties, clubs, banquets, and other celebrations. It changed performers regularly. The next dance offering after Neja Sima and her Hindu belly dance was Camile Rameroz, a "Spanish dancer" who appeared with both a comedian and with "Thelma Twist, Colored Acrobatic and Exotic Dancer." The dancers had two shows nightly, as had Neja. Thelma Twist did not have a photograph included in local press advertisements, nor indeed did most of the women who appeared at the venue that summer. Rameroz, however, was photographed in a classic flamenco-style pose: one arm arched above her head, the other in front of her torso, head held high, one leg extended in front of her with her bare toes pointed and resting lightly, but deliberately, on the floor. She wore her dark hair down, and a ruffled dress, with a fringed sort of scarf draped across her chest. In addition to the two nightly shows, a live band—the Buddy Bonneau Trio—played. Several dances were also being held in the region, including at the Auto Rest Park farther south, which featured a WABI RFD jamboree, show, and dance that weekend. The Auto Rest Park continued to hold dances and offer several celebrated musicians into the late 1950s. One local to or visiting the region could even dance at the Hanger at the Bar Harbor Airport in Trenton, where there would be "hundreds of visiting planes from all over New England," and Charlie Bennett's Orchestra performing.[9]

Thelma Twist, billed then as an "acrobatic exotic dancer," appeared without Rameroz the following week, with a different comedian performing as well as a magician and the Buddy Bonneau Trio at the Anchorage Hotel. The next offering at the Anchorage included a song and dance team. Following them, Betty Larke, a "lovely exotic dancer," appeared at the hotel and restaurant/bar. A number of other female "exotic" dancers would appear at the venue with no specific style of dance noted. They might have been performing burlesque, belly dancing, or dancing another style, but sexiness was clearly part of the offerings. Meanwhile, the Twilight Pavilion opened for the summer season in Hermon and at the Birchmere Inn in Old Town. Diane Dawn, billed as an "interpretive dance-songbird," performed at the close of the month.[10]

As the Fourth of July approached, new dancers appeared at the Anchorage, and new shows were presented elsewhere as well. The Hanger at the Bar Harbor Airport held dances in early July and throughout the summer, as did the other local venues from Dover to Mattawamkeag to Millinocket to Presque Isle to Bar Harbor itself to Bucksport. A few films shown in early July seemed a bit risqué, and one theater in Ellsworth reintroduced a version of the *Follies Revue* along with the *French Follies*, which it billed as "Adults Only" and "Raw! Daring! Spicy!" The special midnight show was held on July 4 and proclaimed as "The Best In Burlesque."[11] Burlesque was still alive and well, but not—at this particular show—live.

However, the Brewer E. M. Loew's drive-in offered a show starring the "Body Beautiful Sutira, Dancer Extraordinaire" in person along with "a bevy of gorgeous beauties live before your eyes." On screen, the film *Parisienne Follies*, perhaps the same show as that in Ellsworth, was advertised as "Adults Only" with a photograph included of a woman who seems to have been a dancer, wearing classic American-style dancing shoes, a skimpy top and bottom, with a lightweight veil streaming out behind her. In another advertisement, the show was billed as "Burlesque at its Best."[12]

Entertainment at the Anchorage was always live and likely, at times, burlesque even if not billed as such. Pattie Dane, billed as an "exotic dancer," performed at the establishment in early July 1954 as did Donna May, a "beautiful exotic dancer" in early August. A few days after Donna May's run at the Anchorage, Lucille Monroe, billed as simply "a beautiful girl dancer," no style indicated, started her run at the hotel and bar, and by August 20, Arlyn Jordan, a "girl dancer," had started performing nightly.[13] Stripteases were not yet legal in Maine, and quite likely at least some of the exotic dancers were doing burlesque, although at times during the era the term "exotic" indicated Eastern dancing.

In terms of more famous acts, Dusty Owens and his Rodeo Boys performed at the Auto Rest Park in early July 1954, the Roxyettes danced at the Bangor State Fair in August, and also in August Gene Autry performed at the Bangor Auditorium on September 11. Tommy Dorsey and his orchestra (including saxophone star Jimmy Dorsey) performed at the Pier in Old Orchard on July 7, and on August 10 they played at the Armory in Augusta, appearing "with 20 star musicians and entertainers."[14]

While locals could visit various venues for dance, music, and entertainment, in the immediate Old Town–Orono–Bangor area the Anchorage seemed to offer the most varied of nightly floor shows featuring female dancers. The Anchorage had had exotic and other dancers before 1954. The establishment advertised more frequently during the late spring and summer months of the early and mid-1950s than during the rest of the year, and to bring in more noteworthy or potentially more lucrative acts during the summer months. The acts did not always include female dancers, although most shows in the summer did do so. In 1953, the Anchorage stated that it brought in new acts weekly, although its owners did not always advertise the specific individuals involved, so during some weeks it was difficult to ascertain just who performed at the venue. The Anchorage also pointed out directly and indirectly that it brought in well-known acts, in one case referring to an act as "Direct from the Most Important Night Clubs in America." Some acts, including female dancers, appeared more than once. For example, Thelma Twist, "Acrobatic Dancer," had danced at the Anchorage in mid-June 1954. She danced there again in mid-June 1955, if not sooner.[15]

The Anchorage did not advertise its entertainers extensively before the mid-1950s, although the hotel itself had opened by 1941. By 1952, the establishment did advertise some of its acts, but they seemed both tamer and longer running than those that followed. For example, the Hawaiian Trio, an instrumental group accompanied by a female singer, appeared for at least three weeks in June and July 1951, and seems typical of the first years of the decade. However, both advertising and the acts offered started to heat up over the next year.[16]

A few summer acts of 1953 indicate that female dancers were becoming popular components of the floor shows at the Anchorage. At the opening of June 1953, for example, the Anchorage featured "Chinese Week." After advertising that "Dorothy Kilgallen, Famous Broadway Columnist" in her article, "A BIG NIGHT IN BANGOR" featured in that month's *Good Housekeeping* magazine, had written "Catch the Show at the Anchorage," the venue's advertisement featured pictures of three performers—a dancer, a juggler, and a magician—of the Anchorage's "Chinese Revue." The first of these was "Ming Cho, Beautiful Oriental Dancer." In this case, the dance style quite likely was Chinese and not one of the more Middle Eastern–based belly-dancing styles that came months later. Ming Cho was photographed leaning into the camera, wearing an ornate robe or kimono, a flower (perhaps a white chrysan-themum) in her hair. Subsequent advertising for the show included only Cho's photograph. She was possibly the leading act. Meanwhile, in Bangor at the Park Theater, locals could see noted actress Paulette Goddard and famed burlesque dancer Gypsy Rose Lee in *Babes in Bagdad*. Gypsy Rose Lee would soon accuse a newly acclaimed belly dancer of stealing her moves from her own burlesque version of belly dancing.[17]

Mitsie Ray, "Parisian Rubber Doll" and a "Beautiful Acrobatic Dancer," next appeared at the Anchorage in summer 1953. A photograph of her appeared in the Anchorage's advertising, with Mitsie shown stretched to her maximum, not in an acrobatic pose but in a ballet one. She wore a classic ballerina's bodysuit and tutu and was en point in her toe shoes, her arms gracefully arched over her head. This is one of Maine's rare examples of a woman dancing in what was essentially a modern-day version of the older dance halls in a classic ballet pose. Others no doubt had classic training, but here was the evidence for such overlap.[18] Had she appeared in the late 1800s, she might have been labeled a "ballet girl" and disrespected on that regard even on a more respected stage.

Other types of acts followed Mitsie's, including a dancing female comedian, and in early July 1953 patrons could see Raye Miles, a "Terrific Girl Dancer," perform as part of the current floor show, while in Brewer one could watch *Salomé, Where She Danced* at the drive-in theater. Salomé, played by Yvonne DeCarlo, wore a jeweled top and a glittery fringed skirt or dance scarf in at least one of the advertisements for the film. Although the belly dancing remained in the film, the story did not follow quite the same lines as had the controversial 1910 film, but rather was set in the Civil War era.[19]

In early May 1954, a burlesque version of a fan or bubble dancer appears to have been performing in northern Maine. The Anchorage advertised "Sony Flores, Girl Dancer," and included a photograph of her wearing high heels and an umbrella, or, rather, an umbrella was used to cover her nudity or any clothing she wore, much as Sally Rand's feathered fans had covered her body in some performances and photographs, and as her bubbles had also strategically covered her at times. Flores was photographed from the side while resting at the edge of a chair or other prop, one long leg spread before her, the other bent, and her face and bare shoulder turned toward the camera. The umbrella was open and photographed straight on, effectively covering the dancer's entire torso. The bar/restaurant also noted that at its floor shows there was "no cover, no minimum," the first referring to the lack of any entrance fee and the last referring to the number of drinks a customer might be required to purchase to earn a seat at the show. The Buddy Bonneau Trio, already a popular band for the venue, performed.[20]

Next up at the Anchorage in May 1954 was "Shanghai, The Lovely Exotic China Doll." Shanghai was photographed in a low-cut garment, only her upper torso shown, with long dark hair and a visage that appeared as Western as it did Eastern, perhaps suggesting that her dancing was not of a classic Chinese style. Appearing at the same stage show was a comedy act and "Ingagi, Famous Hollywood Gorilla." The show was billed as "Beauty and the Beast."[21]

Mary Alice, a "beautiful girl dancer and singer," and making no pretense at being from a different culture, soon appeared on the floor show along with a comedian and, of course, a band. While Mary Alice looked fairly subdued in her publicity photograph, Jane Russell, appearing locally in the film *The French Line*, looked anything but in hers. Unlike the women pictured behind her larger portrait—and who could easily have been wearing only their underwear—Russell was wearing a "show girl" outfit: high dance shoes, a dark bodysuit with sequins and cutouts along the front and halter-style straps, and black opera-style gloves. She wore dangling earrings and a big smile as she struck her pose. The advertisement, as seen in northern Maine, promised that the movie would "KNOCK BOTH YOUR EYES OUT!" It further stated (almost shouted, if words in print could shout), "THAT Picture! THAT Dance! You've heard so much about!" Filmed in Technicolor, locals could see the film at "E. M. Loew's Bangor-Brewer Drive-In Theater" on Route 1 in Brewer. Drive-ins were becoming increasingly popular, and some in Maine were showing films advertised as "Adults Only!" that appeared to be akin to soft porn. However, as with other shows in the past—both on film and those featuring live female dancers—the films could have promised something other than that which they delivered. During the same period, some features at the regular theaters hinted at Eastern themes and women, such as *Slaves of Babylon* and *East of Sumatra* in spring 1954.[22]

It was after the seemingly demure Mary Alice danced at the Anchorage in May 1954 that "Neja the Hindu Dancer" appeared. With her arrival came the new style of belly dance, and it came well before the movie *Fannie* appeared before the American public, and even before the play *Fannie* opened on Broadway. The Anchorage started advertising Neja's appearances in late May, initially not including her photograph and billing her as simply "Neja, Exotic Hindu Dancer." After Neja and the other summer dancers appeared, Loraine White, billed as a "dance stylist," and Bobbie Swan, billed as an "exotic dancer," appeared. Advertising for the Anchorage disappeared for a time during the autumn. However, the movie *King Richard and the Crusaders*, based on Sir Walter Scott's work *The Talisman*, opened in Bangor at the Opera House in late September 1954, and that film featured the soon-to-be celebrated belly dancer Nejla Ates. Oddly, after all the previous illustrations for films that featured female dancers in the Bangor region as in other parts of the state, *King Richard* did not do so.[23]

Nejla Ates, also known as the "Turkish Delight," was born in 1932 in Constata, Romania, and became a belly dancer and an actress in the United States. She later stated that she had "contrived her dance without a lesson after reading in an ancient tome how favorite wives in a harem danced for the Sultan." As she went on from Turkey to Beirut, Cairo, and Baghdad, she may have picked up other pointers on various forms of the dance in her travels. By the time she moved on to Rome and Paris, "she was greeted by growing public and critical acclaim," according to a November 1954 interview with the Associated Press.[24] By November 1954, she had already appeared in the movie *King Richard and the Crusaders*. Perhaps she had also appeared in Maine at the Anchorage as "Neja the Hindu Dancer." The timing and name overlap, at any rate, and Ates had indeed been performing in American clubs for some time before she appeared in the play *Fannie*. Photographs of the two women neither confirm nor deny that the two women were one and the same. The publicity photo of Neja used by the Anchorage shows clear similarities to those of Nejla, but is not clear enough to make a firm identification.

Belly dancers at the turn of the twenty-first century tended to point to Nejla Ates's appearance in the November 1954 (the reason for the AP interview) Broadway debut of *Fannie* as the start of a new era of belly dancing in the United States. The play featured Ates as a belly dancer. An *oud* player, Mohammed El Bakkar, also appeared. The play featured a "rope dance," a "slave dance," and one or two others. Ates became a darling of the media for a short time.[25]

Ates, however, become something of a scandalous figure after a few well-publicized romances, at least a couple of them with married men, including the husband of another belly dancer who was also coming to the attention of the American public, Samia Gamal (also with various spellings, and born Zaynab Ibrahim Mahfuz) of Egypt. Gamal had studied the dance in Egypt with the person credited by some as being the founder of "modern oriental dance." Gamal starred in numerous Egyptian films and in a few international ones, and in 1949 Egypt's King Farouck had proclaimed her "The National Dancer of Egypt." She came to the United States in 1950 and danced in the Latin Quarter in New York, a trendy nightclub. In the United States, she would appear in the film *Valley of the Kings* in 1954. In Egypt, she had worn a filmy fabric over her belly, as it was illegal there for women to show their stomach in public. In the United States, dancers like Samia Gamal and Nejla Ates uncovered their stomachs and favored tight, often sparkly tops—first with wider straps to cover part of the shoulders and then with straps in halter styles—along with skirts of chiffon or other flowing materials, and hip scarves.[26] Other belly-dance styles would continue to feature more covered-up styles, even into the twenty-first century, instead of the "cabaret" style Ates and others favored.

In an interesting twist, Ates would have something of a tiff with burlesque dancer and film star Gypsy Lee Rose, who accused Ates of stealing much of her routine from Rose's own burlesque dance numbers.[27] Apparently, even for dancers, the line could be fine.

Ates did not appear in the film version of *Fannie*, which did not come out until 1961. She did appear in *Son of Sinbad* in 1955, however, as well as in *King Richard and the Crusaders* in 1954. By autumn 1954, *King Richard* was shown in Maine, and Mainers and visitors to the state could see Ates dance in her silver fringed top and hip scarf, a diadem on her forehead, before a bewildered Richard, who initially had no idea where he was. And Mainers had had a chance to watch "Neja the Hindu Dancer" live at the Anchorage just a couple of months previously. In 1955, Mainers could watch Ates dance in *Son of Sinbad*, which by June 1955 had made it out to even rural areas, showing, for example, at the Milo drive-in in late June.[28] Maine was in no way behind the rest of the nation in seeing belly dancers perform.

The *New York Times* in March 1954 ran a short article about the upcoming film *Son of Sinbad*, which starred Dale Robertson, Lilly St. Cyr, Sally Forest, Vincent Price, and Mari Blanchard (whom Mainers had already seen perform in *The Veils of Bagdad*). The *Times* identified four "artists" as lending "their interpretations of oriental dancing" to the film: St. Cyr, identified as a "night club and burlesque star"; Forrest, identified as a "stage and screen star"; Kalantan, "star of Mexico City and American supper clubs"; and "Nejla Ates, international dancing star from Istanbul."[29]

The "curvy, torrid" 4'11" Ates had a nude statue of her placed in Central Park as part of a publicity stunt and danced in American clubs even after beginning her acting. She told reporters that her name meant "sunset fire" in Turkish, and that in Turkey she would not have been allowed to perform in theaters at such a young age. As to her performances in Broadway's *Fannie*, the AP stated, "Her dance is the most unrestrained and intricate exhibition of abdominal versatility since burlesque houses were closed here [in New York City] ten years ago." Moreover, "Later in the night she dances 'very free and comfortable' in a supper club."[30] A supper club was the designation or entertainment venue category that allowed Neja to perform at the Anchorage way up north from New York in Old Town.

Ates stated in 1954 that in many ways women were more interested in what she was doing than were men. Women would come up to her and ask her about her costumes, her makeup, and her dance moves. She had not been home in five years at that point, in part, it seems, because of her public appearances on the stage when she was so young. She stated that in Turkey the women were covered up when they danced, "but here, they come to the theater, they like to see a little leg, no?" She also stated that when she danced, "I only think of the music, and give the best of myself."[31]

No matter which woman one credits with starting a revival of belly dancing in the United States—and there were others besides the three Gamals and Ates involved—after its move to America, American belly dance developed its own dress, movements, lingo, and diversity. Being exclusive to no culture, the dance can adapt to—it would seem—almost any culture, including the most personal ones. And, although many Americans might try to deny the affiliation, there has indeed been an affiliation at various times and places between belly dancing and some forms (depending on the era) of exotic dancing. Belly dancing is in many ways exotic, or certainly can be seen as sensual, and thus questions do arise. As one male recently asked after attending a show in Portland, "What difference is there really between that and exotic dancing, except perhaps the dancer's relationship with the audience?" Although he did not clearly understand all the differences, he may have hit on the crux of the matter: that the connection between dancer and audience, and the intent of the dancer, as well as the fact that in the early 2010s most audience members were other women, may make all the difference.[32] However, this relationship has evolved over time.

In the meantime, places like the Anchorage continued to bring various dancers to the Maine community. After the appearance of "Neja the Hindu Dancer," other women performed a variety of acts at the supper

club. Although other types of acts continued to appear, female dancers continued to receive the greatest advertising space and apparently
brought in the greatest number of customers. Moreover, the advertisements, and seemingly the dances themselves, became more risqué over
the next few years. By the summer of 1957, after a number of other
women performed, a woman would appear at the Anchorage who was
clearly a burlesque dancer and one who apparently performed the more
erotic side of burlesque dancing—almost, one might argue, promising
something of the striptease.[33]

By summer 1957, advertising for the Anchorage's female dancers became increasingly blatant and often resembled the "pin-up girl"
genre of the era or could almost be considered pornographic, although,
of course, the women all seemed to be wearing some type of clothing,
however scanty. Belly dancing continued to receive some sort of a nod,
although supposed Eastern dancers appeared in their photographs (regularly included in advertising for the Anchorage) to be more erotic in
aspect than exotic. For example, a photograph of "SABAH, 'Princess
of the Nile,' Oriental Dancer" appeared in one of the supper club's June
1957 advertisements. Sabah was pictured wearing a very scanty covering
over rather abundant breasts, a boa or other ornament wrapped around
her neck, her hair dark and flowing, her lips heavily painted, her eyes
closed, and her head tilted to the back.[34]

Next up in the offerings was Judy Day, billed as a "Dancing Darling,"
who appeared along with a "Roc-N-Roll Dance Team." It is unclear what
type of dancing Judy Day did, but her photograph shows her in a less
erotic pose than Sabah's, although she was wearing a small, skin-colored
bra top (the 1950s "pointed" type at that, which made the breast almost
conical in shape) plus a low-cut dipping bottom made of feathers or some
fluffy material. An advertisement just above that of the Anchorage, however, shows that the supper club now had more competition: Not far away
in Old Town, the Birchmere Inn was offering a floor show featuring a
comedian and "Suzette, Enchanting Exotic Dancer," and offered "mellow
music" by the Blue Notes, who would play regularly at the venue. After

Suzette, "Carmella, The Irresistible Dancer" appeared at the Birchmere.[35] The Birchmere had been around for a few years, but its advertising and seemingly its dance offerings had increased by 1957.

Carmella seems to have moved over to the Anchorage Hotel in mid-June. The Anchorage began to use a lighthouse on the left side of its advertisements at this time, with its beacon flaring out to the right and the letters of "ANCHORAGE HOTEL" growing in size across the advertisement. Carmella, seemingly the same dancer from the Birchmere, was billed as "Carmella, The Torrid Twister." She was shown smiling provocatively (or what was apparently meant to be that), her long hair down, and wearing a halter top. However, the Anchorage billed it as her "1st Maine Appearance," so she may or may not have been the same woman.[36] Quite likely, she was the same woman who had performed at the Birchmere but was still on her first tour in Maine.

A comedy and burlesque team followed Carmella on the floor show at the Anchorage, while the Birchmere featured "Florence Logan, the flame of the Florida coast." "Juanita, The Miniature Exotic" succeeded Logan at the outset of July, while at the Anchorage, Mabel Childs, "Duchess of the Roaring 20s," started a long run. The duchess, however, had changing acts performing with her, the first being "Joyce Ramee, Dancing Sensation" as well as a female singer. While the duchess made her appearances, a sweep of burlesque appeared on Maine screens as the Fourth of July arrived. For example, north of Mattawamkeag, at the Katahdin drive-in, *Naughty Paris Nights*, billed as "Thrilling Burlesque at its Best," was held over due to "popular demand," while in Milo the drive-in held over *International Burlesque*, billed as "Daring to See," and the Enfield drive-in featured "BURLESQUE, HELD OVER! HELD OVER!"—plus a film starring Marilyn Monroe and Jean Harlow.[37] Live or on film, women dancers were quite popular in some sectors of the north country.

On July 4, Joyce Ramos, billed simply as a Spanish dancer, joined the duchess at the Anchorage, and the following week "Cupcake Carroll, Beautiful Exotic" danced at the Birchmere while Joyce Harvey, an "Oriental Dancer," appeared at the Anchorage. There was no photograph of Harvey. Women who followed Harvey in the floor show included "FRANCINE, Beautiful Exotic Featured at Boston's 'Casino,'" "MONA LEE, Beautiful Queen of the Exotic Dance," and "RITA WRAYE, Beautiful Exotic Dancer." These women also did not have photographs included, unless it were Wraye, shown in a strapless top and blonde curly hair, although the photo may have been of the female emcee who was at the venue for a few weeks. At the Birchmere during these weeks, "MARY JANE, The Beautiful Exotic," performed, followed by, at the same shows, Margie DeVere, billed as an "Exotic Fireball," and Brenda, who performed "The Dance of the Isle." A few exotic dancers followed these acts, and then, at the close of August 1957, Doreen came to the Anchorage.[38]

Doreen was featured in perhaps the most blatant photograph published in the local newspapers for the Anchorage. She was billed as simply "DOREEN, Tassle Tossin' Cutie." And her photograph showed her tassels: long fringed ones sprouting from the front of her seemingly strapless tiny bikini-style top. She wore a very small bottom as well, and her legs and most of her torso were bare. She was photographed with one hand on her hip, leaning slightly forward, her other hand on her opposite thigh, her head tilted back and her darkly painted lips forming a kiss.[39]

Doreen, the "Tassle Tossin' Cutie," seems to have been an erotic dancer. The 1957 photograph was certainly intended to titillate, and Doreen may have looked to promise nudity, although the striptease remained illegal.[40] The "Tassle Tossin' Cutie" resembled a pin-up girl of the more erotic variety of the era, and she was just what the women at the center of the 1943 riot in Portland and some of the early belly dancers feared: a woman who seemed to promise to take it all off, even if she did not. Belly dancers do not take anything off unless it is a veil in a routine, and the women at the center of the 1943 riot never promised to remove a thing either. Neither group posed for such blatant photographs, at least not any located in Maine. Doreen may not have been what some female dancers were accused of being—strippers or prostitutes—but she came closer to the edge—not because of a lack of clothes per se but more because of her pose, her expression, and the tassels in her photograph. And this was a battle a whole new generation and more of belly dancers would continue to fight. In the meantime, one could go to the Anchorage or the Birchmere in the early 1960s and see "exotic" dancers, seemingly ones like Doreen, perform, as well as a few women identified as "Oriental Dancers"—Ginny Loring and Melissa—at the Anchorage. And, while one Eastern or Oriental dancer in the Bangor area danced her husband through seminary school, to the consternation of some people, elsewhere in the state Little Egypt truly grew up and became the Queen of the Coast.[41]

CHAPTER EIGHT

"Little Egypt" Grows Up and Becomes the Queen of the Coast

The Emergence of Modern Ethnic and Belly Dancing in Maine in the 1960s and Beyond

AFTER BECOMING "REDISCOVERED" IN THE 1950S, BELLY DANCING EXPE-rienced a revival in America in the 1960s and 1970s. It purportedly started in both New York and California during that time, and it spread out thereafter. Ethnic nightclubs and restaurants with belly-dance per-formances experienced revitalization along the way, with women making respectable sums of money in the major venues. By 1970, a few dancers were reaching popular acclaim, and in 1972 *Life* magazine interviewed Serene (or Serena) Wilson of New York City. She performed and held workshops to train dancers, and by 1973 at least a few dancers who knew of her—and at least one who had studied with her—began to offer classes in Maine. Wilson herself would come to Maine to perform at least once during the 1970s, performing in the Portland region. She would return to Maine in the 1990s.[1]

Serena Wilson, interestingly, and linking her to some of the other dance genres discussed herein, was from a vaudeville family, and she had performed with her family in vaudeville as a young girl. Her par-ents' troupe was called Blake & Blake, Wilson's birth name having been Serene Blake. She changed the spelling of her first name to Serena as a young woman. The family group performed comedy and dance numbers, and Serena also studied with Ruth St. Denis, the dancer renowned for her sinuous, Eastern dance–inspired moves in the early 1900s, who had herself been controversial. Born August 8, 1933, just a few months before the Hampden marathon fire and the subsequent banning of marathon dancing in Maine, Serena Wilson first belly danced in the early 1950s, after her husband, Alan Wilson, and his band booked a gig that required a belly dancer. Alan Wilson's band was a Dixieland one, but no matter; he quickly gathered the music he needed for the show, and Wilson, already trained by St. Denis, agreed to dance. According to Wilson's husband in 2007, at those first one or two shows, "She carried a vase on her shoulder in order to disguise the fact that she didn't know what to do with her hands."[2]

Alan Wilson learned to play Middle Eastern drums and drum rhythms, and Serena became increasingly involved with belly dancing, honing her moves at the Egyptian Gardens in New York, a nightclub in the trendy Chelsea neighborhood, which at the time featured several Greek and Middle Eastern cabarets. Wilson quickly became a noted belly dancer, and danced for New York mayor John V. Lindsay at the city council chambers. In the mid-1960s, she opened a dance studio—purportedly one of the earliest in the nation devoted exclusively to belly dancing. She trained women, and women only, to dance, and hired out dancers for both public and private performances. According to an interview she gave to the *Wall Street Journal*, her business flourished until 1991, when Americans were fighting in the Persian Gulf War, and, as she put it, "There are people who just don't want to be reminded of things Middle Eastern." In 2007, immediately after her death at the age of seventy-three, Wilson's husband would state that that type of prejudice was no longer a factor.[3]

Wilson published her first of three books written with her husband on belly dancing in 1972, *The Serena Technique of Belly Dancing*.[4] By that time, the dance form had started its revival in other parts of the nation, and national journals started to note the resurgence, and the changes that had come with it. As a short piece accompanying a photo essay in *Life* magazine stated in 1972, "Until now, American belly dancing has always had a certain seedy aura about it, seldom suggesting anything more refined than a county carnival hootchie-cootchie." Now, however, according to *Life* in its "Now You Can Shimmy Like Your Sister Kate," the title from a popular song, "thousands of perfectly respectable women across the country" were finding the dance a good way to exercise and "maybe raise their husbands' eyebrows a notch or two." Sex, it seems, was still a major selling point, even though Wilson apparently tried to guide the interview away from that premise. And, although the piece mentioned that Wilson's Stairway to Stardom studio had an enrollment of 600, double that of the preceding year's and consisting of "grandmothers, schoolteachers, a lady stockbroker, and at least one grimly determined women's liberationist," the major share of the included photos, in terms of space provided, featured a classically beautiful young woman, mostly in her bare-belly dance costume, but also one of her pushing her child's stroller.[5]

Ruth Gibson of London trained in classical ballet and opened a dance school in Brunswick, Maine, in the early 1970s, offering belly dancing as a primary course after having earned part of her living in England as a belly dancer under the name Rebekah, an Arabic spelling of her middle name. (Many belly dancers take Arabic stage names, while some others more recently have adopted more American names with natural or exotic connotations.) Gibson emphasized the *bedi* form, essentially a form danced by rural or hill women in Turkey and other localities, whereas Serena favored the cabaret style more.[6]

Gibson said of Serena Wilson in 1974, "She is accepted in New York Society. She is not as Margot Fonteyn is to ballet, though."[7] To her dancers, however, even though she may not have been as well known or respected in the broader culture as Fonteyn was, she was still extremely influential in the development of modern belly dance, and her reputation would only increase over the years.

Gibson quickly filled up her Maine classes and had about ninety-six students in August 1974. Of these, about ninety were married. She found her students' partners were either all for it, or totally against it. This was especially true for performances. Indeed, she established a performance group but found that "the husbands said no. In front of a lecture group or for a demonstration all right, but in a nightclub, no."[8]

Gibson acknowledged that belly dancing was "degraded" by the general public, and compared its moves to Hawaiian hula dancing, and especially to modern dance as compared to ballet, both of which were generally deemed respectable by the mid-1900s. Of belly-dance performances, Gibson said, "It's fascinating if pleasantly presented rather than sensually presented. Sex is more in the viewer's mind than the dancer's. As far as actual movements, modern dance is a lot worse, a lot more suggestive."[9]

As far as students go, Gibson said, "You are dancing to show what you can do with your body, not to show someone else, regardless of what's in the mind of the viewer." Furthermore, she said, "It is easy to teach the extrovert, but the very secretive and retiring also benefit." She spoke of how women first came in to dance in their jeans or body suits or leotards, and would gradually "start stripping down. At the end you see them just come out of their shells. They're gorgeous. One day a girl comes in and she has made a costume." She considered belly dancing "fun, fascinating, rewarding, and a good way to tone muscles, as well as, at its more professional levels, an art." She said of that art, "It's attractive, people are fascinated. Once the dancer gets over her embarrassment, it's fascinating."[10]

At roughly the same time as Gibson opened her studio on Main Street in Brunswick, the YWCA in Portland, in March 1973, began offering belly-dance lessons. In 1976, the *Portland Evening Express* called belly dancing "one of the most popular dances of the '70s." By that year, the local YWCA had had three years of lessons offered, and the newspaper interviewed the principal belly-dance instructor, Virginia DeKovens Kovensky. The resulting article included a double-page spread of Ruth Frost, an attractive young woman, performing in full belly-dance regalia, playing *zils* or *zagats*—finger cymbals—and doing a veil removal.[11]

According to Kovensky, much of the impetus for beginning the classes was urging for the same by Brenda Frost, who had lived in California when the dance first began its revival and who would become one of the city's most devoted students and practitioners. That—plus a workshop Kovensky took with Serena Wilson—convinced her, as the YWCA's dance instructor, to offer the classes, overcoming much initial hesitancy.[12]

The first class offered had sixty women enrolled, plus a waiting list. The next session saw an intermediate-level class offered as well as the beginner's class. A few months after that, an advanced class was started. The classes continued to be popular, and in 1976 both Kovensky and Frost stressed, as had Ruth Gibson and Serena Wilson and other women, that "belly dancing is an art form, not a nightclub routine," or, as Wilson said most directly, it is "not stripping."[13] Of course, in Maine as elsewhere, belly dancing was and is indeed performed in nightclubs.

On April 25, 1976, the Portland YWCA sponsored a performance by belly dancer Desmeen of Worcester, Massachusetts, and two of her students, performances open to the public. By that time, the local YWCA had its own dance troupe with thirteen performers, including Frost and Kovensky. The local paper deemed belly dancing as now "considered to be the 'fun' way to exercise by today's mothers and grandmothers," and stated, "If the officials who ousted Little Egypt in 1893 from the Chicago World Fair could see us now, they'd shimmy in their graves." "Not only are housewives and career women gyrating and gliding to the 7/8 rhythms of the Middle East, they're doing it in one of America's most respectable institutions, the Young Women's Christian Association."[14] Yet, over the next few decades, the association between belly dancing and stripping would, for many people, continue to exist, and each new generation of dancers and instructors in Maine and throughout the nation would continue to deny that the two are connected. And, of course, a few women have done both, including in smaller cities like Bangor. And some Maine belly dancers would perform burlesque.

Meanwhile, belly dancing became more popular throughout Maine. Additional schools or classes started in various locations in the mid-1970s, and those first few women brought in more famous dancers as the years passed, and held public shows and workshops.

Belly dancing in Maine and elsewhere continued to increase in popularity, and by 1977 it was considered pervasive enough that even *Readers' Digest* acknowledged its current wide appeal. "Every One Is Belly Dancing!" the magazine titled its article, which discussed belly dancing in New York and other cities, as well as mentioning its spread to YWCAs, colleges, and other venues. Its author was enthralled by Serena Wilson and her studio, and her desire to see belly dancing develop its own American style, as opposed to Ibrahim "Bobby" Farrah and his troupe. Farrah wanted to see Middle Eastern dancing preserved in its original forms.[15] Both schools of thought would emerge in Maine.

The movement overall went more in Serena's direction. Although many American belly dancers would visit Egypt, Turkey, and other countries associated with belly dance to advance their techniques, in the United States, American cabaret and eventually tribal or American Tribal styles would become extremely popular over time. The former features classic chiffon, silks, and sequins in its performance costumes, the latter the more ethnic, thicker, and often less revealing outfits, along with more regulated, angular movements. Fusion forms, which often blend belly-dance types, and more recently, the influence of modern dance, ballet, and burlesque, are apparent.

In the 1970s in Maine, however, a woman began to practice who would perform and teach into the new millennium. As such, her story embraces much of the story and culture of belly dancing in Maine from the 1970s on. In the mid-2010s, she was recognized as being perhaps the oldest living dancer in Maine. Colette Poliquin—known as Zeina in the dance world—had had an interest in belly dance for many years, but only at about age thirty did the Lewiston native find a place to study belly dancing in Maine. In 1981 she stated in an interview, "I had always been interested in it. Even when I was a little girl, I used to play at being a dancer." The working-class daughter of French Canadian descent first studied in 1974 under Clara Desjardins in Auburn after the "big surge" in belly dancing had started in Maine. Some of her fellow students had taken classes with Virginia Kovensky, and she would also attend one of

Serena Wilson's workshops and dances in Maine. By 1981, Poliquin was traveling to Boston, which was and remains a center for belly dancers to meet and work on their techniques.[16]

Poliquin soon met dancer Dolly Marie Pomerloau, known also by her dance name Sylina, after watching her dance at the Zapion Taverna. She viewed Sylina as "a real belly dancer" and one gifted on the *zils*. Sylina was teaching in Scarborough at the time. Poliquin studied with Sylina for a couple of years, and in the early 1980s, by now dancing with *zils* herself and often to the melody of an *oud*—a stringed instrument and purportedly the forerunner to the lute—Poliquin started teaching, first in her home studio on Auburn's Western Promenade. Due to a lack of available costumes at the time, Poliquin made most of hers herself and would later help other dancers to do the same, or help them customize purchased costumes or costume components when they became more readily available after the turn of the century.[17]

Poliquin proved most interested in traditional belly-dance moves and practices, in 1981 stating that it was the Arabic style that most suited her. She soon thereafter met an Armenian musician who played with Sylina. The two became friends. Alan Gardiner (née Alan Shavarsh Bardezbanian) helped Poliquin learn about music, secure quality instruments, and so forth. She eventually became "his dancer," the two performing regularly at an ethnic restaurant in Hallowell as well as performing in other places on occasion, primarily in Middle Eastern restaurants.[18]

Patrons sometimes throw money at a belly dancer's feet as they dance, and later, as the years passed, tip jars were sometimes used to collect the money spectators would contribute. Sometimes the money raised proved generous, sometimes not. As the years progressed, in Maine as elsewhere, the "belly-gram" developed. The belly-gram was essentially a dance-on-order venue, wherein a dancer would advertise her availability for shows or personal appearances and be hired by private parties to perform for a specific event, often a birthday or the like, sometimes surprising a guest of honor. Live performances, teaching, and belly-grams all provided income streams for the more talented dancers. Belly-grams allowed a woman to set her own fees, and by the turn of the century, one could order a belly-gram from Ellsworth to Portland, Bath to Lewiston, Bangor to Millinocket. The women would sometimes perform close to home, sometimes hours away. Sometimes, however, the patrons expected more than a regular belly dance.[19]

Colette Poliquin, or Zeina, was one of the women who made belly-gram appearances and other private shows. They were not her preferred venue, however. She stated in 2015 that she would specify that she would only perform in mixed company—not all males—or have her husband accompany her. She received some threatening phone calls and was harassed a few times for her work from people who did not understand what it truly was. "But one summer," she said, "belly-grams saved us. Bath Iron Works [her husband's place of employment] was on strike. I was still living in Auburn and would go to Bath, Portland, Augusta, etc. to do them. I would travel up to about one and a half hours away to perform."[20]

Poliquin turned down some offers, however, because "it was obvious they wanted something else." In one instance, a group of men wanted her to come and stay on Vinyl Haven Island, and said that no husbands were allowed. Another time, a group wanted her and another dancer or two to go to New Hampshire and stay for a few days, and the monetary offering was for far more than the going rates for private belly-dance appearances. "I went to some where they picked me up," she said, "and they turned out fine, but I didn't feel safe." She said that she was shy and afraid of hurting people's feelings, so sometimes did not voice her concerns. Yet, she said, the belly-grams could be far more lucrative than dancing in nightclubs and restaurants, and many dancers liked them for that reason. For her and for some other women, however, teaching was the favored way to make a living from the dance, although teaching generally did not provide a full living wage, at least not in the late twentieth century.[21] Many teachers taught only part-time.

For Poliquin, it was teaching that most appealed, as well as simply the dance itself. She stated in 2015, after only recently giving up teaching, at least for the time being, "I did it for its own sake. I would have liked to have had more people to share it with, but by the time it 'blew up' I wasn't as interested in the form the dance presented itself as." She preferred the more traditional forms of the dance. However, by 2015 she also thought that the older forms were once again being rediscovered.[22]

Dance troupes also became popular over the years, and Colette Poliquin joined one out of Portland. It was one run by Sylina, and, she stated, "I had to audition for it. I was part of the troupe for several years." The group assembled about once a week; they would practice, perform at some shows, and went to a number of workshops in Boston.[23]

Workshops in Maine in the 1990s and beyond allowed Maine dancers to meet, study, and dance with some of the more famous dancers from throughout the country. When Colette saw Serena Wilson of New York perform, it was at a church in Portland, after she had given a workshop or two. Her friend Alan Gardiner played music that night for some of the dancers, and another dancer, Catherine "Kitty" Tambling, known also as Kahas when performing, had her recorded music "die" while she was onstage. Alan Gardiner and some other musicians simply jumped on stage and improvised for her, and she continued her sword routine. Kahas Productions would bring several dancers in from out of state during the late 1900s and early in the 2000s, and stage numerous shows. Kahas also taught in the Bangor region. Poliquin had met Kitty (or Kahas) previously, at Maine workshops and in Boston, and did a few costume adjustments for her. According to Poliquin, "Kahas Productions, for a good ten or twelve years, was very active . . . brought in big names . . . presented big shows." Women from northern Maine and New Brunswick came to some of the shows, sometimes to watch, sometimes to perform or take workshops, thus extending some portions of the dance farther north. Poliquin danced in one of these shows, but soon thereafter her eyes started to trouble her such that she did not want to travel any great distances at night.[24]

Poliquin also met a number of other Maine dancers through Josie Conté, who moved to Portland in about the 1990s and put on a number of workshops. She also taught a number of women who would soon form a network of dancers. And, according to one of her students, Jeanne Handy,

Conté brought Serena Wilson back to Maine in the 1990s, where Handy and other Maine women had a chance to take workshops with her.[25]

In the mid-1990s also, Poliquin moved to Bath where her husband was already working and where Poliquin had performed in the past. She started teaching in Bath—the first woman to work as a belly-dance teacher—at the Bath Dance Works Studio. She taught there for several seasons, usually having six to eight students in any given class, teaching often more than one class per session. She then built a home studio at the edge of the city, and taught about four or five classes per week, squeezing the students in when more than five or six women showed up at a given class. She did this for over a decade, but by 2010 just two or three women came to classes as Poliquin reduced her teaching schedule. By this time, Poliquin was in her mid-seventies but still dancing for the joy of it, teaching some classes, and performing. She particularly enjoyed working with veils and doing dance as a form of meditation. She started to become a bit tired of teaching, however, but felt that she was contributing because she taught the more traditional methods of belly dancing and the reasons why the movement had developed the way it did (although for some movements there is seemingly no reason why they are done the exact way they are). She felt that she taught more about traditional culture and music than some contemporary teachers. She was more interested in the process than in preparing women for the stage, something she feels some other teachers do emphasize, or some students seek—even before they are ready for the stage.[26] And, of course, the quality or preparedness of women who dance publicly or who teach varies greatly.

Some women still wanted to come to her home and dance, even after Poliquin started to taper off her lessons, and come they did, with Poliquin transitioning her formal teaching into dance sessions held without fees for the few women with whom she continued to work. The women formed friendships through these more informal sessions, and they enjoyed themselves.[27]

In answer to critics who might charge that belly dancing was a limited skill or art form, Poliquin stated, "I do it for its own sake, to work towards progression, to keep doing the practice no matter what, to keep learning. There's always more that dancing has to teach us." And she added that, through creating the right environment, "dancing can help us get through the rough stuff in life." Poliquin continues to dance in the mid-2010s.[28]

One of the women who came to dance at those later sessions in Poliquin's home studio in Bath was Josephina Gasca. Poliquin spoke of how on one day it was just lovely outside so she decided to have the women dance outside. "And the mosquitoes just ate Josephina up. The mosquitoes attacked her. She came three or four times, then she never came back. The mosquitoes just ate her up."[29] Poliquin made the statement with amusement; the women remained friends, and Josephina Gasca has in some ways stepped into the role Poliquin had had in Bath, beginning to teach at about the same time as Poliquin was easing out of the role of instructor.

Poliquin stated that she remembered going to other types of dance forums, some with ethnic dancers. At one such event, she stated of a woman who had been trained in classical dance, "I told her what type of dance I did, and she backed off, as though it might contaminate her." Other people who learned what Poliquin did said, "Ooh, I never thought you would do something like that." Some people who called about performances "were worried you would take things off, others wanted you to take things off. Some people were afraid to see you dance, they had a certain mindset about what it [belly dancing] was."[30]

As to overlaps with other forms of dancing, Poliquin stated that she had once won a $50 dance contest (about thirty-five years earlier) at a disco club. The club had decided to hold a belly-dancing contest to try to pull more customers in. The club advertised the contest, and about six to eight women entered to win the prize. The dance was in Lewiston, and one of the other women clearly knew little if anything about belly dancing, but thought that she could muddle through. Poliquin won the contest, even though the woman who did not know the dance was convinced that the prize was hers. Poliquin was surprised that she won the contest, not over the amateurs or impressionists, but over the other experienced belly dancers who had entered. The contest did pull in more customers.[31]

At another juncture, a woman called and asked her about some music. She wanted Poliquin to help her select some Turkish dance music, but Poliquin came to realize that the music was for a strip dance routine. Poliquin ended up not giving the woman the music, not because she was a stripper (many of whom she said were talented in their own way) but because of the struggle that belly dancers have long had trying to convince the public that they themselves are not strippers. The woman worked at the Holly in the Lewiston–Auburn area.[32]

At still another venue, a public fair in Lewiston, a woman came up to her and complained about some other dancers that she had heard would be performing. "They are probably going to do some horrible hootchie-cootchie," the woman said. She also stated that the hootchie-cootchie was some sort of communist plot.[33] Clearly, perceptions of what the hootchie-cootchie or belly dancing was varied greatly, and even at Maine fairs the dancers still danced, and they could still raise an eyebrow or two.

Josephina Gasca came to Maine from Chicago, where she had had previous experiences in belly dancing. Gasca was not one to brag about her past, so Poliquin said of Gasca, "She had some wonderful experience (and talent) already when she came to Maine. She had a very famous teacher in Chicago." That teacher, Jasmin Jahal, would soon have one of the only, if not the only at the time, Eastern dance studios in America, according to Gasca. Gasca, born in the late 1960s, started dancing in Chicago in 1998 and moved to Maine in 2003. "I didn't think I'd be able to find belly dance here," she said in 2015. "But I did. It was sort of word of mouth." She contacted Emma Holder in Portland, a dancer from Canada who would later transition partially to the tango, and soon started taking classes with her. She had already taken a few classes with Poliquin in Bath, her new home, but at the time Poliquin was not teaching frequently enough to meet Gasca's commitment level. "I wanted something more," she stated.[34]

Gasca soon started taking classes first with Josie Conté, and then with Jeanne Handy of Maine Belly Dance in Portland. One of the later renowned Maine dancers, Rosa Noreen, also took some classes with

Jeanne Handy as a young woman. Rosa Noreen would start Star Bright Studios in Portland, bring in numerous well-known—in the belly-dance world—dancers for shows, give and perform in numerous shows in the 2010s in Maine and internationally, and record belly-dance videos. Yet another woman who would take classes with Handy, Anne Beal or Ana-bee, would establish a practice in the Lewiston–Auburn area and also perform in numerous venues in and outside of the state.[35]

Gasca started performing in 2006 and in the winter of 2007 started teaching belly dance in Bath and elsewhere in coastal Maine. One of her teachers had told her that she needed to teach and to perform to further develop her dancing. A writer also, Gasca would eventually find a way to blend the two, offering an ongoing workshop for dancers that combined belly dance, meditation, and storytelling. In the meantime, her Chicago teacher Jasmine wanted her to perform in Chicago, but at the time Gasca did not feel ready to do so. By 2006 she was. Then Jeanne Handy called her and asked, "Why aren't you teaching?" So by 2007 she was doing both.[36]

As a dancer and teacher, Gasca sought to create more venues that celebrated women and the beauty of belly dancing. For her, the dance was "very sensual and beautiful, and also very spiritual." Her words echoed some of Poliquin's.[37] None of the women interviewed for this book viewed belly dance as something less than other forms of dancing.

Gasca also created a writing program in Chicago that continued into the late 2010s. From a family that she classifies as working class, or even "sub-working class," Gasca attended Columbia College in Chicago a decade after attending secretarial school and studying business. She eventually taught fiction writing at Columbia College for three years before moving to Maine, and it was there that she established an ongoing writing program. In writing, dancing, and her other interests, what she sought most was to "create community." She started taking belly-dance lessons after taking other dance classes, while she was teaching creative writing, and said of it, "I just fell in love, and the love affair continues." She eventually went to graduate school for dance.[38]

As a performer, Gasca has danced in Maine at various shows in various places, from Bangor to Portland, including ones in Portland hosted by Rosa Noreen, and performed at the Greek Acropolis Restaurant and occasionally performed at the Dobra Tea House, both in Portland in the 2010s. She did not do belly-grams, however, and by the mid-2010s the term had largely become antiquated, although in essence some dancers still performed them. Gasca performed in several of Jeanne Handy's shows, and said in 2015, "I've done private shows," too. "I'm very selective. I know I will not get paid for the amount of money and education I've put into this, so I want to make sure that when I perform I'm going to enjoy myself." When she returns to Chicago to visit, she sometimes performs there also.[39]

Gasca prefers to focus on her classes and her shows, however. In the mid-2010s, she continued to put on a belly-dance show every year in Bath at the Bath Dance Works Studio, as well as to hold "Belly Balls," a large dance open to anyone featuring live musicians, a potluck buffet, and a wonderful time overall with perhaps fifty to one hundred women talking and dancing, and with all levels of dancing and costuming in evidence. As she said of performances in general, "There is something really powerful about a group of women dancing and creating art."[40]

Class sizes vary depending upon the season and the year. Josephina Gasca generally taught four to five classes a session in the 2010s, with about twenty-eight to thirty-five students per session. Students were of varied ages, from mothers with their daughters to a woman in her eighties. She did not feel a need to advertise, as noted, and stated, "I think what really sells my classes are the women in my classes." She has had students who have started to teach in their own right. She also has had students regularly come from Portland to her classes, and Gasca has also taught in Portland.[41]

Gasca stated of her students, "I do not have to produce the best students in the world who go out and teach and perform." Instead she looks for growth and creativity in her students, and seeks to create a community that can help make changes in the world. As she likewise said of herself, "I do not need to be the best dancer there is. I just need to be at my best." As to when women should start belly dancing, she stated, "It's for every age. It's for every point in your life. Whenever you start is the right, the perfect, time."[42]

As to changes in belly dancing in Maine, she stated, "I feel as if I came during a kind of Renaissance period" in terms of "who was in my classes alongside me, and who was teaching. Some of the people who were teaching then have pulled back or quit teaching altogether. It just felt like a Renaissance." But, she concluded, "Maine is small. There are only so many opportunities. There are a lot of good dancers on the professional level, but only so many venues. I've tried to create some, but you can only do so much." Yet she continues to teach and dance, and in autumn 2015 offered classes in Bath, Lisbon, and Portland, with upcoming shows and events planned for late 2015 and through 2016.[43]

The woman who taught Gasca most intensely in Maine was Jeanne Handy, and Handy taught a number of other women who became active entertainers and teachers. Gasca also studied with Josie Conté, who in turn taught Jeanne Handy.

Josie Conté—who would take the stage name Joselle, but whom Serena Wilson introduced as either Fatima or Judeah—had previous dance experience, including ballet, modern dance, tap, and jazz. She earned her college degree at Brockport University in dance, before beginning to study belly dancing in 1984. She studied first with Dianne McPherson (Dunya) in New York City. "She was a beautiful dancer, and heavily influenced by the Sufi tradition," Conté stated in 2015. In her first experiences of Eastern dance, "I fell in love with the music and the dance." In 1989, Conté began studying with the famed Serena Wilson in her New York studio. She became a dancer in Wilson's company, and later, after she moved to Maine, Conté kept in touch with Serena, visited her in New York, and eventually brought her to Maine.[44]

Serena's second visit to Maine gave Maine dancers a chance to study with the renowned dancer, as well as an opportunity for Mainers in general to watch her perform. Belly-dancing workshops are generally open to everyone, including students of various skill levels, and ticket sales to performances are open to the general public, even those associated with a day or weekend of specialized workshops, which became increasingly popular in the 1990s and beyond. Having Serena Wilson return to Maine was a major event. Serena, who had helped revitalize Eastern dance in America, like belly dancers in America and elsewhere, had continued to dance and perform into her later years.

Conté also performed in a number of highly respected venues, including the Lincoln Center, and danced with the Ramzi El Edlibi Dance Company. As with Serena Wilson, Conté would also bring Edlibi—celebrated both for his choreography and his theatrical sense— to Maine. He visited several times, giving Maine dancers and their audiences new experiences.[45]

Josie Conté, born in the 1960s, moved to Maine from New York in 1992. She joined the Perennial Dance Collective, a multigenerational dance group established by Betsy Dunphy, and began teaching soon thereafter, in 1993. She formed the dance troupe "Dancers of the Eternal Crescent," in 2004 "so I wouldn't have to dance alone," she stated. The troupe was hired for a number of performances at locations ranging from the Children's Museum of Maine to the Maine Art festivals. (The troupe was also referred to as Baraka! when it performed with musicians.) The *Maine Times* stated of Baraka! that "the dances create an atmosphere of mystery and beauty (on a stage transformed into an exotic realm), where the female body becomes an example of power and pride."[46] Her teaching and her dancing gained more followers, "and it just took off," Conté stated—not just her work, but belly dancing in the region in general.[47]

She stated, "Colette [Poliquin] danced with us or we had some collaboration, Cassandra [Hoover, a talented dancer who "performed belly-grams"] joined with me, Jeanne [Handy] joined in 1994, Josephina [Gasca] found me in about 2003, and then Anabee [Anne Beal] joined." Other women who became known as belly dancers in the state also worked with her, as students or in performances. Conté brought other dancers and musicians to Maine, not only Serena Wilson and Ramzi El Edlibi.[48]

However, there were some problems. Conté arranged to hold her first *hafla*—a gathering of belly dancers in which they share food, dance, and music, and sometimes work on their moves, costumes, and so forth—in Maine at the local VFW. "On the day we were to have it, they wouldn't let us do it. They saw some posters, looked at the costumes and such, and said, 'No.'" So, after some finagling, the group moved the event to the Quaker Meeting House nearby.[49]

Like other dancers, Serena Wilson was well aware of the controversy her students might encounter. Conté stated that Serena had made a point of talking to the dancers about the differences between exotic dancing (which belly dancers did) versus erotic dancing (which most did not, and some others did but with humor).[50] Some women did both exotic and erotic dancing over the years, but Wilson tried to instruct her students as to the differences.

Conté understood this difference, noting that belly dancing has "circular, sinuous moves" that are often not accepted even in places like gyms where women sometimes wear less clothing than the typical belly dancer and engage in very physical "but angular" movements. Belly dancing allows women a place to dance in a sensuous way "that is very healthy," she pointed out. It "creates a space where you can do this." Of her teaching, she said, "I loved teaching. Women would change, and make such friendships together. It always turned into something beautiful and supportive, and I miss that so much. . . . We don't really value women's wisdom and bodies as much as we can. It's ok to dance in small costumes in ballet," but not in the more-covering costumes of the belly dancer, with its less angular movements.[51]

In 2002, Conté began pre-med classes at the University of New England in Biddeford. She finished her medical studies in osteopathy, and in 2015 started a residency in Waterville. She continued to dance, including teaching a class in Portland that May, and had taught a class in Hallowell earlier in the year.[52] But as her medical work increased, she clearly cut back on her belly-dance practice. Her students, however, did not.

Anne Beal, or Anabee, a dancer teaching in Lewiston, also danced with Colette Poliquin. However, this would have been only a few times, and at the beginning of Anabee's career. While Josephina Gasca in some ways took over Poliquin's teaching venue in the Bath area, Anabee would eventually take over some of the area in Lewiston–Auburn where Poliquin had once taught. And all three would be linked by one belly dancer in the Portland region.

Anne Beal, born in the 1970s, spent much of her youth in Connecticut. Her mother and father both worked. Beal moved to Maine in the early 1990s and started her study of belly dance in the mid-1990s with no other dance background. She had attended broadcasting school and secured work with Maine Public Broadcasting as a video editor and producer. (One of the videos she edited in the 1990s was about dancer Molly Spotted Elk.) A fan of heavy metal music, Beal, who had moved to Maine in her twenties, simply wanted to feel more comfortable with her body and decided that belly dancing would be a means to that end. She decided to undertake the dance as a New Year's resolution. She did not expect to become a performer or teacher. She initially contacted someone in Bangor—perhaps Catherine Tambling—who recommended her to Jeanne Handy, who, being in Portland (as well as teaching in Brunswick and other locations), was much closer to Beal, who lives in Poland and runs an animal boarding kennel from her home.[53]

"I just fell in love with it [belly dancing] for a number of reasons," she stated in 2015. "Many people say it's very meditative; the energy that you are tapping into." She specializes in *raqs beledi*—an Egyptian form of the dance. She said, "You can dance by yourself in the kitchen, as well as up on a big stage. It doesn't have to be about performing, but it can be."[54]

Although she started out thinking that she would never perform for an audience, Beal has performed extensively in Maine, Vermont, and New Hampshire. She started out in a group piece and then moved on to solos. She adopted "Anabee" as her performance name; it was also her childhood nickname. In 2014–2015, Anabee performed in Boston once a month. And as with many other dancers over the decades, Maine restaurants and clubs have also provided opportunities. She has danced at Narls, a Greek and Mediterranean restaurant and bar in Auburn regularly, and previously performed at two other area restaurants that had frequently brought in belly dancers. Beal has performed at other such venues, including Blue Restaurant in Portland. Blue has a very small and dark dance area, and dancers would perform sandwiched between the dining/audience members. Anabee feels that such an intimate environment provides a good starting place for dancers. Dobra Tea House in Portland also offered belly dancing once a month for its diners in the mid-2010s, and a number of dancers, including Beal, performed there.[55]

Beal prefers to dance in these smaller types of venues, where she can get close to her audience and focus on them one at a time, something echoed by a few of the other belly dancers interviewed. She stated, "Some dancers like to be on a stage, some like it better up close. When I'm dancing in restaurants I'm focused on just the person in front of me. On a stage I feel more pressure to perform." She also noted that Jeanne Handy was one of the rare dancers who could truly function well in the bright lights of a big stage from which one can see only a part of the audience. Beal considers herself largely an introvert but still found that she enjoys performing. "I work with dogs all day, belly dancing awoke something in me that I didn't know was there. I like dancing for an audience and performing."[56]

In terms of the monetary aspects, some restaurant/club/bar venues paid the dancers directly, and tip jars were available, and sometimes, especially in more recent years, they paid only the musicians directly, with the dancers either being paid indirectly or depending only on tips to earn a decent wage. In terms of payments, Anabee stated, "It's hard to make a living as a belly dancer in Maine. I'm thankful that I'm not trying to do it for a living." Beal wanted to create a future in which she could pursue more belly dancing, unhindered by her other current responsibilities.[57] As in other eras and dance forms, earning a living wage remains problematic in most parts of the state.

Beal began teaching in the early 2000s. She taught primarily in the Lewiston–Auburn area in the mid-2010s and taught a course at the University of Southern Maine. In addition, she has taught at various health and wellness venues. She said that she teaches her classes in much the way her teacher Jeanne Handy taught her: She teaches a movement, breaks it into parts, and then breaks the class into small groups so that they can work together at their own level. "It's very fluid, very relaxed."[58]

Like many other contemporary dancers who also teach, watching other women find joy in the dance is most rewarding. She said she had one student who did not want to perform, then she discovered American Tribal Dance—a trademarked form—"and she loved it, perhaps because it is done in a group. . . . She found the type that was right for her." The student subsequently taught American Tribal Style (ATS) for a time.[59]

However, Beal did feel that there has been something of a decline in belly-dancing opportunities in recent years, as some women discovered Zumba and other exercise forms. Lewiston–Auburn remains largely a mill town, and some people do not feel comfortable with the way she teaches, she said, and it is hard to get some types of arts established or widely embraced. Most of her classes remained small in the mid-2010s, at least those taught at the Dance Center in Auburn. Her University of Southern Maine and adult education classes were understandably larger. Yet, although enrollment might not be sky high, she stated, "When I was able to start teaching and making some money, I was really excited. I'm always thankful and honored that the women choose to spend their time with me. So many women fall in love with it [belly dancing] for so many different reasons."[60]

Beal also, like so many dancers—belly dancers and others through the years—gave private performances. She did some bachelorette parties, some birthday parties (including one for a ninety-year-old man who loved the party), and so forth. Sometimes she goes to a private venue to give such a performance, and sometimes has people come to the studio. "You have to be careful. Some people expect it to be burlesque or stripping. I try to be modest in my dress." She considers belly-grams to be just shortened versions of private performances (as usually one would just show up as a surprise and perform just one dance or two), but she has given a few short shows herself. She has also performed at a major event in Toronto, Canada, where she went three times for practice sessions as well as for the performances, and performed at weddings and other events there where belly dancing is a big event. She also danced at larger venues in New York, another popular city for belly dancing. "But that is just not here."[61]

Anabee, like many belly dancers, continues to take classes and workshops to further her professional development. She also started taking modern dance and physical theater classes in the mid-2010s.[62]

Beal's classes with Handy overlapped in time with those of Josephina Gasca. The two remained in contact over the years, such that Beal's students would dance at Gasca's shows or recitals, and vice versa. "It's a nice belly-dance community," Beal commented.[63]

Another dancer who became friends with both Beal and Gasca through her training with Josie Conté was Jeanne Handy. Handy's background and thus her reasons for starting belly dance were different from those of Poliquin, Gasca, and Beal, however. Handy—who performs under the name Jamileh—came from a Lebanese heritage. She had regularly seen her mother and other members of her family dance at various gatherings such as weddings, not professionally but socially, as part of their culture.[64]

Handy grew up in Boston where her father was a teacher, and moved to Portland in 1993. In order to keep in touch with her Lebanese background, she decided to start belly-dance lessons, but she wanted these to be a good fit with her heritage, so she made several inquiries before selecting a teacher. The teacher she chose was Josie Conté, who had studied Lebanese dance and the Egyptian style, and had been a student of Serena Wilson in New York. Handy would have had the opportunity to take workshops with Serena Wilson when she returned to Maine in the 1990s as well as taking workshops with Wilson in New York City when she traveled there with Conté.[65]

Handy studied with Conté for a number of years, and she considered Conté her primary teacher. However, Handy also went to workshops in various places, including New York, where she sometimes went with Conté. She said in 2015, "I definitely chose the right person [teacher], but then Josie cut back on her own classes, and I started teaching. Colette had already cut back, Maryann Butts [another talented teacher and dancer] had also cut back—she and I had studied with Colette together.

We all came from different perspectives," she stated. "Rosa Noreen was trained in ballet, and new to belly dancing at that time. She took classes with me. It happens a lot; women find that they can't move past a certain point [in traditional dance], cannot get past a certain body type. Then she found belly dancing, and that was it."[66]

After studying for three or four years, Handy began teaching part-time, while still studying. She would eventually teach not just in Portland (in the mid-2010s at the Maine Center for Taijiquan) but also in Scarborough, Falmouth, Brunswick, and Gray, and teach regularly at Bowdoin College where she directed the Bowdoin College Middle Eastern Dance Ensemble. She also taught a workshop in Massachusetts on a regular basis. "I would find ways to get my name out. When I was trying to make it as a dancer, I was able to support myself." This was before her family obligations prevented her from traveling more than occasionally, and she moved much of her focus to her interior design business. She said of these classes, and perhaps of her own lessons, "The friendships that formed in these classes were amazing. The sisterhood that developed in these classes was great. You can't ask for more than that."[67]

"I teach Middle Eastern belly dance because that is my connection to it," Handy stated in 2015. "But there are so many offshoots; there is no one definition of belly dance and that has been a struggle for it," for belly dancing as a whole. "But it's also made it more acceptable. In the Middle East, big-name belly dancers are like Hollywood stars. I think it's less so now." In America, at least when she started dancing, dancers were still struggling with misperceptions about what belly dancing is.[68]

Handy performed at various functions, including some private women's parties and celebrations, and occasionally danced at men's parties—but only if the men were much older and of Middle Eastern descent, such that they would know what belly dancing was all about. She danced at a ninetieth birthday party for one such man, and, she said, "He was a grandpa and he loved it. The kids loved it too. It was like dancing with my family."[69]

Jeanne Handy as Jamileh performed at several large shows in Boston, including the Arabic Belly Dancing Celebration. She also put on shows with her own students and other dancers, called the Fantabulous Shows. She would designate specific charities for the show's profits—such as the Preble Street Homeless Shelter. "It was always a benefit show, and we'd have a ball. We had a great time, and at one point there would be over 300 people in the audience."[70]

Handy also danced with Al Gardiner (Alan Shavarsh Bardezbanian), with whom Colette Poliquin had danced years before. She danced to his music for a number of years, and the two became close friends. She held a memorial show for him in 2014. Earlier they had taken part in the Middle Eastern Suitcase Project, a project that originated in Portland and aimed to help break down the walls between various cultures. "Alan and I handled the music part of it. One of the schools had us come in for a week. We did Middle Eastern dance and music," she stated in 2015. "On the last night, we had the parents come. The kids danced, and we did a show. I had to win these people over. At the end of the show, I asked who wanted to try it. The parents just poured off of the bleachers to try it. It was a riot."[71] Certainly it was a better riot than those seen in the Portland region in 1849 and 1943.

One of Jeanne Handy's most memorable experiences as a performer occurred when she was two days past her due date for her son. The show in which she performed was the national tour of the *Vagina Monologues*. The show had been scheduled for a few months earlier, and then had to change its date. Handy told them of the impending birth, but they still wanted her to perform. She did, although she had a backup dancer ready just in case. However, the day came, and Handy—who carried her pregnancy weight all in the front of her torso—went on. "I started with my back to the audience, they didn't know, and when I turned in profile," they were all just simply stunned. "You could have heard a pin drop. When it was over, they just erupted. It was beautiful. And it was a gift for me to be part of it." Some people were afraid she would have the baby that night, "but my son didn't come for another two weeks." A woman in the audience wrote a poem about the performance and had it published, and a minister wrote a sermon about the event, of which she later received a copy. And, in this case, the dancer was viewed in a very positive light.[72]

Many of Handy's students (and in some cases co-students) were teaching in the mid-2010s, including "Josephina, Anabee, Rosa Noreen, and Jessica Means who founded Nanya's Trance [a performance group]." Other dancers she has worked with are doing fusions of belly dancing with other forms of dance. She summed up her experience of belly dance by stating in 2015, "I do not have the time and place in my life now to be doing more, but I know the benefits of it. I know that we really need to get back to our bodies, to feeling confident with them." Belly dancing does these things, and Jeanne Handy plans to be dancing for all of her life. She took a break for about a year in the early 2010s, and found that her body really missed it, that her energy levels had changed. That fixed itself when she resumed dancing and teaching, and in 2015 she taught about two classes at a time, one in Portland and the other at Bowdoin College.

Still, Handy's focus had shifted by the mid-2010s, and she stated in 2015, "I say no to a lot of performance requests now. I will not do an event unless it is something I really care about." That caring may be for the musicians (like many dancers, she prefers live music), the other dancers, if there are any, or the cause behind the event.[73]

Other women continued to teach belly dance in Maine, although classes and shows, in terms of the number spread throughout the state, seemed to reach a pinnacle in about 2010. For example, one could study with one of at least four teachers in Bangor at the time, as well as take classes at Unity College, in Ellsworth, Belfast, Waterville, and in other nearby towns. By 2016, the number of women actively teaching dancers in the northern part of the state seems to have declined, as had the number of belly-dance performances. Yet the dance continues.

American belly dancers hold performances and celebrations at which only women are present in the audience. This may not have been true in the 1950s to 1990s, but by the 2000s, in Maine and elsewhere, it certainly was. At the 2010s "Belly Balls" in Bath, hosted by Josephina Gasca—essentially extravagant *haflas*—for example, one could watch close to one hundred women dancing, some dancing together, some in groups, and some alone. Women also make up the majority of general belly-dance audiences, including those at the dance shows held throughout Maine and in urban America each year. Furthermore, American belly dancers generally do not perform for groups of men, but they frequently perform for groups of women. Women who belly dance may well be dancing in a manner that can be interpreted as sensual or exotic, but they are often doing it primarily for women, and when they cross into the area of burlesque, they generally do so in a rather tongue-in-cheek manner.

Belly dancers do perform in public venues also, and there the audiences are often mixed in terms of gender. This adds a complexity to the interpretations of what belly dancing is, but it is clear that for many American women it is a dance form that they have made their own, derive both social and artistic pleasure from, and have in many ways taken out of the shadows of history. Although there are all levels of belly dancing, to become a professional takes many years of experience, as well as physical stamina and strength, and artistic skill. Yet, at its basic level, it remains largely working class and accessible to the working class in terms of dancing and watching performances.

Belly dancing in modern America also developed into a form of dance whose practitioners are frequently above the average age of other types of dancers, both at the entry level and beyond. Starting to belly dance at mid-life is not at all uncommon, and women perform in America and in Maine, as they do in the East, late into life. Yet Americans generally do not send their young girls to learn the dance as they might ballet, jazz, and modern dance. A stigma does remain, regardless of its validity.

And then, just as acceptance was beginning to be acquired, at least among women, some belly dancers started to perform burlesque in Maine and elsewhere. In Maine, some of the women in the northern sections started to bring burlesque into their movements in local shows and performances, but in a more casual way than would occur in the southern portions of the state in the early 2000s. In some ways, just accentuating a hip or chest movement can be seen as bringing a burlesque element into the dance, especially when accompanied by a wink or flirty toss of the head, but, as stated previously, this is often done in a tongue-in-cheek manner, meant to amuse, although it also often shows off a great deal of control and flexibility in the dancer.

In southern Maine, a small group of women and a few entertainment venues started to offer burlesque. One of them, with the stage name Vivian Vice, had studied belly dancing with both Josie Conté and Jeanne Handy, as well as with Jessica Means, the founder of Nanya's Trance, after coming to Maine in the early 1990s. Vice started, with Jolene Divine, a "vintage burlesque" troupe called Whistlebait Burlesque.[74]

Other burlesque troupes also formed during the era, and some burlesque or "neo-burlesque" dancers came from out of state to perform. In Portland, by 2011, these included the Dirty Dishes Burlesque Revue and Atomic Trash! That year, the Pontari Sisters of New York City performed burlesque in Westbrook, and in November 2010 famed Tempest Storm held her Las Vegas Burlesque Review in Portland, as part of a national tour. While emphasizing the freedom the dance gives women of different shapes and sizes, much like belly dancing does, the women generally did get down to a G-string and pasties for a brief part of their routine. Still, with its emphasis on humor and performance, and at least some body coverage, its advocates point out that burlesque is not stripping, nor does it draw the same audience as modern-day strippers do.[75]

Most belly dancers did not become burlesque dancers, however. Belly dancers did perform various dances for various audiences in Maine in the late 1900s into the 2000s. They formed a network—and for some a community—of women spanning the state, although the more populated regions saw more opportunities for women to study the dance and to work at belly dancing as a job or career, or as a source of some of their income. As time passed, belly dancing became increasingly respected and specialized but retained some of its mystique from earlier years. And, even in the mid-2010s, not everyone respected the dancers.

CHAPTER NINE

Conclusion

The Same Old Moves with New Respectability, at Least in the Eyes of Many: Maine's Transformed Belly Dancers, Taxi-Dancers, and Burlesque Performers of the Late 1900s and Early 2000s

ONE CAN ARGUE THAT THE HURDY GURDY EVOLVED INTO TAXI-DANCING and that taxi-dancing has evolved into the ballroom dancing pay-per-dance instruction studios of today, that marathon dancing in some ways is reflected in modern endurance contests and in the small local dance marathons held from time to time, and that burlesque has undergone a metamorphosis or resurgence also, becoming more popular in recent years as its performers tend to mimic the routines seen a few decades ago, but making, in some ways, the same separation from stripping as belly dancing has made. Belly dancing has perhaps survived in America with the greatest direct connection to its past but, although the dance is becoming increasingly professional in terms of modern shows and dance instruction, it, like burlesque, retains much of its image of being something different, something unique, something of a subculture, and, perhaps, something scandalous. Yet, unlike burlesque in terms of entertainment, it is geared primarily toward women, not men, and that has perhaps made all the difference.

The evidence for pay-by-the-dance forms like hurdy gurdy and taxi-dancing is scarce for Maine, but Mainers clearly knew what they were, and no doubt some women did perform these in Maine, especially northern Maine for the hurdy gurdy or related dances, and southern Maine for taxi-dances and related forms. Furthermore, Mainers who traveled to the West or to the larger cities would have had experience with both types of dancers, depending on the era. And there were clearly females performing dances as part or all of their pay in Maine saloons and dance halls in the 1800s and early 1900s, at the fairs and circuses of the era, and on the stages and dance floors of later venues in the 1900s and thereafter.

By the late 1800s, vaudeville had brought a bit of everything to the state. Some women also left Maine for the stage, women like Molly Spotted Elk and Lucy Nicolar, and countless other women came to the state to perform, and then, for most, traveled on. Here, as elsewhere, wages were often small, and some dancers, like those who died in Hampden in 1933, even paid for dancing with their lives. Marathon dancers included both experienced dancers and inexperienced ones, some natives of the state, some coming to Maine to perform. In the 1990s and beyond, some dancers came to Maine to teach as well as to perform, especially in belly dancing, and the new burlesque queens also put in appearances in the 2000s.

And what Mainers did not see live, they saw in films and in advertisements. Those who did not have the opportunity to dance with a taxi-dancer or hurdy gurdy girl still knew that they existed. Maine was seldom as insular as some people assumed, even though it is located on the far northern East Coast of the nation and has a relatively small population. And in the 1900s, every form of dance that came to America seems to have made an appearance in Maine. The trend continued into the 2000s.

Dancing for money was never easy work, but it was what some women loved, and it helped feed so many others. It may not have reached the artistic levels and freedoms some dancers might have desired, but it still provided them with work, and sometimes with food, lodging, and extra money or prizes or a chance in show business. It seldom became mainstream, but it did—overall—become increasingly respectable as the decades passed. And yet, with just a wink and a toss of the head, the burlesque queen, the dance hall diva, and the whirling dervish send out the words, "Look at me, I have something you do not want to miss," and all of a sudden, the audience is no longer certain.

NOTES

CHAPTER ONE: THE ROAD TO PERDITION

1. Works Progress Administration (WPA), *Portland City Guide*, part of the American Guide Series, Forest City Printing Co., Portland, Maine, 1940.

2. Ibid.

3. Ibid.

4. *Bangor Daily Whig & Courier* (*BDW&C*), August–September 1882. See also other years.

5. Quote, *BDW&C*, 4 April 1882; also see *BDW&C*, 5–30 April 1882; see also Trudy Irene Scee, *City on the Penobscot: A Comprehensive History of Bangor, Maine*, The History Press, Charleston, South Carolina: 2010, for examples.

6. *BDW&C*, 4 April 1882; *BDW&C*, 5–30 April 1882; and Scee, *City on the Penobscot*.

7. See note 12, and Jacquie Rogers, "The Entertainer: Hurdy Gurdy Girls," posted on http://unusualhistoricals.blogspot.com as posted in 2011 and 2015.

8. Ibid.

9. Ibid.

10. Ibid. See also, as quoted in "Barkerville: A Guide to the Fabulous Cariboo Gold Camp," *Canada West Magazine*, special issue no. 7, 1987. Also see the *Sentinel*, "The Cariboo Gold Rush Women, Hurdy Gurdy Girls," posted on http://bcheritage.ca/cariboo/people/hurdy.htm, 2012.

11. Jacquie Rogers, "The Entertainer: Hurdy Gurdy Girls," http://unusualhistoricals .blogspot.com, as posted in 2011 and 2015. See also William McConnell, *Early History of Idaho*, 1913.

12. As quoted in "Barkerville: A Guide to the Fabulous Cariboo Gold Camp." See also the *Sentinel*, "The Cariboo Gold Rush Women, Hurdy Gurdy Girls."

13. From author's previous research. See Scee, *City on the Penobscot*, for examples. The author has a doctorate in history from the University of Maine majoring in American social history (as well as writing a number of Maine history books) and a master's in history majoring in western history from the University of Montana, and has thus encountered evidence for the above numerous times, although the specifics are often vague. Also see *Bangor Daily News* (*BDN*), 1907.

14. Ibid.

15. Ibid.

16. See Scee, *Rogues, Rascals, and Other Villainous Mainers*, Down East Books, Camden, Maine, 2014. Also from research by author for another project, see also Scee, *City on the Penobscot*, for further information on Fan Jones and her life and business.

17. Ibid. Also see *Eastern Argus* for July–September 1849, especially 8–9 September, and Scee, *Rogues, Rascals, and Other Villainous Mainers*. It is possible that the house and the hotel were one and the same, or that King used part of the hotel as his residence.

18. Ibid.

19. *Eastern Argus*, 9 September 1849.

20. *Eastern Argus*, 8 September 1849.

21. *Eastern Argus*, 9 September 1849.

22. Ibid.

23. *Portland Advertiser*, 10 September 1849.

24. *Eastern Argus*, 9 September 1849 and *Portland Advertiser*, 10 September 1849. Also see Scee, *City on the Penobscot*, on the House of Corrections as a local institution in New England and in particular Bangor's House of Corrections, which regularly held prostitutes, drunks, and so forth.

25. *Portland Advertiser*, 10 September 1849.

26. *Portland Advertiser*, 7 September 1849.

27. *Eastern Argus*, 9 September 1849.

28. *BDW&C*, 13 September 1849.

29. *Portland Advertiser*, 17 September 1849.

30. See Chapter Six.

31. *BDW&C*, 26 May 1849.

32. Scee, *Rouges, Rascals and Other Villainous Mainers*; Scee, *City on the Penobscot*; and Scee, research for another project; see also *Portland City Directory* for 1900 on population numbers.

33. On the 1830s dance hall and the Kemp family, see H. H. Price and Gerald E. Talbot, *Maine's Visible Black History, The First Chronicle of Its People*, Tilbury House, Gardiner, Maine, 2006.

34. *BDW&C*, 12 September 1849.

35. *BDW&C*, 2, 3 July 1849; *Portland Advertiser*, 4 July 1849; Scee, *City on the Penobscot*, on the 289 deaths. These deaths occurred during the 1849 fiscal year, which started in March.

36. Scee, *City on the Penobscot*.

37. Ibid. See also *Portland Advertiser* and *BDW&C*, 5–10 June 1855, for coverage of the Portland Rum Riot.

38. Information on children in schools taken from Elizabeth Kendall, *Where She Danced*, New York, Alfred A. Knopf, 1979. Balance from author's previous studies and numerous books on women in the 1800s.

39. *Portland City Directory* for 1866–1867; *Portland Evening Express* (*PEE*), 31 December 1908; and *BDN*, 1907–1908 advertisements.

40. *Bangor City Directory* for 1907, see also previous years; card as posted by the Maine Memory Network, Maine's Online Museum. Established by the Maine Historical Society and Maine State Museum, www.mainehistory.org, retrieved 2015.

41. *Bangor City Directories* for 1868–1910; Scee, *City on the Penobscot*.

42. *BDN*, August 1907, quote from 27 August 1907.

43. *BDW&C*, 18 August 1897, sample advertisement.

44. *BDW&C*, 20 August 1897.

45. *BDW&C*, 18 August 1897, sample advertisement; plus *BDW&C*, 20–24 August 1897; for fair coverage, as sent in from Portland, see 24 August 1897, especially on the battle for fairs.

46. *BDW&C*, 21 and 23 August 1897; and 31 August 1897, for quote about midway.

47. *BDW&C*, 31 August 1897 and 1–4 September 1908.

48. *BDW&C* for 1890s; see 1880s also.

49. *BDW&C*, 26 and 29 August 1899; see also following pages.

50. *BDW&C*, 3 and 31 August and 1 September 1899.

51. *BDW&C*, 31 August 1898.

52. *BDW&C*, 30 and 31 August 1898; see also advertisements of surrounding days.

53. *BDW&C*, 1 September 1898; see also surrounding days and years.

54. From author's previous research. See note 12, and see Kendall, *Where She Danced*. For examples of these "Indian camps," see *BDW&C*, 30 and 31 August 1898.

55. From author's previous research; see also note 12.

56. Bunny McBride, *Molly Spotted Elk: A Dancer in Paris*. University of Oklahoma Press: Norman and London, 1995. Other works on Nelson exist, but most are derivatives.

57. *BDW&C*, 30 and 31 August 1898; see also advertisements of surrounding days.

58. McBride, *Molly Spotted Elk: A Dancer in Paris*.

59. From author's previous studies; see also Kendall, *Where She Danced*, as well as following pages and sources.

60. Ibid.

61. Ibid.

62. Ibid.

CHAPTER TWO: SCANDAL ON THE STAGE AND THE SEARCH FOR MUCH MORE

1. See local 1908–1909 newspapers on advertising; *Portland City Directories* for 1907–1909, on the theater's existence and address; see also WPA, *Portland City Guide*, on the purported initial financial problems at Keith's.

2. See advertisement from 1908–1914 for examples. In some cases the venue was called Keith's, in other places, the B. F. Keith Theater.

3. General sources; see also *New York Times* (*NYT*), 30 November 1913 and Obituary, 26 March 1914. Also see Abel Green and Joe Laurie, *Show Biz, from Vaud to Video*, New York, Henry Holt and Company, 1951, for some often garbled and undocumented, but generally accurate, background on show business and vaudeville.

4. Kendall, *Where She Danced.*

5. General sources; see also *NYT*, 30 November 1913 and Obituary, 26 March 1914; Green and Laurie, *Show Biz, from Vaud to Video*; and see Wikipedia, posting of 2015.

6. *Lewiston Daily Sun* (*LDS*), 22 January 1908.

7. *PEE*, 24 January 1908.

8. *PEE* and *Portland Press Herald* (*PPH*), 26–30 January 1908.

9. *PEE*, 27 January 1908.

10. Ibid.

11. Ibid.

12. Ibid.

13. *PEE*, 28 January 1908.

14. *PEE*, 31 December 1908.

15. *BDW&C*, 1 August 1899.

16. *BDW&C*, 1 and 15–27 August 1899.

17. See following chapters.

18. *Cambridge Chronicle*, 12 October 1901.

19. Ibid.

20. See Theda Perdue, editor, *Shifters: Native American Women's Lives*. Oxford University Press, New York and Oxford, 2001; and "Lucy Nicolar," www.penobscotculture.com, retrieved in 2015.

21. McBride, *Molly Spotted Elk: A Dancer in Paris.*

22. *PEE*, 31 December 1908; see also *Portland City Directory* for 1908.

23. *PEE*, 25–30 December 1908.

24. *Portland City Directories* for 1907 to 1940, general sources; see also following pages. Both the Nickel and Keith's in Portland appeared in city directories first in 1908 (but the Nickel was located in newspapers well before Keith's grand opening); the Nickel disappeared the following year, while Keith's remained open and in city directories until 1938.

25. *BDN*, 27 July and 12–15 August 1907.

26. *LDS*, 22 January 1908; see also surrounding weeks.

27. Green and Laurie, *Show Biz, from Vaud to Video.*

28. See *BDW&C-BDN* (cited hereafter as simply the *BDN*). Also see *BDC* for the era, as well as other Maine papers.

29. *BDN*, 9 August 1907.

30. For examples, see *BDN*, 12 and 13 August 1907 and subsequent days.

31. *BDN*, 13 August 1907.

32. *BDN*, 13 August 1907.

33. *BDN*, 27 August 1907.

34. *BDN*, 28 August 1907.

35. Ibid.

36. Ibid.

37. Ibid.

38. Ibid. Also see a dictionary of Eastern instruments for those commonly used to accompany the dancers.

39. See previous pages and Greene and Laurie, *Show Biz, from Vaud to Video*. Their source, once again, seems to have been *Variety Magazine*.

40. Ibid.

41. *BDN*, 5, 22, 26, and 27 October 1908, and *BDC* for same period; quote, *BDC*, 27 October 1908. Also see Scee, *City on the Penobscot*.

42. Ibid. Quote, *BDN*, 5 October 1908.

43. *BDN*, 5, 26, and 27 October 1908 and 19–22 November 1963. Quotes, *BDN*, 26 and 5 October 1908 and *BDC*, 26 October 1908. Also see Scee, *City on the Penobscot*; and see Wayne E. Reilly, *Hidden History of Bangor: From Lumbering Days to the Progressive Era*, The History Press, Charleston, South Carolina: 2013.

44. *BDN*, 3 October 1908.

45. *BDN*, 27 October 1908.

46. Ibid.

47. Ibid.

48. *BDN*, 28 October 1908.

49. Ibid.

50. *BDN*, 15 December 1908.

51. *BDN*, 15 and 16 December 1908.

52. *BDN* and *BDC,* 15–16 January 1909; BDC, 18 January 1909; and longer quote, *BDN*, 16 January 1909.

53. See *BDN* and *BDC* advertisements of late January and early February 1909, and *BDN*, 1 March 1909.

54. *BDN*, 14 January and 17 and 20 February 1909.

55. *BDW&C*, 26 August 1899; *BDN*, 10 August 1907. See also *BDC* and *Ellsworth American* for these years; Scee, *City on the Penobscot*; and see Reilly, *Hidden History of Bangor*.

56. *BDN*, 5 and 12 August and 26 and 28 July 1907.

57. *BDC*, 2 January 1911; and *BDN*, 3 January 1911.

58. *BDC*, 2 January 1911; and *BDN*, 3 January 1911 and 21 December 1910.

59. Quotes from Commissioner Gilman quoted in both the *BDN*, 3 January 1911 and *BDC*, 2 January 1911.

60. Ibid.

61. *BDN*, 21 December 1910.

62. *BDN*, 21–27 August 1910; quote 25 August 1910.

63. *BDN*, 21 December 1910.

64. *BDN*, 21–27 August 1910; quote 25 August 1910.

65. Quoted in Green and Laurie, *Show Biz, from Vaud to Video*.

66. Ibid. See also Kendall, *Where She Danced*, on the events of 1907–1910.

67. Kendall, *Where She Danced*.

68. *BDC*, 2 January 1911, on the various theaters; *BDN*, 2 January 1911, on the trio of dancers.

69. See Scee, *City on the Penobscot*, for more information on the fire.

70. *Bangor City Directories* for 1909–1912.

71. For an advertising example, see *PEE*, 10 November 1913. Quote from *PEE*, 7 November 1913.

72. Quote from *PEE*, 7 November 1913.

73. As quoted in Green and Laurie, *Show Biz, from Vaud to Video*.

74. For an early advertisement for an amateur night at the Jefferson, see *PEE*, 17 December 1908.

75. As quoted in Green and Laurie, *Show Biz, from Vaud to Video*.

76. *PEE*, 11 November 1913.

77. General sources; see also *NYT*, 30 November 1913 and Obituary, 26 March 1914. Also see Wikipedia, posting of 2015.

78. For examples, see *BDN*, July to August 1917 and 1918.

79. *BDN*, 4, 10, and 11 July 1918.

80. For examples, see *Ellsworth American*, 7 August 1918; *BDC*, 24 August 1918; and *BDN*, 25 August 1918.

81. Ibid.

82. *BDC*, 26 and 27 August 1918; and *BDN*, 27 August 1918.

83. *BDN*, 4, 6, 7, and 10 July 1923. Quote from *BDN*, 10 July 1923.

84. *BDN*, 26 August 1923.

85. *BDN*, 21 August 1923.

86. Kendall, *Where She Danced*.

87. *PEE*, 11 and 13 November 1913. For a later example of the "All Acts Appear in Person" statement, see *PEE*, 5 September 1928.

88. Also see Wikipedia, 2015 postings on Keith's and the two theaters in Boston and New York on the company merger.

89. General sources; see also Green and Laurie, *Show Biz, from Vaud to Video*.

90. Ibid.

91. *PEE*, 1928. Also see *Portland City Directories* for 1927–1930.

92. *PEE*, 4 September 1928.

93. Green and Laurie, *Show Biz, from Vaud to Video*.

94. General sources; Green and Laurie, *Show Biz, from Vaud to Video*.

95. On the week of November 1913, see *PEE*, 11 and 13 November 1913. For an example of the "All Acts Appear in Person" statement and on the marathon advertisement, see *PEE*, 5 September 1928.

CHAPTER THREE: OH, FOR THE SATIN SLIPPERS AND THE GOLD AND THE SILVER PURSES

1. "The Citizens' Committee of Portland," 1914 printed report, Southworth Printing Co., Portland, Maine. (It may be worth noting that a Constant Southworth served on the Board of Directors.)

2. Ibid.

3. Ibid.

4. Ibid.

5. Ibid.

6. Ibid.

7. Ibid.

8. Ibid.

9. Ibid.

10. Ibid.

11. Portland's *Daily Advertiser and Express*, 10 November 1933.

12. Ibid.

13. *Portland Daily Advertiser and Express* (which was also the *PEE*), 1 and 10 November 1913.

14. *PEE*, 7 November 1913.

15. *PEE*, 10 November 1913.

16. Ibid.

17. *PEE*, 1 and 7 November 1913.

18. *PEE*, 4 September 1928.

19. Ibid.

20. For examples, see *PEE*, *LSD*, *BDN*, and *BDC* for era.

21. Paul G. Cressey, *The Taxi-Dance Halls: A Sociological Analysis*, University of Chicago Press, Chicago, 1932.

22. Earnest W. Burgess's foreword to *The Taxi-Dance Halls: A Sociological Analysis*.

23. Cressey, *The Taxi-Dance Halls: A Sociological Analysis*.

24. Ibid.

25. Ibid; see also previous pages.

26. Ibid.

27. Lyrics by Lorenz Hart.

28. Green and Laurie, *Show Biz, from Vaud to Video*.

29. *PEE*, 31 December 1908.

30. *Portland City Directories* for 1920–1935, Cressey; *The Taxi-Dance Halls: A Sociological Analysis*. See also following pages.

31. *Portland City Directories* for 1920–1935.

32. "The Citizens' Committee of Portland," 1914 report.

33. For examples, see *PEE*, 18 and 23 July 1923.

34. *PEE*, 15 and 16 August 1928.

35. *PEE*, 21 and 31 August 1928, 14 July and 16 July 1928, and 8 and 30 August 1928.

36. For example, see *PEE*, 21 September 1928.

37. *PEE*, 4 September 1928.

38. *PEE*, 5 September 1928.

39. *BDN*, August 1923 and 1925.

40. *BDN*, 3–5 July 1923.

41. *BDN*, August and September 1925. See *BDN* 26 August 1925 for quotes.

42. *PEE*, 3 January 1934.

43. Cressey, *The Taxi-Dance Halls: A Sociological Analysis*.

44. McBride, *Molly Spotted Elk*. Quote from Molly's diary of June 1922.

45. Ibid. Quotes from diary entries of June and July 1922. Other sources on Molly Nelson exist, but they are largely derivative.

46. McBride, *Molly Spotted Elk*.

47. *Cambridge Chronicle*, 12 October 1901.

48. Ibid.

49. Ibid.

50. Ibid.

51. Ibid. See also Greene and Laurie, *Show Biz, from Vaud to Video*, and following pages.

52. Ibid.

53. Greene and Laurie, *Show Biz, from Vaud to Video;* and Calabria, *Dance of the Sleepwalkers: The Dance Marathon Fad*, Bowling Green State University Popular Press, Bowling Green, Ohio, 1993.

54. McBride, *Molly Spotted Elk*. Also see *BDN*, 1 March 2008, although this too is rather derivative, it does discuss Molly's daughter, her statement that her father had been enamored of American Indians and cowboys, and information on Molly's writing being donated years after her death.

55. PR flyer as quoted in McBride, *Molly Spotted Elk*.

56. See Perdue, editor, *Shifters: Native American Women's Lives*; and "Lucy Nicolar," www.penobscotculture.com, retrieved in 2015.

57. McBride, *Molly Spotted Elk*. Combined quote from her journal of November and December 1929.

58. McBride, *Molly Spotted Elk*; see also general sources; and Greene and Laurie, *Show Biz, from Vaud to Video*.

CHAPTER FOUR: AND THE VICTROLA PLAYED ON

1. Green and Laurie, *Show Biz, from Vaud to Video*; Carol Martin, *Dance Marathons, Performing American Culture in the 1920s and 1930s*, University of Mississippi, Jackson, 1994; and Frank M. Calabria, *Dance of the Sleepwalkers*.

2. Calabria, *Dance of the Sleepwalkers*; Martin, *Dance Marathons*.

3. *Portland Sunday Telegram/Portland Press Herald*, 7 December 1958; and *PEE*, 18 July 1923.

4. *PEE*, 18 July 1923.

5. Ibid.

6. *PEE*, 18 August 1928; *Portland Sunday Telegram/Portland Press Herald*, 7 December 1958.

7. *PEE*, 15 and 16 August 1928.

8. *PEE*, 17 and 18 August 1928.

9. Ibid.

10. *PEE*, 18 August 1928.

11. Ibid.

12. *PEE*, 20 August 1928.

13. *Portland Sunday Telegram/Portland Press Herald*, 7 December 1958; and *PEE*, 23 August 1928.

14. *PEE*, 22 and 23 August 1928.

15. Undated, unnamed source, but as determined by internal evidence published ca. mid–1920s, titled "The New Palace Ballroom, Famous Old Orchard Beach Where the Sea Breezes Blow." Available at the Old Orchard Beach Historical Society, Old Orchard Beach, Maine.

16. Ibid.

17. Ibid.

18. See following pages.

19. *PEE*, 5 September 1928; *Portland Sunday Telegram/Portland Press Herald*, 7 December 1958. Sources vary on the exact amount of the second prize awarded.

20. *PEE*, 1 September 1928.

21. *PEE*, 4 September 1928.

22. *Portland Sunday Telegram/Portland Press Herald*, 7 December 1958.

23. Ibid.

24. Horace McCoy, *They Shoot Horses, Don't They?* New York, Avon Books, 1935. See also Martin, *Dance Marathons*, for a critique of McCoy, whom she believed was trying to establish himself as the existential writer of America through his novel.

25. See Daniel E. Blaney, *Old Orchard Beach, Postcard History Series*, Arcadia Publishing Company, Charleston, South Carolina, 2007.

26. *PEE*, 15 September 1933.

27. See Blaney, *Old Orchard Beach, Postcard History Series*, on the dual names. He identified both venues as being the Marathon Arena; perhaps this was just a "working

title" for the venues in question. The book also has a photograph supposedly of at least some of the contestants, but the winners are not pictured, so it is difficult to ascertain when or where the photograph was actually taken.

28. *Portland Sunday Telegram/Portland Press Herald,* 7 December 1958.

29. Evelyn Middleton, 1933 autograph book. Held by the Old Orchard Historical Society.

30. Ibid.

31. Ibid.

32. Ibid.

33. Ibid.

34. Ibid.

35. Ibid.

36. Ibid.

37. Ibid.

38. Ibid.

CHAPTER FIVE: DANCING IN PARADISE, BURNING IN HELL

1. *BDC,* 28 October 1933.

2. *BDN,* 28 October 1933.

3. *BDC,* 31 October 1933.

4. Ibid.

5. Ibid.

6. Ibid.

7. Ibid.

8. *BDC,* 31 October 1933.

9. *BDC,* 1 November 1933.

10. Ibid. There may be some misspellings of names; information on Pelletier and Beck's being a boxer from *BDC,* 11 December 1933.

11. Ibid. Also see "Preliminary Hearings into the Fire at the Hampden Paradise Dance Pavilion," 11, 12, and 14 December 1933. In storage at the Maine State Medical Examiner's Office, Augusta, Maine, in the late 1990s. Also included in the file are twelve letters concerning the case and three other legal documents that have been used herein.

12. *BDC,* 1 November 1933.

13. Ibid.

14. Ibid.

15. Ibid.

16. Ibid.

17. Ibid.

18. Ibid.

19. *BDN*, 6 November 1933.

20. Chapter 135, Section 29, "Revised Statutes of Maine," 1933.

21. *BDN*, 6 November 1933.

22. Ibid.

23. Ibid.

24. Ibid.

25. Ibid.

26. Ibid.

27. *BDC*, 11 December 1933.

28. Compiled from pages 57 to 178 of "Preliminary Hearings into the Fire at the Hampden Paradise Dance Pavilion," 11, 12, and 14 December 1933; and *BDC*, 11 December 1933, on Sousa's age.

29. Ibid.

30. Ibid.

31. "Preliminary Hearings into the Fire at the Hampden Paradise Dance Pavilion," 11, 12, and 14 December 1933. Testimony of Sidney Curtis in transcript.

32. Ibid.

33. Ibid.

34. Ibid.

35. "Preliminary Hearings into the Fire at the Hampden Paradise Dance Pavilion," 11, 12, and 14 December 1933. Location of Sousa's body taken from *BDN*, 11 December 1933.

36. "Preliminary Hearings into the Fire at the Hampden Paradise Dance Pavilion," 11, 12, and 14 December 1933.

37. Ibid.

38. *BDN*, 11–12 and 13 December 1933. Death certificate of Helen Francis Emery, on file with the State of Maine Archives, Augusta. The certificates of death for John Ryan, Gertrude Sousa, and Emile Pelletier are not on file.

39. Ibid. See also *BDC*, 11 December 1933, on the men's ages.

40. Ibid. See also "Preliminary Hearings into the Fire at the Hampden Paradise Dance Pavilion," 11, 12, and 14 December 1933.

41. Ibid.

42. *LDS*, 11 December 1933.

43. *BDC*, 11 December 1933; and *LDS*, 11 December 1933.

44. *PEE*, 11 December 1933.

45. "Preliminary Hearings into the Fire at the Hampden Paradise Dance Pavilion," 11, 12, and 14 December 1933.

46. Ibid.

47. Ibid.

48. Ibid.

49. Ibid.

50. Ibid.

51. Ibid.

52. Ibid.

53. Ibid. And for quotes, see *BDC*, 11 December 1933.

54. Ibid.

55. Ibid. See also Frank Calabria, "The Dance Marathon Craze," *Journal of Popular Culture*, XI, 1987.

56. "Preliminary Hearings into the Fire at the Hampden Paradise Dance Pavilion," 11, 12, and 14 December 1933.

57. *LDS*, 11 December 1933.

58. "Preliminary Hearings into the Fire at the Hampden Paradise Dance Pavilion," 11, 12, and 14 December 1933.

59. Quote from *BDN*, 11 December 1933; see also *BDC*, 11 December 1933.

60. Interview with Stan West, 1997. Carol Martin also had the opportunity to interview West for her *Dance Marathons* book.

61. Ibid.

62. "Preliminary Hearings into the Fire at the Hampden Paradise Dance Pavilion." See also *BDC*, 1 November 1933, on the Winn siblings. There may have been mistakes in the list in the paper, however. See *BDC*, 15 December 1933, on the people who left within five days of the fire.

63. *BDN* and *BDC*, 11–18 December 1933.

64. *BDC*, 14 December 1933.

65. *LDS*, 11 December 1933.

66. *PEE*, 11 December 1933.

67. *BDN* and *BDC*, 11–18 December 1933; and *BDN*, 28 October 1933.

68. *BDN*, 28 October 1933; see also 12 December 1933.

69. *BDN*, 12 December 1933.

70. *BDC*, 12–14 December 1933.

71. *BDN*, 5 January 1934; and *BDC*, 13 December 1933.

72. Ibid.

73. On the $250 fines, see *BDC*, 11 December 1933.

74. *BDC*, 11 December 1933.

75. *BDC*, 14 December 1933.

76. Ibid.

77. *BDN*, 14 December 1933; *BDC*, 13 December 1933 and 8 January 1934; and *LDS*, 13 December 1933, on the sum of $5,000 set for bail; the *PPH* reported it at $50,000. Also see letters included with the "Preliminary Hearings into the Fire at the Hampden Paradise Dance Pavilion." For quotes, see *PEE*, 13 December 1933; also see *PPH*, 11 and 13 December 1933.

78. "Preliminary Hearings into the Fire at the Hampden Paradise Dance Pavilion."

79. Letters included with the "Preliminary Hearings into the Fire at the Hampden Paradise Dance Pavilion"; and *BDN*, 13 December 1933.

80. *BDC*, 11 December 1933.

81. *BDC*, 13 December 1933.

82. *BDC*, 13 December 1933.

83. Advertisement as printed in *BDC*, 14 December 1933. Also see its regular coverage on same day.

84. *PPH*, 11 December 1933.

85. Trudy Irene Scee, "Dancing in Paradise," *Bangor Business Weekly*, September 1997.

86. Ibid.

87. *PPH*, 2 March 1976. Dance to be held that Friday night.

88. See Blaney, *Old Orchard Beach, Postcard History Series*, on the Speedathon "Bill" and the dance's location. See also the *PPH* and *PEE* on the continuing acts at the venue over the year.

89. Ibid. See also Evelyn Middleton, 1933 autograph book, held by the Old Orchard Historical Society.

90. List as printed in Blaney, *Old Orchard Beach, Postcard History Series*.

91. Author's interview with Stan West, 1997. See also Carol Martin, *Dance Marathons*.

92. *BDC*, 12 December 1933.

93. *BDC*, 14 December 1933.

CHAPTER SIX: THE DANCE DIDN'T GO ON,
AND THEY REALLY WEREN'T STRIPPERS

1. *PEE*, 9 January 1934; see also *Portland City Directories* for 1930–1935.

2. Ibid.

3. Ibid.

4. Ibid.

5. Ibid.

6. Ibid.

7. *PEE*, 1 January 1934.

8. *PEE*, 2 January 1934.

9. *PEE*, 3 January 1934.

10. *PEE*, 4 and 5 January 1934.

11. *PEE*, 9 January 1934.

12. *PEE*, 10 January 1934.

13. *PEE*, 15 December 1933.

14. *PEE*, 10 and 14 December 1933.

15. *PEE*, 14 December 1933.

16. See previous pages.

17. *BDC*, 1 November 1933; *BDN*, 20 October 1933; *PEE*, 5 March 1934; *PEE*, 26 October 1933; and *BDN*, 3 July 1941.

18. *NYT*, 26 November 1935.

19. *PEE*, 26 May 1937.

20. *PEE*, 27 and 28 May 1937.

21. *PEE*, 28 May 1937.

22. *PEE*, 2 and 3 July 1937.

23. *PEE*, 3 and 4 July 1937.

24. *PEE*, 6 and 9 July 1937.

25. *PEE*, 30 July to 25 September and 11 October 1937.

26. *PEE*, 7 and 8 October 1937.

27. *PEE*, 9 October 1937.

28. Ibid.

29. Ibid.

30. *PEE*, 11 October and 13–17 December 1937.

31. *PEE*, 11 October 1937. See previous editions for similar advertisements for the Colonial Theater.

32. *PEE*, 11 to 13 October 1937.

33. *PEE*, 12 October 1937.

34. *PEE*, 13 and 14 October 1937.

35. *PEE*, 15 and 18 October 1937.

36. *PEE*, 15 and 18 October 1937.

37. For examples, see *PEE*, 3 July, 9 October, and 24 December 1937.

38. *PEE* on news for entire year; *PEE* 23, 25, and 27 October 1937, on new show.

39. *PEE*, 29 October, and 1 and 4 and November 1937.

40. *PEE*, 4–8 and 23 and 29 November 1937.

41. *PEE*, 31 October 1937.

42. *PEE*, 21–23 November 1937.

43. McBride, *Molly Spotted Elk*. Also see *PPH* and *PEE* for May 1937.

44. McBride, *Molly Spotted Elk*.

45. *BDN*, 29 October 1935; see also the rest of month, as well as the *BDC*; and McBride, *Molly Spotted Elk: A Dancer in Paris*.

46. *BDN*, 12 and 2 October 1935.

47. *BDN*, 14 and 7 October 1935.

48. *BDN*, 1 October 1935.

49. For examples, see *BDN*, 18 April 1923.

50. *BDN*, 21 October 1935 and subsequent days.

51. *BDC*, 31 October 1935.

52. *BDN*, 31 October 1935.

53. *BDC*, 2 November 1935. See McBride, *Molly Spotted Elk*, for the more famous 1930 photograph of Molly Nelson.

54. *BDN*, 29 October 1935; see also the rest of month, as well as the *BDC*; and McBride, *Molly Spotted Elk.*

55. As quoted in McBride, *Molly Spotted Elk.*

56. McBride, *Molly Spotted Elk.*

57. Nelson's diary of April 1937 as quoted in McBride, *Molly Spotted Elk*; *PEE*, 6 May 1937.

58. *PEE*, 18 May 1937.

59. *PEE*, 19 May 1937.

60. Ibid; see also *PEE*, 22 May 1937.

61. *PEE*, 19 May 1937.

62. *PEE*, 22 May 1937.

63. Ibid. Also see *PPH*, 22 May 1937; and McBride, *Molly Spotted Elk.*

64. McBride, *Molly Spotted Elk*; *BDN*, 1 March 2008.

65. *PEE* and *PPH* for November and December 1937; and *Portland City Directories* for 1935–1939.

66. *BDN*, 31 October 1937.

67. *BDN*, 19 November 1937.

68. For example, see article as printed in *PEE*, 24 May 1937.

69. Ibid.

70. Ibid.

71. For an example of the amateur shows, see *PEE*, 1 November 1937.

72. *BDN*, 3 July 1941.

73. Ibid. See also Trudy Irene Scee, *Public Enemy No 1: The True Story of the Brady Gang*, Down East Books, Camden, Maine, 2015.

74. *BDN*, 3 July 1941.

75. *PEE*, 25 January, 6 March, and 15 March 1943.

76. *PEE*, 15 March 1943.

77. *PPH*, 16 March 1943.

78. *PPH*, 16 and 17 March 1943; and *PEE*, 16 March 1943.

79. *PPH*, 16 March 1943.

80. *PPH*, 17 March 1943; see also *PEE*, 16 March 1943.

81. *PEE*, 16 March 1943.

82. *PPH*, 16 March 1943.

83. *PPH*, 17 March 1943; see also *PEE*, 16 March 1943.

84. *PPH*, 16 and 17 March 1943.

85. Quotes from *BDC*, 17 March 1943.

86. *PEE*, 16 March 1943.

87. *PEE*, 16 March 1943; and quotes from *BDC*, 16 March 1943.

88. *PPH*, 17 March 1943.

89. *PEE*, 17 March 1943.

90. Ibid.

91. Ibid.

92. *PEE,* 18 March 1943.

93. *PEE,* 19 March 1943. See also other papers for the day.

94. Ibid.

95. Ibid.

96. Ibid.

97. *PEE,* 7 May 1943. The Colonial did not appear in any newspapers as advertising shows of any sort for at least several months after the riot and the grand jury decision.

98. See *Portland City Directories,* 1943–1955; and local newspapers for these years.

99. *PPH,* 17 March 1943.

100. From author's previous research. Also see *BDC,* 16 March 1943, on the figures for women workers in Bath, Maine; newspapers in general for the era; and Scee, *City on the Penobscot,* for in-depth coverage of the war's effects in northern Maine.

CHAPTER SEVEN: BRING BACK THE HOOTCHIE-COOTCHIE

1. *BDN,* 27 September 1975.

2. See general sources; Serena and Alan Wilson, *The Secret Technique of Belly Dancing,* Pocket Books, 1975; Serena and Alan Wilson, *The Belly Dance Book,* McGraw-Hill, 1983; Helen Waldie, "A History of Modern US Belly Dance," www.bellydance.org, as posted in 2012 and 2015; see also following pages.

3. Ibid.

4. For example, see *BDN,* 22 June 1954; see also *NYT* article as printed in *Pittsburgh Post Gazette,* 10 March 1954.

5. Ibid.

6. See *BDN* for these years; also discussion with local native Ralph Doble, August 2015, whose older cousins used to frequent the Anchorage; and author's previous knowledge of the era.

7. *BDN,* 1–4 June 1954.

8. *BDN,* 2 June 1954.

9. *BDN,* 12–13 June 1954.

10. *BDN,* 18, 22, 25, and 26–27 June 1954.

11. *BDN,* 1–4 July 1954.

12. *BDN,* 1 and 3–4 July 1954.

13. *BDN,* 5 July and 5, 6, 10, 20 August 1954.

14. *BDN,* 5 July, 3 and 10 August, 10 September 1954.

15. See *BDN,* 1953, especially summer months. See also *BDN,* 18, 22, and 25 June 1954 and 13 and 17 June 1955, on Twist.

16. *Bangor City Directories* for 1940–1955 (these included surrounding towns, including Old Town, for most years), available at the Bangor Public Library; and *BDN,* 1950–1953, see especially 10 June to 15 July 1952.

17. *BDN*, 1 and 3–5 June 1953.

18. *BDN*, 12 June 1953.

19. *BDN*, 15 June and 1–6 and 20 July 1953. DeCarlo would be remembered, too, for her roles as the wife of Moses in the epic *The Ten Commandments*, and as Lily Munster, wife of Herman Munster in the television show *The Munster Family* during the 1960s.

20. *BDN*, 1–2 May 1954.

21. *BDN*, 4–9 May 1954.

22. *BDN*, 12–15 July 1954; see also 1953–1954 newspapers for examples of the Adults Only films advertised in Maine.

23. *BDN*, without photograph, see 24 May 1954; with photograph, *BDN*, 26 and 31 May 1954; *BDN*, 7–10 July and 13–16 September 1954, for White and Swan; and *BDN*, 12–15 July 1954, on *King Richard and the Crusaders*.

24. AP article as printed in *Lima News*, November 1954.

25. Ibid. Also see "Fannie," www.wikipedia.com/Fannie, retrieved in 2015.

26. Ibid. Also see "Samia Gamal," www.worldbellydance.com/SamiaGamal, retrieved in 2015. Various sources differ on some of the details of the 1950s dancers. The goal here, however, is not to define belly dancing globally or nationally but to highlight some of its features and parameters in Maine.

27. "Najla Ates," www.wikipedia.com/NajlaAtes.

28. General sources; the film *King Richard*; see also the above citations, as well as *BDN*, 28 June 1955.

29. *NYT* article as printed in *Pittsburgh Post Gazette*, 10 March 1954.

30. AP article from New York as printed in *Dayton Beach Morning Journal*, 20 November 1954; and *Life* magazine, 6 June 1955, on the statue of Ates created by sculptor Albino Manca.

31. AP article from New York as printed in *Dayton Beach Morning Journal*, 20 November 1954.

32. Comment from one of author's friends, Johnny Robinson, 2012, while author was herself dancing (but not at that show), and researching the subject.

33. *BDN*, 1954–1957.

34. *BDN*, 1–2 June 1957.

35. *BDN*, 3–11 June 1957.

36. *BDN*, 20 June 1957.

37. *BDN*, 26 June and 1 July 1957.

38. *BDN*, 4, 13–14, 16, 19, 23 July and 1–10 and 29 August 1957.

39. *BDN*, 29 August 1957.

40. Ibid.

41. See *BDN* for early 1960s, especially see 19–26 November 1963; and Records of the Bangor Theological Seminary, currently unavailable to the public but to be available in 2016.

Chapter Eight: "Little Egypt" Grows Up and Becomes the Queen of the Coast

1. Serena and Alan Wilson, *The Secret Technique of Belly Dancing*; Serena and Alan Wilson, *The Belly Dance Book*; Helen Waldie, "A History of Modern US Belly Dance"; *Life* magazine, 4 February 1972; interview with Colette Poliquin, August 2015, on Wilson's performing in the Portland region, also mentioned in the *Life* article; and interview with Jeanne Handy, September 2015, on Wilson's 1990s time in Maine.
2. *NYT*, 24 June 2007; *San Diego Union-Tribune*, 7 July 2007.
3. Ibid.
4. Ibid.
5. *Life*, 4 February 1972.
6. *Maine Times*, 16 August 1974. See also Serena Wilson, *The Serena Technique of Belly Dancing*, 1972.
7. Ibid.
8. *Maine Times*, 16 August 1974.
9. Ibid.
10. Ibid.
11. *PEE*, 12 April 1976.
12. Ibid.
13. *PEE*, 12 April 1976; and *NYT*, 24 June 2007, on Wilson.
14. *PEE*, 12 April 1976.
15. *Readers' Digest*, August 1977.
16. Interview with Colette Poliquin, August 2015. Interview with Josephina Gasca, August 2015, on Poliquin's being the oldest living dancer in the state, and the author's own observations. Quotes from *PEE*, 23 June 1981, and from 2015 interview with author.
17. Interview with Colette Poliquin, August 2015. Also see *PEE*, 23 June 1981.
18. Ibid.
19. General observations from the author's attendance at various shows and interactions with various dancers over the years.
20. Interview with Colette Poliquin, August 2015.
21. Ibid.
22. Ibid.
23. Ibid.
24. Ibid. Also, although not figured into the above, the author studied with Catherine Tambling as well as a couple of other Maine belly dancers.
25. Interviews with Colette Poliquin, Josephina Gasca, and Josie Conté, August and September 2015.
26. Interview with Colette Poliquin, August 2015.
27. Ibid.
28. Ibid.

29. Ibid.

30. Ibid.

31. Ibid.

32. Ibid.

33. Ibid.

34. Interview with Josephina Gasca, August 2015.

35. Ibid. The author has also taken a workshop at Rosa Noreen's studio and attended one of her shows.

36. Interview with Josephina Gasca, August 2015.

37. Interviews with Josephina Gasca and Colette Poliquin, August 2015.

38. Interview with Josephina Gasca, August 2015.

39. Ibid.

40. Ibid. The author attended a couple of Gasca's "Belly Balls" and found them delightful, and the information about the same is taken from the author's experiences there; the author subsequently took a few classes with Gasca.

41. Interview with Josephina Gasca, August 2015.

42. Ibid.

43. Interview with Josephina Gasca, August 2015; and Gasca's website as posted in 2015.

44. Telephone interview with Josie Conté, September 2015.

45. Ibid. See also *NYT*, 14 September 1986.

46. Quote taken from *Maine Times*, 1996, from Conté's website.

47. Telephone interview with Josie Conté, September 2015.

48. Ibid.

49. Ibid.

50. Ibid.

51. Ibid.

52. Ibid.

53. Interview with Anne Beal, September 2015.

54. Ibid.

55. Ibid. The author watched Beal perform at Narls in 2015.

56. Ibid.

57. Ibid. See also other interviews of this chapter.

58. Interview with Anne Beal, September 2015.

59. Ibid.

60. Ibid.

61. Ibid.

62. Ibid.

63. Ibid.

64. Interview with Jeanne Handy, September 2015.

65. Ibid.

66. Ibid.

67. Ibid.

68. Ibid.

69. Ibid.

70. Ibid.

71. Ibid.

72. Ibid.

73. Ibid.

74. *Portland Phoenix*, 23 April 2015; and interview with Jeanne Handy, September 2015.

75. *PPH*, 14 March 2011.

Selected Bibliography

Bangor City Directories, 1850s–1960s.

Bangor Daily Commercial, 1890s–1950s.

Bangor Daily News, 1907–2015.

Bangor (Daily) Whig & Courier, 1880–1907.

Blaney, Daniel E. *Old Orchard Beach, Postcard History Series*. Arcadia Publishing Company, Charleston, South Carolina, 2007.

Calabria, Frank M. *Dance of the Sleepwalkers: The Dance Marathon Fad*. Bowling Green State University Popular Press, Bowling Green, Ohio, 1993.

———. "The Dance Marathon Craze." *Journal of Popular Culture*, XI, 1987.

"The Citizens' Committee of Portland." Southworth Printing Co., Portland, Maine, 1914 printed report.

Cressey, Paul G. *The Taxi-Dance Halls: A Sociological Analysis*. University of Chicago Press, Chicago, 1932.

Dayton Beach Morning Journal, 20 November 1954.

Eastern Argus, 1840s–1900s.

Ellsworth American, assorted years.

"Fannie." www.wikipedia.com/Fannie.

Green, Abel, and Joe Laurie. *Show Biz, from Vaud to Video*. Henry Holt and Company, New York, 1951.

Interview with Anne Beal, September 2015.

Interview with Josephina Gasca, August 2015.

Telephone interview with Josie Conté, September 2015.

Interview with Jeanne Handy, September 2015.

Interview with Colette Poliquin, August 2015.

Telephone interview with Stan West, 1992.

Kendall, Elizabeth. *Where She Danced*. Alfred A. Knopf, New York, 1979.

Lewiston Daily Sun, 1908–2000s.

Life, assorted issues.

"Lucy Nicolar," www.penobscotculture.com, retrieved in 2015.

"Maine Memory Network; Maine's Online Museum." Historical Society and Maine State Museum, www.mainehistory.org.

Maine Times, 16 August 1974.

Martin, Carol. *Dance Marathons: Performing American Culture in the 1920s and 1930s.* University of Mississippi, Jackson, 1994.

McBride, Bunny. *Molly Spotted Elk: A Dancer in Paris.* University of Oklahoma Press: Norman and London, 1995. Other works on Nelson exist, but most are derivatives.

McConnell, William. *Early History of Idaho*, The Arthur H. Clark Company, Glendale, California, 1913.

McCoy, Horace. *They Shoot Horses, Don't They?* Avon Books, New York, 1935.

Middleton, Evelyn. Personal 1933 autograph book. Held by the Old Orchard Historical Society.

"Najla Ates." www.wikipedia.com/NajlaAtes.

"The New Palace Ballroom, Famous Old Orchard Beach Where the Sea Breezes Blow." Undated, unnamed source, but as determined by internal evidence published ca. mid-1920s. Available at the Old Orchard Beach Historical Society, Old Orchard Beach, Maine.

New York Times, 30 November 1913; 26 March 1914; 24 June 1907, and assorted other dates.

"Now You Can Shimmy Like Your Sister Kate." *Life*, 4 February 1972.

Perdue, Theda, editor. *Shifters: Native American Women's Lives.* Oxford University Press, New York and Oxford, 2001.

Portland Advertiser, 1840s–1950s.

Portland City Directories, 1866–1966.

Portland Evening Express, 1900–1950s (also as Portland's *Daily Advertiser and Express and Advertiser).*

Portland Sunday Telegram/Portland Press Herald, various years.

Portland Umpire, 1849.

"Preliminary Hearings into the Fire at the Hampden Paradise Dance Pavilion," 11, 12, and 14 December 1933. In storage at the Maine State Medical Examiner's Office, Augusta, Maine, in the late 1990s. Also included in the file were twelve letters concerning the case and three other legal documents.

Price, H. H., and Gerald E. Talbot. *Maine's Visible Black History: The First Chronicle of Its People.* Tilbury House, Gardiner, Maine, 2006.

Readers' Digest, August 1977.

Reilly, Wayne E. *Hidden History of Bangor: From Lumbering Days to the Progressive Era.* The History Press, Charleston, 2013.

"Revised Statutes of Maine," Chapter 135, Section 29, 1933.

Rogers, Jacquie. "The Entertainer: Hurdy Gurdy Girls," http://unusualhistoricals.blog spot.com. as posted in 2011 and 2015.

"Samia Gamal." www.WorldBellyDance.com/SamiaGamal, retrieved in 2015.

San Diego Union-Tribune, 7 July 2007.

Scee, Trudy Irene. *City on the Penobscot: A Comprehensive History of Bangor, Maine*. The History Press, Charleston, 2010, for examples.

———. "Dancing in Paradise." *Bangor Business Weekly*, September 1997.

———. *Rogues, Rascals, and Other Villainous Mainers*. Down East Books, Camden, Maine, 2014.

Sentinel, "The Cariboo Gold Rush Women, Hurdy Gurdy Girls," http://bcheritage.ca/cariboo/people/hurdy.htm, 2012.

Waldie, Helen. "A History of Modern US Belly Dance," www.bellydance.org, as posted in 2012 and 2015.

Wilson, Serena, and Alan Wilson. *The Belly Dance Book*, McGraw-Hill, New York, 1983.

———. *The Secret Technique of Belly Dancing*, Pocket Books, New York, 1975.

Works Progress Administration (WPA). *Portland City Guide*. Part of the American Guide Series, Forest City Printing Company, 1940.

Index

Abanaki or Wabanaki Tribes, 24, 25, 27, 36, 88
Abbe Indian Museum, Bar Harbor, 163
Acker's Family Theater, Bangor, 46, 56
Acropolis Restaurant, 216
aerial, dancing, 19, 59, 60
Albee, Edward Franklin II, 30, 32–33, 59
Albee Vaudeville Circuit, 39, 89
Alice, Mary, 194–95
amateur nights, 2, 50, 58, 85, 164, 174
American Legion Hall, Westbrook, 156
American Tribal Dance, 208, 222
Anchorage Hotel, Old Town, 188–202
Archambaud, Jean, 167, 169–70
Argentine tango, 57
Armstrong, Louie, 155
Aroostook, 22
Assembly Hall, Portland, 2
Ashford, Edward, 114
Atlantic Casino, Bangor, 163–65, 171, 174
Ates, Nejla, 186, 195–98
Atomic Trash!, 228
Auburn, 13, 39, 75, 82, 208, 220, 222
Augusta, 12–13, 40, 144, 191
Auto Rest Park, Carmel, 175, 190, 191
Aztec Theater, Texas, 89

B. F. Keith Theater, Boston, 30, 33, 64
B. F. Keith Memorial Theater, Boston, 64
Babes in Bagdad, 193
bachelorette parties, 222
Bailey, James A., 19
Bakkar, Mohammed El, 196
ballet, 25–26, 189, 193, 206, 208, 217, 227
"ballet girls," 26, 193

ballrooms, 67, 76, 79–80
Bangor Athaeneum, 3
Bangor Band, 23
Bangor-Brewer Ministerial Association, 120, 137
Bangor Dancing Fraternity, 16–17
Bangor Eastern Maine Fair, 18, 20, 21, 22, 24, 42–44, 51–54, 60, 62, 85
Bangor Fire Department, 136
Bangor Fire of 1911, 46, 56–57
Bangor House, the, 45
Bangor Law, the, 15
Bangor Opera House, 2, 3, 18, 42, 56–57, 152, 171, 189, 195
Bangor Police Department, 118
barker, 22, 27, 51, 62, 151
Barker, The, 151
Bar L Ranch, Newport, 175
Barnum, P. T. (Phineas Taylor), 23
Barnum & Bailey, circus, 19, 23, 30
Bass Park, Bangor, 61
Bath, 183, 210, 212, 213, 215–16, 220
Bath Dance Works Studio, 212, 216
Bar Harbor, 20, 40, 50, 85, 163, 174, 190
Beal, Anne "Anabee," 215, 218, 219–23, 226
Beck, Martin, 59
Beck, Russell "Ginger," 114, 126, 139
bedi (dance), 205
Belfast, 40, 50, 226
"Belly Balls," 216, 226
belly dance, xiii–xv, 43–44, 150, 151, 161, 185–88, 192, 193, 195–99, 201–2, 203–28, 229, 230
belly-gram, 209–10, 216, 222

Berry, Reverend Wilbur F., 51–54
"Betty Babette, French Nudist," 154–55
Big Band Era, 100
Bijou Theater, Bangor, 57, 59, 62, 144–45, 152–53
Bijou Theater, Boston, 30
Birchmere Inn, Old Town, 190, 199–200
Black and White Revue, 154–55
Blair, Howard, 62–63
Blake & Blake, 203–4
Black Satin Revue, 176
Blanchard, Mari, 187, 197
Blaney, Daniel E., 105
Blue Restaurant, Portland, 221
Boston & Maine Railroad, 97
Botti, Mae, 42
Bow, Clara, 151
Bowdoin, 224, 226
Bowdoin College Middle Eastern Dance Ensemble, 224
Brady, Al, 160, 175
Brazilian tango, 64
Brewer, 13, 190–91, 193, 194
Broadway, New York, 172, 173, 186, 195–96
Brownville, 85
Brunswick, 144, 205–6, 220, 224
bubble dance, 66, 173, 193
Bucksport, 22, 50, 175, 190
Burgess, Earnest W., 76
burlesque, dancing, xv, 29, 63–63, 65, 145, 147, 149–51, 153, 161, 171–75, 183, 185, 188, 190–91, 192–93, 199, 207, 208, 222, 227–28, 229
Burley, Edward, 114
Butts, Maryann, 223

cabaret style, American, 205, 208
Calabria, Frank, 94
Camp Benson, 84–85
Caribou, 19
Carmel, 175
Carmella, 200
carnival, 78, 151, 205
Carson and Kams Revue, 150
Casino, the, Bar Harbor, 85

Casino Theater, Westbrook, 73
Cella, Connie, 158, 159
Central Maine Fair, Waterville, 18, 23, 54, 60
Charleston, the dance, 66, 74, 84
Chateau Ballroom, Bangor, 85, 134, 144
Chesterfield cigarettes, 153–54
Chicago Pirates, 84–85
Chicago World Fair, 1893, xiv, 44, 186, 207
Chicago World Fair, 1934, xv, 66
Cho, Ming, 192
cholera, 14
Christian Civic League of Maine, 141
circus, 1, 2, 18–19, 23, 26, 30, 50, 51, 59–60, 61–62, 88, 230
Citizens' Committee of Portland, 67–72, 81
City Hall, Bangor, 2, 3, 56
City Hall, Portland, 2, 101, 168
Clifford, Cassie, 46
clog dancing, 20, 31, 46, 132, 164
Cocoanut Grove Fire, Boston, 178–79
Colonial Theater, Portland, 159, 174, 175–80
concert hall saloon, 78
Conchita, 161
Congress Theater, Portland, 37
Conté, Josie "Joselle," 211–12, 214, 217–19, 223, 228
Corio, Ann, 173
corsets, 16, 27
Count Basie, 168
Craig, Joseph, 16, 80
Cressey, Paul G., 76
Criterion Theater, Bar Harbor, 153, 174
Crystal Ballroom, Dover-Foxcroft, 174
Cumberland County Sheriff's Department, 71, 181
Cummings, Alma, 93–94
Curtis, Sidney, 111–12, 122, 123, 126–28, 129–30, 133, 135, 138–39

Dance Center, the, Auburn, 222
dance contests, 67, 75, 81–85, 86, 92, 93, 130, 155, 213
dance exhibitions, 82, 84, 85, 95, 144

dance marathons, xiv–xv, 66, 76, 82, 90, 93–109, 111–44, 171, 229
Dance of the Seven Veils, 55, 187–88
dance pavilions, 80–81, 84, 137
dancing academies, 77, 81
"dancing girls," 53–54
Dancing Lady, 150
Dane, Pattie, 191
Dawn, Diane, 190
Day, Judy, 199
DeCarlo, Yvonne, 193
Desjardins, Clara, 208
Devalery's 12 Dancing Tambourines, 65
Devil's Half Acre, Bangor, 6–7, 17
dime-a-dance halls, 77
Dirty Dishes Burlesque Revue, the, 228
Divine, Jolene, 228
Dobra Tea House, Portland, 216, 221
Doreen, "Tassle Tossin' Cutie," 201–2
Dorothy Martin Revue, 150
Dorsey, Fifi, 162
Dorsey, Tommy, 191
Dow, Neal, 15
Dreamland Theater, Portland, 37
Duncan, Isadora, 27, 63

Earhart, Amelia, 155–56
Earl Taylor's Glorified Revue, 157–58, 160
Eastern Argus, 8
Eastern dance, 43, 44, 55, 62, 150, 186–88, 191, 199, 202, 204, 214, 217–18
Eastern Maine General Hospital, Bangor, 124–25
Eastern Maine State Fair, Bangor, 18, 20, 21, 22, 24, 42–44, 51–54, 60, 78
Edison, Thomas, 30, 39
Egyptian Ballroom, the, Lewiston, 75
Eighteenth Amendment, 75
Elk's Home, club, Portland, 71
Ellington, Duke, 156–57
Ellsworth, 13, 40, 51, 85, 190–91, 210, 226
Ellsworth American, 50, 60
E. M. Loew's Bangor-Brewer Drive-In, Brewer, 190–91, 194
Emery, Helen Francis, 124–25, 131, 134

endurance dancing, xiv–xv, 66, 76, 82, 93–109, 111–44, 172, 185, 229, 230
Everand, Mable "Bubbles," 104–5
exhibition dancing, 82, 84, 85, 95, 144

Fairfield, 38
fairs, 1, 2, 18–19, 22, 24, 27, 43, 45, 50, 51, 55, 59, 60–63, 73, 214, 230
fakirs, 21, 22, 62
fan dance, 66, 173, 193
Fannie, film, 195, 197
Fannie, play, 186–87, 195–96
Farrah, Ibrahim "Bobby," 208
Farrar, Sheriff John K., 118, 138, 140
Fatima, xiv, xv, 44
Faulkingham, Ann, 114
female impersonators, 62, 162
Fitzgerald, Ella, 156, 158
flapper, 62
Flores, Sony, 193–94
"Follies Begere [*sic*]," 155
Footlight Parade, 152, 171
Forepaugh & Sells Circus, 19
Forrest, Sally, 197
Fort Fairfield, 19
Foster Girls, the, 88, 89, 92
fox-trot, 74, 81, 82, 83, 95, 96
Frankfort, 174
"free" dance, 27, 35
Freeport, 108, 144
French Follies, 161, 190
French Line, The, 194
Frost, Brenda, 206–7

G-string, 155, 173, 228
Gaiety Theater, Bangor, 48–49, 56–57
Gamal, Lys and Lyn, 186
Gamal, Samia, 196
Gardiner, 38, 144
Gardiner, Alan (né Alan Shavarsh Bardezbanian), 209, 211, 225
Gardner, Harry M., 45
Garry, Thomas Jr., 126
Gasca, Josephina, 213, 214–17, 218, 219–20, 223, 226

Gem Theater, Bangor, 46, 57
Gibson, Ruth, 205–6, 207
Gilbert, Vesta, 49
Gilman, Augustus W., 52–53
Girdellers Models, 159
Girl without a Room, 151
Goddard, Paulette, 193
go-go dancing, 185, 188
Golden Slipper Producing Company, 111, 119, 130
Golden Slipper Dance Hall, Old Orchard Beach, 106–8
Goodman, Benny, 168
Gorham, 54
Gorman's Alabama Troubadours, 44–45
Gorman's New York Vaudeville Club, 35
Gorman's Operetta Company, 35
Graham, Martha, 63
Graphic Theater, Bangor, 47, 49
Gray Road Inn, Portland, 75, 82, 98
Great Depression, xiv, 92, 101, 103, 143, 171
"Great White Way," Bangor, 48–49, 56, 59
Greely's Theater, Portland, 57
Gruaman, Sid, 93
Guinan, "Texas" (Mary Louise), 90, 92
gypsies, 35
Gypsy Rose Lee, 173, 193, 196–97

hafla, 218–19, 226
Halloween, 1933, xiii, 111, 113–14
Hallowell, 12, 209, 219
Hampden, 35, 50, 51, 84, 103, 109, 111–44, 147, 151, 230
Hampden dance marathon, 111– 44, 147, 179, 204
Hampden Dance Pavilion, xv, 103, 109, 148
Handy, Jeanne "Jamileh," 211–12, 214–15, 216, 217, 218, 220, 221, 223–26, 228
Hanger, the, Trenton, 190
Harry Berry Sunkist Vanities, 161
Healy, Connie, 114
Hedlund, Viola and Harold, 104
Hermon, 85, 190
Hindu dance, 26, 188–89

Hippodrome Theater, NYC, 88
Holder, Emma, 214
Hoopla, 151
hootch kooche, 54–55
hootchie-cootchie, xv, 23, 43–44, 133, 171, 185, 205, 214
houchie couchee, 21, 22, 23
Hoover, Cassandra, 218
Houlton, 13, 40
House of Corrections, 10
hula dancing, Hawaiian, 206
hurdy gurdy, 3, 229–30
hurdy gurdy girls, xi, xii, xiv, xv, 1, 3–6, 17, 18, 21, 23, 27, 29, 42, 185

illustrated songs, 38, 39, 41
Indian Island, 24, 25, 35, 87, 91
Indian Lake Pavilion, Machias, 84
I'm No Angel, 162, 171
interpretive dance, 27, 63, 89, 91, 190
Island Park, Portland, 75

Jack-O-Lantern, Portland, 75
Jahal, Jasmin, 214, 215
James Carroll Players, 62–63
jazz, 66, 217, 227
Jefferson Theater, Portland, 2, 37–38, 56, 58
Jimmy Hodges Revue, 160
John the Baptist, 51, 55
Jones, Fan, 7
Jordan, Arlyn, 191
Judd, Loyde (also spelled Lloyd or Loyd), 108–9, 143

Kahas Productions, 211
Kay, Al, 117
Keith-Albee Circuit, 89
Keith-Albee-Orpheum Circuit (KAO), 64
Keith, A. Paul (Andrew), 32, 59
Keith, Benjamin Franklin "B. F.," 30, 32, 59
Keith's theater, Portland, 30, 31–35, 38, 64–65, 66, 148–51, 152, 154–62, 168–69, 171
Kemp family, 13
kick-waltzing, 156

kinetoscope, 30, 32
King, Augustus, 7–12, 13
King Richard and the Crusaders, 195, 197
"kitty," dancers, 122, 123, 132–33, 139–40
Knowles, Dorothy, 57
Kovensky, Virginia DeKovens, 206–7, 208
Kurtz, Myer, 130

Lady Godiva Revue, 162
Larabee, Edward, 114
Larke, Betty, 190
LaRose, Catherine, 104
Las Vegas Burlesque Review, 228
Lee, Miss Stella, 35
Legere, Irene, 96
Lewiston, 13, 19, 20, 31, 38–39, 41–42, 50,
    54, 56, 75, 85, 134, 142, 144, 208,
    210, 213, 214, 219
Lewiston-Auburn, 13, 85, 143, 152, 214,
    215, 220, 221, 222
Lewiston Dailey Sun, 31, 39
Lewiston State Fair, 18, 19, 20, 60, 85
Life magazine, 203, 204
Little Egypt, xi, xiv, xv, 22, 42–44, 55, 150,
    151, 162, 186, 202, 203, 207
Loew, Marcus, 22
Loew vaudeville circuit, 39, 64
Long Lake Sporting Club, 84
Loring, Frank, 24
"Lovely Lane, Sepia Nudist," 154
Lyka, Marjorie, 118, 125
Lyman, Mitzie, 114

Machias, 40, 84
Maguire, Police Captain Harold K.,
    178–79
Maine Belly Dance, 214
Maine blue laws/Maine Sunday Laws,
    118–19, 121–22, 137
Maine Center for Taijiquan, Portland, 224
Maine Central Railroad, 22
Maine Constitution, 141
Maine Highway Police, 118
Maine Law, the, 14–15
Maine, 1846 liquor law, 7, 14

Maine State Legislature, 135, 142, 183
Maine State Police, 118
Majestic Rink, Peaks Island, 73
Maliseet, 24
Maplewood Park, Bangor, 20, 22, 42, 61
Marathon Arena, Old Orchard Beach, 105,
    106
marathon dancing (endurance dancing),
    xiv–xv, 66, 82, 93–109, 111–44, 171,
    185, 229, 230
marathon road dances, 96–102
Martin, John, 17
McBride, Bunny, 25, 86, 90
McCormack, Joe, 113
McCoy, Harold, 124, 126, 139
Manhattan Merry-Go-Round, dance revue,
    161–62
May, Donna, 191
Means, Jessica, 226, 228
Micmac, 24
midway, fair, 18, 20–23, 29, 40, 43, 44, 51,
    52, 53, 60–62, 151
Middle Eastern dance, 192, 208, 225
Middle Eastern Suitcase Project, 225
Middleton, Evelyn, 106–9
Miles, Raye, 193
Miller, Glenn, 158, 170
Miller, Nadia, 62
Millinocket, 190, 210
Milton Goodhue's "Indian revue," 87
Ministers' Union of Portland and Vicinity,
    141
Miss Helene, 161
modern dance, 27–28, 63, 206, 208, 217,
    223, 227
Molly Spotted Elk (Molly Nelson), 35–36,
    67, 88, 92, 162–63, 165–71, 220, 230
"monkeys," 87
Monroe, Lucille, 191
Moore, James E., 30, 32
Morgan, J. P., 55
Mt. Desert Island, 22, 50
Munjoy Hill, Portland, 8, 10, 13–14, 17, 78
Music Hall, Bangor, 3
Music Hall, Bar Harbor, 50

Nanya's Trance, 226, 228
Narls Restaurant, Auburn, 220
National Marathon Dance Association, 113
Native Americans, 1, 23–25, 27, 36, 91
Nautch, dance, 26–27, 167
"Neja the Hindu Dancer," 195, 197, 198
Nelson, Molly Alice, 35, 37, 86–92, 162–63, 165–71,
"neo-burlesque," 228
Neptune, Clara, 24
New Bijou theater, 144, 153
New England Fair, Portland, 18, 19–20
New Palace Ballroom, Old Orchard, 100–101
Nickel Theater, Bangor, 38, 40–42, 45, 46, 49, 56–57
Nickel Theater, Lewiston, 38
Nickel Theater, Portland, 37, 38
Nickelet Theater, Lewiston, 39
nickolodians, 38
Nickel Theaters, Maine and general, 38–39
Nicolar, Lucy (also spelled Nicola and Nicolas), 24, 36–37, 67, 87, 88, 89, 91, 230
Noreen, Rosa, 214–15, 216, 224, 226
Norombega Hall (also Norembega Hall and Norumbega Hall), 3, 47–48, 56
Northern Maine Fair, Presque Isle, 60
Northern Maine Junction, 85
Norway, Maine, 54

Oakdale Pavilion, Lewiston-Auburn, 82, 84–85
Old Orchard Arcade, Old Orchard Beach, 103, 106
Old Orchard Beach, 13, 50, 79, 81, 84, 94, 95, 98, 103–9, 123, 143
Old Orchard Historical Society, 106
Old Port, Portland, 7
Old Town, 24, 25, 35, 50, 87, 91, 169, 187–88, 191, 198, 199
Oriental dance, 23, 89, 150, 196
Orono, 188, 191

Packard, Wyman, 176–77, 179–82
Palace Ballroom, Old Orchard, 75, 79, 82, 96, 98–101, 143
Pantages Vaudeville Circuit, 63
Paradise Club, New York, 66
Paradise Dance Pavilion, Hampden, 109, 111, 114, 118, 121, 126, 152
Paradise Dance Pavilion Fire of 1933, 111–44
participatory dance, 74
Passamaquoddy, 24
pasties, 145, 149, 154, 155, 228
Pavilion, the, Portland, 72
Peaks Island, 73
Pelletier, Emile, 114, 125, 131, 132, 134
Penobscot County Jail, Bangor, 119
Penobscot County Sheriff's Department, 118
Penobscot tribe, 24–25, 88
Penobscot nation, 24, 88
Persian Gulf War, 204
Philadelphia Centennial, 1876, 186
(Ocean) Pier, Old Orchard, 75, 82, 155, 156, 168, 191
Pine Tree Pavilion, Ellsworth, 85
Pitt Street, dancing hall, Portland, 72–73
Pleasant Lake Pavilion, Stetson, 175
Pomerloau, Dolly Marie "Sylina," 209, 211
Poliquin, Colette "Zeina," 208–14, 218, 219–20, 223, 225
Pontari Sisters, the, 228
Portland Advertiser, 9, 10,
Portland Evening Express, 31, 32, 34
Portland's Great Fire, 1866, 2
Portland Municipal Court, 71, 74, 181
Portland Press Herald, 160, 169, 177
Portland Rum Riot, 15
Portland Sunday Telegram, 56
Portland Theater, New, 2
Portland Umpire, 12
Prairie Pavilion, Brownville, 85
Presque Isle, 60, 190
Princess Spotted Elk, 89

Princess of the Tarrantines, 23, 24–25
Princess Watawaso (also spelled Watahwaso), 24, 37
Princess Watawaso Indian Troupe, 89
Proctor, Frederick Freeman, 31, 59
Prohibition, Maine, 7, 14–15, 17, 74, 182–83
Prohibition, National, 75, 111, 182–83
Puritan, 1

Radha dance, 26, 55
Radio-Keith-Orpheum (RKO), 64
Rameroz, Camile, 189–90
Ramzi El Edlibi Dance Company, 218
Rand, Sally, xv, 66, 173, 193
raqs beledi, 220
Ray, Mitsie, 193
Readers' Digest, 208
Recreation Building, Portland, 147–48
Redpath Chautauqua Bureau, 37
Renault, Francis, 162
revues, dance, 89,
Revue Fantastic, 149
Revue Glorified, 157–60
Revised Statutes of Maine, 118
rumba, 167
Ricker Gardens, Portland, 152, 156–57, 158, 170
Rigby Park, Portland, 19
Riverside Park, Hampden, 35, 50, 111
Riverside, Portland Park and Pavilion, 74, 82–83
Riverside Dance Pavilion, Riverton, 101–2
Robinson Circus, 59–60
Rockland, 50
Rogers, Ginger, 145, 162
Rogers, Jacquie, 5
Roland, Jeff, 164
roller-skating dances, 144, 175
roller-skating rinks, 111, 160
Roxyettes, 191
Russell, Jane, 194
Ryan, Eleanor, 125, 131, 134, 139
Ryan, John, 125, 131, 132, 134

Sabah, "Princess of the Nile," 199
Saco, 96
St. Louis Exposition, 1904, 44
Salomé, 55
Salomé, play, 55
Salomé, movie, 55, 193
Salomé dances, 54–55
Sam Cohen's Golden Girls, 61
Sanford, 144
Savoy Theater, Portland, 37
Scarborough, 209, 224
scarf dance, 155
Schubert, J. J., 91
Schubert's Vaudeville Circuit, 39
Sentinel, 5
Serena Technique of Belly Dancing, The, 204
Shanghai, 194
Shaw, Artie, 170
Shawn, Ted, 63
shimmy, 66, 151
Shipyard Workers Riot of 1943, 147, 175–83, 201
Sima, Neja, 188–89
skirt dance, 46
Skowhegan Fair, 18, 23
Smith, Helen, 114
Snow, Mildred, 106
solo dancer, marathon, 111, 115, 121, 129, 144
Son of Sinbad, 197
Sousa, Gertrude, 121, 124, 131, 134
South Portland, 13
"Spanish" dance, 51–52, 89
Spark Circus, the, 61–62
speakeasies, 75, 88
specialty dances, 156
Speedathon, Old Orchard Beach, 143–44
speed derbies, 143–44
Spyropoulos, Farida Mazar (Fatima), xiv
stag, 177, 179, 180
Star Bright Studios, 215
Stairs, Gertrude W., 101
State Ballroom, Portland, 80, 147–48, 152
State Theater, Portland, 65, 151, 160, 162

Steep Falls, Maine, 82
Strand Theater, Portland, 65, 162
stripping, dance, xiii, 7, 185, 207, 214, 222, 228, 229
striptease, xii–xiii, 65–66, 173, 176, 180, 182, 185, 191, 199, 201
St. Cyr, Lilly, 197
St. Denis, Ruth, 26–27, 30-31, 55, 63, 91, 204
Sunset Ballroom, Portland, 82
supper club, 185, 188, 197–98
Swan, Bobbie, 195
Swan Lake Pavilion, 84

Tambling, Catherine "Kitty," "Kahas," 211, 220
tango, 57, 70, 72, 74, 81, 83, 214
Tango Dancing Lesson, 57
tap, 217
Taylorettes, 159
taxi-dancing, xi, xiv, 27, 67, 70, 75–81, 84, 85–87, 148, 185, 229–30
Temperance Committee, 183
Tempest Storm, 228
Thelma Twist, 189–90, 192
Thomas, Dick, 114
tribal or American Tribal, dance, 208, 222
Twilight Pavilion, Hermon, 190

Uncle Ezra Stebbens and His Radio Barn Dance Follies, 155
Union Hall, Bangor, 45–46, 56–57
Union Hall theater, Bangor, 45–46, 56–57
Union Hall, Portland, 2
United Booking Offices of America, 58–59

Valley, Rudy, 156
Valley of the Kings, 196
vaudeville, dance, xv, 1, 13, 20, 26, 27–28, 29– 39, 45, 46–48, 50, 51, 57–59, 61–65, 73, 86, 123, 145, 147, 149–51, 153, 170, 173, 183, 185, 230
Veils of Bagdad, 187–88, 197
Vinyl Haven Island, 210
Vivian Vice, 228

Wabanaki or Abanaki tribes, 24
Wabe, Ashea, xiv
Walker, Lew ("dancing girls"), 53–54
walkathon, dance, 109, 142
waltz, dance exhibits and contests, 81, 82, 83
Watawaso's Indian Troupe, 89
Webb, Chick, 157, 158
Waterville, 38, 51, 54, 85, 226
West Bath, 114
Westbrook, 73, 156, 228
West, Mae, 58, 65–66, 162, 171
West, Stan, 131–32, 144
Wahaletka Indian Revue, 167
White, Loraine, 195
Whistlebait Burlesque, 228
Whorehouse Riot of 1849, 1, 11, 12
"Wiggle Dance," 29, 54, 56
Wildwood Pavilion, Steep Falls, 82–83
Wilson's Dance School/Academy, Portland, 16, 80
Wilson, Alan, 204
Wilson, George, 16
Wilson, Samuel Payne, 54–55
Wilson, Serena, 203–5, 207, 208, 209, 211, 212, 217–18, 219, 223
Winterport, 174
Wise, Kay (also spelled Kay Wice), 118, 121, 124, 125, 129, 130, 131
World War I, 150
World War II, 168, 183
World Fair, 1893, Chicago, xiv, 44, 186, 207
World Fair, 1934, Chicago, xv, 66
Wynne, Lee, 121, 124

YMCA, Portland, 141
YWCA, Portland, 206–7

Zapion Taverna, 209
Ziegfeld, Florenz, 55
Ziegfeld Follies, 89
Zorita, 162
Zubelda Dancing Girls, 60–61
Zumba, 222